THE ITALIAN COOKBOOK

THE ITALIAN COOKBOOK

BY MARIA LUISA TAGLIENTI

RANDOM HOUSE
NEW YORK

FOR MY HUSBAND

COPYRIGHT, 1955, BY MARIA LUISA TAGLIENTI

All rights reserved under International and Pan-American Copyright Conventions. Published in New York by Random House, Inc., and simultaneously in Toronto, Canada, by Random House of Canada, Limited.

LIBRARY OF CONGRESS CATALOG CARD NUMBER: 55-5813

MANUFACTURED IN THE UNITED STATES OF AMERICA

INTRODUCTION

Italians are not only gourmands but also gourmets. Italian gastronomical art was born in the luxury of Imperial Rome, and all through the centuries it has been one of Italy's national treasures. But somehow *grande cuisine*, or the art of fine cooking, is nowadays almost entirely associated with France. Yet, as a matter of fact, it actually stems from Italy, and a wealth of what are thought of as French dishes are really Italian in origin. *The Columbia Encyclopedia* states: "Modern cookery derives from Italy and dates from the Renaissance. When Catherine de' Medici went to Paris she took Italian cooks, and so great was the interest aroused in the revival of an ancient art that noblemen took to cooking, and cooks were enriched and honored."

Catherine de' Medici when leaving Florence in 1533 to become the bride of the Duke of Orléans and the future Queen of France not only brought along Italian cooks, but also a battery of utensils, molds and other items not to be found in France, including the fork. She adored pastry, and many were the delicacies her well-trained chefs prepared for her and the court of France. And I think that she would have felt amused had she been able to foresee that some day in practically every good restaurant in the world trays would be passed bearing, in some instances the originals, in others derivations, of her desserts—and all called "French Pastry!"

Marco Polo and other Italian traders had brought strange and exotic foods and spices from the Orient and the Middle East. Columbus and other Italian and Spanish explorers later brought from the New World tomatoes, potatoes, corn and cocoa, all of which were incorporated into Italian cuisine. It therefore today embraces an outstanding variety of dishes, most of which are still practically unknown outside of Italy. Moreover, each region and each town has developed its own way of preparing food, and in one place one kind of food is naturally more popular than in others. For example, in northern Italy from Milan to Turin to Venice, a greater amount of rice and polenta is consumed than in any other region. Also, in that region, butter is much more used in cooking than olive oil. In Bologna, milk or cream are used more often in the preparation of many dishes than elsewhere. From Rome down to Sicily, tomatoes and garlic are used more frequently in cooking than in the North. However, all Italians use plenty of spices, and wine is in widespread use for seasoning.

This is a collection of recipes from *all* sections of Italy. Some are from famous restaurants, secrets of noted chefs; some are from prized collections of family and friends; and some are from ancient cookbooks long out of print. And, naturally, all classic Italian dishes are included.

The recipes thus gathered from various sources have, when possible, been compared with all of the best Italian cookbooks currently in print in Italy in order to insure the authenticity of every regional specialty. And, as with every recipe in this book, they have been carefully tested and have been set down in a form of measurement and direction that will be familiar to the American housewives and hostesses for whom this book is intended.

Recipes have been simplified and substitutions suggested or made *only* when the preparation or cooking processes were too elaborate or when an occasional ingredient might not be easily obtained. In cases of substitutions, I have made careful and repeated tests of the recipes involved, for it is not my aim in this book ever to give recipes which would result in a pale replica of a savory Italian dish. As an example, in many communities it may not be possible to obtain prosciutto, the Italian cured ham, called for in some recipes. When this is needed in small amounts—such as in a sauce or in veal birds—good lean bacon or Canadian bacon may be used and the taste of the original dish retained. In some of the recipes, the cook may want to alter the amount of seasoning—more basil?, less sage?—and, of course, this is the prerogative of a good cook. Many of the readers will find less of a taste of garlic in most of these recipes than they are accustomed to find in most Italian-American restaurants, which generally feature either Southern Italian or Sicilian specialties, or even less than recipes from some magazines or other cookbooks. I have used garlic as it is generally used by most good cooks in Italy—with discretion. A faint taste of garlic is an asset to many a dish, but when used out of proportion, it tends to smother or kill all other flavors. But for those readers who desire a stronger garlic flavor, by all means use more; and for those who do not take to garlic at all, it can generally be omitted entirely without complete disaster. The same holds true for olive oil. If its taste is not favored, either butter or any good salad oil can easily be substituted.

I have tried in this volume to cover all phases of Italian cooking—from antipasto to desserts and candy making—selecting from the thousands of regional specialties those I felt would appeal most to the American homemaker and her family. I have also included a chapter on wines and a group of menus, including formal dinners and a large buffet selection. In addition, I have thought it well worthwhile to put in a casserole reference page which will enable busy readers to find quickly the pages where these ever more and more popular dishes are located. There, also, I have listed other recipes which, although not strictly casserole, are nonetheless particularly suitable for quick and tasty one-dish meals.

The purpose of this book has been to share with the American cook, homemaker and hostess all my knowledge and to initiate her into the not-so-obscure or difficult mysteries of authentic Italian cooking.

MARIA LUISA TAGLIENTI

CONTENTS

INTRODUCTION	v
Antipasti	3
Soups	17
Sauces	31
Macaroni, Rice and Corn Meal	42
Egg Dishes	75
Fish	79
Meat	89
Poultry	114
Vegetables	127
Salads	146
Pizza, Bread, Rolls and Batters	154
Desserts and Candy	160
Cakes, Pastries, Pies and Icings	181
Coffee	206
Wines	208
Preserved and Pickled Vegetables	212
Jams and Jellies	217
Cheese	220
Menus	222
Casseroles	228
STANDARD MEASUREMENTS	230
INDEX	231
ITALIAN INDEX OF RECIPES	241

ACKNOWLEDGMENTS

In addition to members of my own family, and especially my mother, who furnished me much help and encouragement over the years, I should like to make grateful acknowledgment for valuable suggestions, assistance and contributions to the following: John and Marguerite Fornacca, Luigi Barzini, Jr., Emma Agee Ling, Nina Stroop, Charles Criswell, Shirley Neitlich and Hector Spagna.

M. L. T.

THE ITALIAN COOKBOOK

HORS D'OEUVRES

ANTIPASTI

Truffled Canapés

CROSTINI CALDI AI TARTUFI

- 10 slices French bread, sliced thin (about ¼ inch)
- ¼ pound butter
- ½ cup Heavy White Sauce (page 35)
- 2 ounce can of truffles
- ½ cup grated Parmesan cheese

Cut each slice of bread in half. Sauté bread slices in butter till golden and crisp. Slice truffles very thin and sauté over low flame in the same butter for about 5 minutes. Spread sauce on bread slices, add truffles and sprinkle with Parmesan cheese. Place in 375° oven for about 5 minutes. Serve hot. Serves 4-6.

Rice Croquettes Roman Style

CROCCHETTE DI RISO ALLA ROMANA

- 2 cups rice
- 3 tablespoons ready-cooked tomato sauce
- 4 tablespoons butter
- ½ cup grated Parmesan cheese
- 2 eggs, beaten
- 1 cup diced mozzarella cheese
- about 1½ cups bread crumbs
- 2 cups olive oil

Cook rice in salted boiling water until tender but still firm, about 15 minutes. Drain and let cool. Mix with tomato sauce, butter, Parmesan cheese and eggs. Shape into an oblong croquette by spreading 1 tablespoon of rice in palm of hand; place in the center one piece of mozzarella cheese; top with one tablespoon of rice. Roll in bread crumbs. Repeat until all rice is used. Fry a few at a time in hot oil until golden on all sides. Serve hot as part of antipasto or with meat or fowl. Serves 6-8.

Mozzarella in Carozza

This is a very rich Neapolitan dish.

- 20 slices white bread, one day old
- 10 slices mozzarella cheese about ¼ inch thick (one medium-size mozzarella)
- ½ cup milk
- ½ cup bread crumbs
- 2 eggs, beaten with ½ teaspoon salt
- 1 cup olive oil or butter

To make this dish more attractive, cut bread with metal cookie cutters of different shapes.

Cut two pieces of bread is the same shape. Cut a slice of mozzarella to match. Place slice of mozzarella between two slices of bread. Dip edges of sandwich in milk, then in bread crumbs; dip the entire sandwich in beaten eggs. Fry in hot oil or butter in 5-inch frying pan. If you use a larger frying pan, use more oil or butter. The fat in the frying pan should be nearly an inch deep, or enough to cover sandwich. Fry a few at a time till golden. If necessary, turn sandwich over with the help of two forks and fry on other side. Remove and place on a piece of paper towel until all are fried, then serve immediately in hot serving dish. Serves 6.

Miniature Pizza di Sciullo

PIZZA ALLA DI SCIULLO

- 2 cups sifted flour
- ½ teaspoon salt
- 1 teaspoon yeast dissolved in ¼ cup lukewarm water
- 1 egg
- 2 tablespoons butter
- ¼ cup and 1 tablespoon milk at room temperature
- ½ cup finely diced mozzarella cheese (any mild white cheese may be substituted)
- 8 anchovy fillets, chopped fine
- ¾ cup sliced fresh mushrooms
- 1 ripe tomato, diced fine
- ½ teaspoon oregano or 1 tablespoon finely chopped parsley (optional)
- about ½ cup olive oil
- salt and pepper

Sift flour and salt together. Place in mixing bowl and cut

in butter. Make a depression in middle of flour and in it place yeast mixture, egg and milk. Beat with fork, gradually working in flour. When ¾ of flour is used begin to mix with hands. Place dough on floured board and knead until smooth. Remove to a floured bowl, cover with damp towel and let stand for 2 hours. Roll dough on floured board into a strip not more than ⅓ inch thick. Cut dough into circles 2 inches in diameter or use metal cookie cutters of different shapes. Place on greased baking sheets about 1½ inches apart. Brush top of each pizza with a little olive oil. Cover top of each with a few pieces of mozzarella cheese, tomato, anchovy fillets and mushrooms. Sprinkle lightly with salt and pepper, add oregano or parsley and rest of olive oil. Bake in 400° oven for 10 to 12 minutes. Pizza should be light golden in color. Makes about 24 miniature pizzas. Serve with drinks.

(*Recipe from Ristorante Cavaletto & Doge Orseolo, Venice*)

Deviled Eggs

UOVA PICCANTI

- 6 hard-boiled eggs
- 6 anchovy fillets, chopped
- 1 tablespoon chopped parsley
- ½ teaspoon horseradish
- 4 tablespoons seafood cocktail sauce
- 2 tablespoons mayonnaise
- ¼ teaspoon vinegar
- salt and pepper

Peel eggs and cut lengthwise. Mash the yolks, season with salt and pepper, and mix with rest of ingredients. Place mixture in pastry bag or cookie press and refill the whites. Chill slightly. Use as part of antipasto or as canapés.

Eggs with Pâté

UOVA CON PÂTÉ

- 6 hard-boiled eggs
- 3 tablespoons purée de foie gras (liver pâté) with truffle
- 2 tablespoons whipped sweet butter
- 2 tablespoons mayonnaise

Peel eggs and cut lengthwise. Mash the yolks, season with salt and pepper and mix with butter, mayonnaise and liver pâté. Fill the egg whites with this mixture. Chill. Use as part of antipasto or as canapés.

Pickled Eggs

UOVA SOTTO ACETO

- 1 dozen large hard-boiled eggs
- 1½ quarts wine vinegar
- 8 peppercorns
- ⅓ teaspoon crushed red pepper
- 2 small onions, peeled and sliced
- 1 clove garlic
- ½ teaspoon rosemary
- ½ teaspoon salt
- 4 one pint jars

Place vinegar in saucepan with peppercorns, red pepper, onions, garlic, rosemary and salt. Bring to a boil and cook for 10 minutes. Peel eggs carefully so as not to break or bruise. Place four eggs in each jar, sterilized in advance, strain the vinegar and pour over eggs. Seal jars and store in cool place. Let stand one week before using. These eggs are delicious as part of antipasto. Chill before serving. Serves 6-12.

Stuffed Eggs with Anchovies

UOVA ACCIUGATE

- 6 hard-boiled eggs
- 5 anchovy fillets, mashed
- 1½ tablespoons butter
- 1 tablespoon finely chopped parsley
- 2 tablespoons mayonnaise
- pinch of pepper

Peel eggs and cut them in half lengthwise. Mash the yolks and add anchovies, butter, parsley and mayonnaise. Mix into a smooth paste and refill the whites with mixture. Serve slightly chilled. Use as part of antipasto or as canapés.

Veal in Tuna Sauce

VITELLO TONNATO

- 2 pounds boneless leg of veal
- ¾ cup canned tuna in olive oil
- 1 onion, chopped fine
- 8 anchovy fillets, chopped
- 2 cups dry white wine
- ⅓ cup olive oil
- juice of two lemons
- 2 tablespoons minced pickles
- salt and pepper to taste

Tie meat to hold it in shape. Place in saucepan together with tuna, onion, anchovies, salt, pepper and wine. Cover and cook over low flame for about 1 hour and 45 minutes.

Remove meat to a bowl. Put ingredients left in saucepan through a sieve. Add the oil, lemon juice and pickles. Pour over meat, cover and place in refrigerator for two days. Serve at room temperature, sliced thin, with some of the marinade. Serves 8.

Pork in Tuna Sauce

MAIALE TONNATO

2 pounds lean boned pork
¾ cup canned tuna in olive oil
1 onion, peeled and chopped
8 anchovy fillets, chopped
2 cups dry white wine
¼ cup olive oil
juice of 2 lemons
3 tablespoons mixed Italian pickles (optional)
salt and pepper to taste

Place meat in saucepan together with tuna, onion, anchovies, salt, pepper and wine. Cover and cook over low flame for 2 hours. Remove meat to a bowl. Put ingredients left in saucepan through a sieve and add to them the oil, lemon juice and pickles. Pour over meat, cover and let stand overnight. Serve at room temperature sliced very thin. This will keep in refrigerator for more than a week. Serves 8.

Snails Marchigiana

LUMACHE ALLA MARCHIGIANA

1 pound live snails
salt
vinegar
2 tablespoons olive oil
2 tablespoons butter
¼ cup chopped onion
2 cloves of garlic, minced
1 cup dry white wine
¼ teaspoon thyme
2 tablespoons tomato paste diluted in ½ cup water
salt and pepper to taste

Place snails in large bowl or pan of cold water with 1 tablespoon salt and one of vinegar. Stir with hands. Repeat operation, changing water four times or until water is clear. Rinse snails in clear water. Place them in pan of cold water over high flame, bring to a boil and cook for 10 minutes, skimming foam from top. Drain and cool. Remove snails from shells. Discard shells and rinse snails in cold water. Cut each snail in two. Sauté onion and garlic in a mixture of oil and butter. Add wine and snails. Cover and simmer for 20 minutes. Add tomato paste, thyme, salt and pepper to taste, and simmer 30 minutes longer. Serve hot on toast. Serves 4.

Saint John's Snails

LUMACHE DI SAN GIOVANNI

A traditional Roman dish. On the night of June 21st, Romans celebrate the feast of Saint John with songs, wine, music and snails. The snails bought at fish markets have gone through the period of purging.

1 pound live snails	1 cup tomato paste diluted in 3 cups water
salt	
vinegar	5 leaves of fresh mint, or ½ teaspoon dried mint
¼ cup olive oil	
1 large clove of garlic	⅛ teaspoon crushed red pepper
4 anchovy fillets, chopped	
	salt and pepper to taste

Sauté garlic in oil, discarding garlic when golden. Add anchovies, tomato paste, water and mint. Simmer for 30 minutes. In the meantime, place snails in large bowl or pan of cold water with 1 tablespoon of salt and one of vinegar. Stir with hands. Repeat operation, changing water four times or until water is clear. Rinse snails in clear water. Place them in pan of cold water over high flame. Bring to a boil and cook for 10 minutes, skimming foam from top. Drain and cool. Remove snails from shells and rinse both in cold water. Drain.

Season tomato mixture with salt and pepper to taste and add crushed red pepper and snails. Simmer for 30 minutes. Remove snails from sauce, place back in shells, return to sauce and serve hot. Serves 4.

Prosciutto and Melon

PROSCIUTTO CON MELLONE

2 cantaloupes, iced   ½ pound prosciutto, sliced very thin

Cut cantaloupe in half and remove seeds. Pare off rind and slice each cantaloupe into ten slices. Place 4 slices of cantaloupe on each plate and cover with slices of prosciutto. Serve with chilled dry white wine. Serves 5.

Cantaloupe Rolled in Prosciutto

FAGOTTINI DI MELLONE E PROSCIUTTO

1 medium-size cantaloupe, iced   ½ pound prosciutto, sliced very thin

Cut melon into 4 wedges, remove seeds and peel. Cut each wedge into 1-1½ inch squares, wrap a slice or half a slice of prosciutto around each wedge, secure with a toothpick and serve. An ideal dish to serve with cocktails in hot weather. Serves 6.

Oysters Veneziana

OSTRICHE ALLA VENEZIANA

2 dozen oysters
black pepper
juice of 2 lemons
caviar
2 lemons cut into wedges
parsley

Clean oyster shells thoroughly. Open oysters and remove from shell. Rinse shells and oysters separately in cold salted water. Drain and place oyster in deep half of shell. Sprinkle lightly with lemon juice and pepper. Surround the meat in each shell with about one teaspoon of caviar. Arrange oysters on 4 plates of cracked ice. Decorate each dish with lemon wedges and sprigs of parsley. Serves 4.

Molded Tuna

SFORMATO DI TONNO

1 7-ounce can of salmon
2 7-ounce cans of tuna fish
¼ cup melted butter
¼ cup heavy cream
3 eggs, lightly beaten
½ teaspoon black pepper
1 tablespoon parsley, chopped fine
1 cup Mayonnaise with Gelatine (page 37)
1 hard-boiled egg
1 teaspoon capers
1 black truffle, sliced thin

Drain salmon and remove skin and bones. Drain tuna. Place fish in large mixing bowl. Mash thoroughly with fork. Add butter, cream, eggs, pepper and parsley. Beat with rotary beater or electric beater till you have a smooth paste (5 minutes by hand or 2 minutes by electric beater at potato-mashing speed). Place fish mixture in top of double boiler, which has been greased and the bottom lined with greased waxed paper. Level off top with a spoon. Cook over boiling water for about 1 hour and 20 minutes. Remove from stove and let cool. When fish is at room temperature remove carefully from double boiler as you would a cake. Place on serving dish and remove waxed paper. Place in refrigerator for an hour. Cover sides and top with 2/3 of the mayonnaise. Decorate with the rest of mayonnaise, using cake decorator. Decorate with a few capers, slices of hard-boiled egg and black truffle. Place in refrigerator for 1½ hours before serving. Serve cut in wedges. Serves 8.

Mussels in Anchovy Sauce

COZZE ACCIUGATE

- 4 dozen mussels
- ½ cup olive oil
- 2 cloves garlic
- 8 anchovy fillets, chopped
- 1 cup dry white wine
- 1 cup wine vinegar
- ¼ cup parsley, chopped
- ¼ teaspoon black pepper

Scrub mussels thoroughly. Open shells with a knife. Rinse in cold salted water, if necessary removing and discarding the horny "beard." Drain. Sauté garlic in oil in large saucepan. Remove garlic when golden; do not allow to brown. Add mussels and anchovies. Cook over medium flame, covered, for 8 minutes. Add wine and vinegar. Cook uncovered for 5 to 7 minutes longer. Liquid should be reduced by more than half. Add parsley and pepper. Cool. Place in refrigerator in large covered bowl for 24 to 36 hours. Serve chilled with the sauce. Serves 4.

Eels Marinara

MARINARA DI ANGUILLA

- 2 pounds eels, skinned and cut into 2½ inch pieces
- 2 slices onion, minced
- 1 clove garlic, chopped
- 1 bay leaf
- 3 tablespoons brandy
- red wine as needed
- ½ pound fresh sliced mushrooms boiled in salted water for 5 minutes
- 12 very small onions, boiled
- 1 tablespoon flour
- 4 tablespoons butter
- salt and pepper to taste

Place garlic, chopped onion and bay leaf in saucepan together with eels. Place over low flame; as soon as pan is hot, add brandy. After 2 minutes add enough red wine to cover eels. Simmer uncovered for 20 minutes. Place butter in saucepan over low flame, stir in flour and mix into a smooth paste. Drain eels and add to butter in saucepan, together with boiled onions, mushrooms, salt and pepper to taste; simmer for 5 minutes, stirring occasionally. Serve hot. Serves 4.

Eels Carpionata

ANGUILLA CARPIONATA

- 2 large eels, about 1 pound each
- 2½ tablespoons olive oil
- 4 black peppercorns
- 3½ cups wine vinegar
- 2 large cloves of garlic
- ½ teaspoon rosemary
- 4 cloves
- 4 small bay leaves
- ½ teaspoon salt
- salt and pepper

Have eels cleaned and cut crosswise in 3-inch pieces. Discard heads. Rinse thoroughly in cold water and dry. Place in single layer in large baking pan which has been greased with the oil, together with 2 bay leaves. Sprinkle lightly with salt and pepper. Bake at 300° for one hour, turning eels occasionally. Remove to a bowl. Place vinegar, salt, 4 peppercorns, 2 bay leaves, garlic, rosemary and cloves in saucepan, bring to a boil and boil for 2 minutes. Pour hot vinegar over eels. Cover and marinate for 3 days before using, turning eels occasionally. Delicious as antipasto.

Pepper Relish

PEPERONATA

- 2 pounds yellow or green sweet peppers
- 1 pound ripe Italian egg tomatoes or regular tomatoes, peeled and diced
- 1 pound onions, peeled and sliced
- ¼ cup olive oil
- ¾ cup wine vinegar
- 1 teaspoon salt

Remove stems and seeds from peppers and slice lengthwise into 8 slices. Rinse. Place peppers, tomatoes, onions, salt and oil in saucepan. Cover and simmer for one hour, stirring occasionally. Add vinegar, and simmer uncovered until excess liquid has evaporated. Place in bowl or jar, cover and keep in refrigerator for 2 days before using. Serve cold as part of antipasto, or with cold roast meats. Will keep in refrigerator for more than a week. Serves 6.

Sicilian Eggplant Relish

CAPONATINA ALLA SICILIANA

- 6 cups eggplant, peeled and diced
- 2 cups celery, diced
- ½ cup olive oil
- 2 tablespoons olive oil
- 1 large onion, minced
- ⅓ cup wine vinegar
- 1 tablespoon sugar
- 2 tablespoons tomato paste diluted in 1 cup water
- 1 tablespoon capers
- 1 dozen large green olives, pitted and coarsely chopped
- 1 tablespoon parsley, chopped

Sauté celery in ½ cup olive oil for 7 minutes, stirring occasionally. Remove celery, add eggplant to oil in skillet and sauté for 10 minutes, or until lightly golden, stirring often. Remove eggplant to a plate covered with paper toweling or other clean absorbent paper. Sauté onion in 2 tablespoons olive oil until soft. Do not brown. Add vinegar, sugar, diluted tomato paste, cover and simmer for 15-20 minutes. Add eggplant, celery, parsley, olives, capers, salt and pepper to taste, cover and simmer for 10 more minutes. Serve cold with roast meats and fowl, or as part of antipasto. If stored in refrigerator in a covered container, it will keep for a week or ten days. Serves 6.

Salmon-Stuffed Tomatoes

POMODORI RIPIENI DI SALMONE

- 8 large ripe firm tomatoes
- 1 tablespoon wine vinegar
- 1 pound canned salmon or tuna, well drained and chilled
- 4 tablespoons whipped sweet butter
- 3 heaping tablespoons Mayonnaise (page 37)
- 1 teaspoon lemon juice
- 1 bunch parsley
- salt and pepper to taste

Remove from the stem end of each tomato a slice about ½ inch thick. Remove carefully the center of each tomato, taking care not to break the wall. Sprinkle the inside of each lightly with salt, pepper and vinegar, and place in refrigerator for 45 minutes. Then turn them upside down to drain. This will take only 10 to 15 minutes. In the meantime, blend into a smooth paste the salmon, butter, Mayonnaise and lemon juice. Stuff tomatoes with salmon mixture and sprinkle top of each with a little chopped parsley. Arrange tomatoes on large platter on a bed of parsley, and serve. Serves 8.

Cheese Puffs

BIGNÈ AL FORMAGGIO

½ recipe Cream Puff Paste (page 191)
⅓ cup grated Parmesan cheese
¼ cup prosciutto, minced
1 cup olive oil

Blend cheese and prosciutto with Puff Paste, then drop batter in hot olive oil by the teaspoonful. Fry until light brown. These can be served with drinks, also with roast meats, or, when made smaller (about ⅛ of a teaspoon of batter of each puff), they can be served with a clear chicken or beef consommé. Makes about 2 dozen large puffs and about 3 dozen small ones.

Parmesan Cream Spread

CREMA DI PARMIGIANO

1 cup heavy cream, beaten stiff
4 tablespoons freshly grated Parmesan cheese
2 small white or black truffles, minced fine

Blend Parmesan with whipped cream, then pile mixture in center of a large round platter, and sprinkle evenly with truffles. More cheese should be used if a stronger flavor is desired. Arrange cheeses and crackers all around it. This makes an unusual looking dish; cream filling can also be used on canapés or for sandwiches.

Gorgonzola Cream Spread

CREMA DI GORGONZOLA

¼ pound Gorgonzola cheese   ¼ pound whipped sweet butter

Remove rind from Gorgonzola and place it in a bowl together with butter and beat with electric beater or pastry blender until a creamy smooth mixture is obtained. Place in any small mold lined with waxed paper and place in refrigerator until ready to use. Remove cheese from refrigerator, invert mold on serving dish, carefully removing waxed paper. Serve with crackers, or use for canapés.

Chicken Liver Spread

FEGATO DI POLLO

½ pound chicken livers, diced
½ pound best quality salt pork, minced
1 tablespoon onion, minced
1½ tablespoons parsley, minced
¼ teaspoon poultry seasoning
⅛ teaspoon freshly ground black pepper
salt to taste

Place salt pork in small skillet and sauté gently until it has expelled as much fat as possible. Add chicken livers and brown over medium high flame, stirring constantly. Add rest of ingredients and sauté gently for 2 minutes. Let cool completely, put mixture through a food chopper, then through a sieve. Keep in refrigerator, covered, until ready to use. Delicious as a canapé spread or for stuffing game. After the mixture has been put through a sieve, one or two minced black truffles may be added. Makes about 1½ cups.

Canapé Suggestions

1. Split Sandwich Rolls (page 157) and spread with whipped sweet butter, then top with one or two anchovy fillets (preserved in olive oil) for each roll.
2. After spreading rolls with whipped sweet butter, fill with a slice of mortadella (a kind of bologna) or ham or prosciutto and one of mozzarella, cut the same size as the roll.

3. Spread Sandwich Rolls with Parmesan Cream Spread (page 13) or Gorgonzola Cream Spread (page 14).
4. Spread Sandwich Rolls with whipped sweet butter and Chicken Liver Spread (page 14).

Antipasto Platter

- 1 recipe Bread Sticks (page 157) or 2 dozen store-bought bread sticks
- 1 pound prosciutto, sliced very thin
- 2 recipes Deviled Eggs (page 5)
- 1 recipe Eels Carpionata (page 11)
- 2 dozen Artichoke Hearts in Olive Oil (page 215)
- 2 dozen olives
- 3 small finocchi (fennel), cleaned and cut in wedges

Break each bread stick in two, then wrap a slice of prosciutto around each half. If slices of prosciutto are too long, cut in half. Sliced prosciutto should be just long enough to go around the bread sticks one-and-a-half times. Arrange ingredients on two large platters and serve slightly chilled. Serves 6.

Fritto Misto

This is one of the classic, tasty Italian dishes, consisting of vegetables, meats and croquettes, all either rolled in flour and dipped in beaten eggs, or dipped in a batter and then deep-fried in hot fat. It is served as an antipasto or as a main dish, each group offered separately piled on a round platter with parsley and lemon wedges all around.

- 1 recipe Potato Croquettes
- 1 recipe Fried Cauliflower
- 1 recipe Golden Artichokes
- 1 recipe Fried Apples
- 1 recipe Rice Croquettes Roman Style
- 1 recipe Mozzarella in Carrozza
- 1 pound chicken livers, rolled in flour, dipped in a beaten egg and fried in deep fat
- 1 pound small shrimps, rolled in flour, dipped in a beaten egg and fried in deep fat

This quantity serves 8 as an antipasto and 4-6 as a main dish. The above is a basic assortment. In Rome one or more kinds of small fish are added, such as tiny cuttlefish, or fresh sardines, whiting, etc., and thick Pasticcera Cream (page 168), cut in small squares, rolled in bread crumbs and fried like everything else. In Milan calf liver, brains, sweetbreads and cockscombs are added. Also other vegetables, like zucchini, eggplant, celery, etc. may be added or used instead of some of the other ingredients. A *fritto misto* can be made with as few or as many ingredients as desired.

Bagna Cauda

A famous sauce of Piedmont that literally means "hot bath" because raw vegetables such as celery, carrots, endive, peppers and especially cardoons are dipped or bathed in it while the sauce is hot.

The original recipe calls for butter (or half butter and half olive oil), garlic, anchovies and white truffles, but many people in Italy add some heavy cream or, in summer, even some basil leaves. I have found that this cream version is more popular with gourmets in the United States. More garlic may be used if desired.

Bagna Cauda not only makes a tasty, varied and unusual antipasto, but it also will garner superlatives when served with cocktails or drinks.

¼ pound butter	1 canned white truffle the size of a walnut, minced (optional)
2 large cloves garlic	
8 anchovy fillets, finely minced	1 cup heavy cream, scalded

Place butter and garlic in small saucepan and simmer for five minutes. Do not allow garlic or butter to brown. Remove garlic. Add anchovies and mix with a wooden spoon until mixture is well blended. Add truffles and scalded cream. Blend and serve. It is very important to keep sauce hot while it is being served. A small chafing dish over a low flame or even a coffee warmer is ideal. The above recipe is enough for 3 hearts of celery; 4 large carrots, sliced lengthwise; 2 endive; 1 bunch cardoons; 2 green or red sweet peppers, cleaned and sliced in thin strips.

All vegetables should be crisp. (Cardoons are young and tender artichoke plants. They should be cut in 4-inch pieces and placed in a bowl of cold water to which the juice of two lemons has been added for at least one hour before serving.)

Bread sticks dipped in the hot sauce are also delicious.

SOUPS

MINESTRE

Beef Broth

BRODO DI MANZO

2 pounds lean beef
1 pound soup bones
2 carrots
1 small turnip
2 leeks
1 stalk celery
3 sprigs parsley
1 teaspoon tomato paste
salt and pepper to taste

Place meat and bones in 4 quarts cold water. Bring slowly to a boil, remove scum, cover and simmer for 2 hours. Add vegetables, season to taste, cover and simmer for one more hour. Strain broth before using. Makes about 9 cups.

Chicken and Beef Broth

BRODO MISTO

1 pound boneless, lean beef
1 pound chicken necks and backs
1 pound soup bones
1 stalk celery
3 sprigs parsley
2 carrots
1 leek
2 very ripe Italian egg tomatoes, peeled and diced (optional) or 1 tablespoon tomato juice
3½ quarts water
salt and pepper to taste

Place meat and bones in cold water. Bring slowly to boiling point, remove scum, cover and simmer for 2 hours. Then add vegetables, season to taste, cover and simmer for one hour more. Strain before using. Makes about 2 quarts.

Egg Bows in Broth

BRODO CON TRIPOLINI

4 cups chicken or beef broth
¾ cup small egg bows (Tripolini)

2 tablespoons grated Parmesan cheese

Cook egg bows in one quart of salted water for 10 to 12 minutes. Meanwhile scald broth. When egg bows are cooked, drain and add to broth. Sprinkle with cheese. Serves 4.

Broth with Egg Flakes

BRODO CON TAGLIARINI

1 cup chicken broth per serving

½ tablespoon egg flakes per serving

Bring chicken broth to a boil. Add egg flakes and cook 3 or 4 minutes more.

Broth with Toasted Croutons

BRODO CON CROSTINI

8 cups of broth (beef or chicken), well seasoned
4 slices white toast

4 tablespoons grated Parmesan cheese

Cut toast into ½-inch squares. Bring broth to a boil, then pour into soup dishes and add toast squares. Sprinkle with cheese and serve immediately. Serves 6-8.

Egg Drop Soup

STRACCIATELLA

6 cups beef or chicken broth
3 large eggs, separated

4 tablespoons grated Parmesan cheese
dash nutmeg (optional)

Beat egg whites until almost stiff. Fold in yolks, cheese and nutmeg. Bring broth to a boil and add egg mixture. Remove from stove immediately. Serves 6.

Soup Pavese Style

ZUPPA ALLA PAVESE

4 slices white toast, buttered
4 eggs
2 tablespoons grated Parmesan cheese
4 cups beef or chicken broth, very hot

Place slices of toast in four individual casseroles. Break egg on top of each slice, sprinkle with ½ tablespoon cheese and add broth. Place in 375° oven for about 7 minutes or until eggs look lightly poached. Serves 4.

Onion Soup

ZUPPA DI CIPOLLE

4 medium-size onions, sliced fine
3 tablespoons butter
1½ cups water
5 cups milk or broth
2 eggs, beaten
4 tablespoons grated Parmesan cheese
3 slices white bread, toasted and diced
salt and pepper to taste

Gently sauté onion in butter, until soft but *not* brown. Add water and simmer slowly until ¾ of water has evaporated. Put onion with pan juice through a fine sieve, return to saucepan, add milk or broth and simmer until it comes to a boil. Season to taste. Place eggs and cheese in a tureen, add onion soup and serve with diced toast. Serves 6-8.

Mushroom Soup

ZUPPA DI FUNGHI

1 pound mushrooms, sliced thin
2 slices bacon, minced
2½ tablespoons butter
1 tablespoon parsley, chopped
1 egg, beaten
¼ cup grated Parmesan cheese
6 cups chicken or beef broth
salt and pepper to taste

Sauté bacon with butter and parsley until bacon is slightly crisp. Add mushrooms and simmer for 5 minutes. Place broth in saucepan and bring to a boil, then add mushrooms, season to taste, and simmer for 15 minutes more. Place egg and cheese in a tureen, blend, add soup and serve. Serves 6-8.

Potato Soup

ZUPPA DI PATATE

- 3 slices of bacon, minced
- 2 pounds potatoes, peeled and diced
- 1 large onion, sliced fine
- 2 cups water
- 2½ cups hot broth or milk
- salt and pepper to taste
- parsley (optional)

Place bacon, onion and potatoes in saucepan with water. Bring to a boil, cover and simmer for 20 minutes or until potatoes are very tender. Put through a sieve, add to them the water in which they have been cooked, milk or broth and salt and pepper to taste. Place over low flame and bring to a boil. Serve sprinkled lightly with minced parsley if desired. Serves 6-8.

Caps Romagnola Style

CAPPELLETTI ALLA ROMAGNOLA

DOUGH:
- 2 cups sifted flour
- 2 eggs
- ¼ cup water
- ½ teaspoon salt

STUFFING:
- ½ breast of a 4-pound broiler, sautéed in butter and put through a food chopper
- ⅔ cup ricotta cheese
- 2 tablespoons freshly grated Parmesan cheese
- 2 egg yolks
- 1 egg white
- ⅛ teaspoon nutmeg
- ⅛ teaspoon grated lemon peel
- salt and pepper to taste
- 2½ quarts chicken broth

Mix all ingredients for stuffing into a smooth paste. Place in refrigerator till ready to use.

Place flour on board. Make depression in center and place eggs, water and salt in it. With fork gradually beat eggs and water with flour till about one half the flour is used up. Add remaining flour by hand and knead into a smooth firm paste. If dough is too soft, add a little flour. Knead for 10 minutes. Cut dough in two and roll out on floured board into two very thin round sheets. With a round cookie cutter about 2¼ or 2½ inches in diameter, cut both sheets of dough, wasting as little dough as possible. Place ¼ teaspoon of stuffing in center of each disk of dough. Dampen edge of disk facing you with finger dipped in water. Fold disk, closing in stuffing, by pressing with finger tips. Bring the two corners together and, if necessary, dampen one corner lightly with wet finger to make it stick. Repeat this operation (see illustration) till all

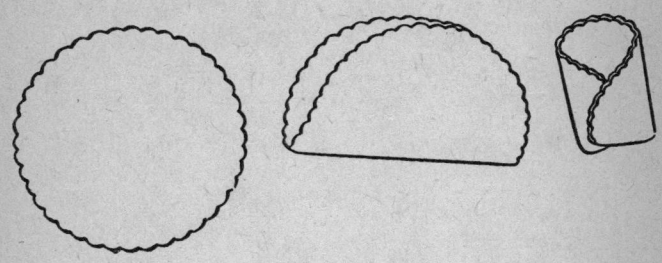

ingredients are used (makes about two dozen caps). Bring broth to boiling point, add cappelletti and cook 15 to 20 minutes. Serves 8. It is quite possible that a few tablespoons of stuffing will be left over, depending on the thickness of the dough sheets. If desired, the filling left over can be used as a spread for canapés.

The cappelletti can be made in advance and kept in refrigerator between sheets of waxed paper, until ready to cook. This soup is usually served during the Christmas holidays.

Fondue, Piedmont Style

FONDUTA ALLA PIEMONTESE

Fonduta is a delicious Piedmontese soup. The original recipe calls for Fontina, a cheese from Piedmont exported to this country, but when Fontina is not available, Swiss or Muenster cheese can be substituted.

1 pound imported Fontina cheese, diced	⅛ teaspoon white pepper
5 egg yolks	2 canned white truffles, size of a walnut, minced fine, or sliced paper thin
milk	
4 tablespoons butter	4 slices of toast, diced

Place cheese in bowl, add enough milk to cover and let stand overnight. Then place cheese and milk in double boiler. Water in bottom of double boiler should be hot but not boiling. Beat with egg beater or stir vigorously with wooden spoon until cheese is dissolved. Then stir in yolks and pepper and cook for another minute or two, stirring constantly. Fonduta should have the consistency of thick cream. Correct seasoning and serve with diced toast, sprinkled with truffles. Serves 6.

Spinach Soup

MINESTRA DI SPINACI

1 pound fresh spinach, cleaned or 1 package frozen spinach	1 tablespoon flour
3 tablespoons butter	1 quart milk
	½ cup heavy cream

Cook spinach in salted boiling water until tender. Drain and put through a sieve. Melt butter in saucepan, blend in flour and add milk. Bring to a boil, add spinach, heavy cream and salt to taste. Bring to a boil and serve. May be served with croutons of Cheese Puffs (page 13). Serves 6.

Minestrone Milanese

- ¼ pound butter
- ⅓ cup diced salt pork
- 1 onion, chopped
- 2 medium-size potatoes, diced
- 1 large carrot, diced
- ⅓ cup diced celery
- 2 small zucchini, diced
- ½ head of small cabbage, shredded
- ½ pound red kidney beans, soaked overnight in cold water, or ½ pound fresh shell beans, shelled
- 3 quarts beef broth
- 1 cup uncooked rice
- 1 level tablespoon parsley, chopped
- 1 clove garlic, chopped very fine
- 1 leaf sweet basil or ⅛ teaspoon dried basil
- ¼ teaspoon powdered thyme
- ⅓ cup grated Parmesan cheese

Sauté onion with salt pork in 5 tablespoons butter in large saucepan. Do not allow onions to brown. Add carrot, celery, zucchini, cabbage and beans. Cover and simmer 15 minutes, stirring occasionally. Add broth and potatoes and cook slowly for 1½ hours if using fresh beans, or 3 hours for dry beans. If soup becomes too thick add a little water. Add rice and cook for 10 minutes over high flame. Add parsley, garlic, basil and thyme. Cook 8 minutes more. Remove from stove, add rest of ingredients and serve. Serves 6-8.

(*Recipe from Caffè Ristorante Savini, Milan*)

Cauliflower Soup No. 1

MINESTRA DI CAVOLFIORE NO. 1

1 small cauliflower	3 quarts beef or chicken broth or water
¼ cup prosciutto, minced or ¼ cup salt pork, minced or ¼ cup bacon, minced	1 cup ditali, cut spaghetti or small macaroni
¼ cup olive oil	⅓ cup grated Parmesan cheese
1 small onion, chopped	salt and pepper to taste
1 tablespoon tomato paste	

Remove leaves of cauliflower and cut off any bruised or dirty spots. Place it top downward in a deep bowl of cold salted water for half an hour. Drain and break cauliflower into flowerets. Sauté onion with prosciutto (or salt pork or bacon) in oil in a large saucepan. Add tomato paste dissolved in ⅓ cup broth or water. Let it simmer for 5 minutes. Add cauliflower and simmer for 10 minutes more. Add broth or water, cover and cook for 30 to 45 minutes. Season to taste. Add spaghetti and cook till tender, about 10 minutes. Serve sprinkled with cheese. Serves 4.

Cauliflower Soup No. 2

MINESTRA DI CAVOLFIORE NO. 2

8 cups beef or chicken broth	4 tablespoons freshly grated Parmesan cheese
1 cauliflower, about 2½ pounds	3 egg yolks
1 recipe Thin White Sauce (page 35)	salt and pepper to taste

Remove leaves from cauliflower, leaving the very small tender ones. Break cauliflower into flowerets and rinse well in cold water. Place cauliflower and broth in pan, cover and simmer for 45 minutes. Remove cauliflower from broth and put through a fine sieve. Replace it in broth together with seasoning, White Sauce and the cheese. Bring to a boil, remove from stove and add well-beaten egg yolks, stirring constantly. Serve immediately. Serves 6.

Lentil Soup

MINESTRA DI LENTICCHIE

½ pound dried lentils, soaked overnight
2½ quarts water
rind from one pound of salt pork
1 teaspoon tomato paste
½ cup ditalini macaroni
salt and pepper

Wash lentils. Cook until tender (about 2 hours) in 2½ quarts water to which the tomato paste and pork rind have been added. Add salt and pepper to taste. Remove rind when lentils are soft. Add more water or milk if necessary. Add ditalini macaroni and cook 10 minutes. Serves 4-6.

Shell Bean Soup

MINESTRA DI FAGIOLI FRESCHI

1 slice prosciutto, minced (optional)
5 tablespoons olive oil
1 clove garlic
½ onion, minced
¼ cup diced celery
2 basil leaves or ⅛ teaspoon dried basil
½ pound Italian egg tomatoes, peeled and diced
2 pounds shell beans
1½ cup ditali macaroni
½ cup grated Parmesan cheese
salt and pepper to taste

Shell beans. Place prosciutto, garlic, onion and olive oil in large suacepan. Sauté gently until garlic is golden. Discard garlic. Add tomatoes, celery and basil. Simmer, stirring occasionally for 8 to 10 minutes. Add beans and 3 quarts water. Cover and cook slowly for about 1½ hours or until beans are very tender, adding more water if necessary. Season with salt and pepper. Add ditali macaroni and cook for 10 to 12 minutes, stirring occasionally. Serve sprinkled with cheese. Serves 6-8.

Bean Soup Venetian Style

PASTA E FAGIOLI ALLA VENETA

- 1 cup white beans soaked in cold water overnight
- 1 beef marrow bone about 5 inches long
- ¼ cup olive oil
- 2 cloves of garlic
- 2 tablespoons fresh parsley, chopped
- ⅓ teaspoon rosemary
- 1 tablespoon flour
- 1 tablespoon tomato paste diluted in ⅓ cup lukewarm water
- 1 cup ditalini macaroni
- salt and pepper to taste

Place beans and marrow bone in 3½ quarts cold water, cover and cook for 1½ hours. Sauté garlic, parsley and rosemary in oil, and add flour, stirring constantly. Simmer for 6 minutes. Add tomato paste. Simmer for 10 minutes, stirring. Remove garlic and add sauce to beans together with salt and pepper. Simmer 2 hours more, until beans are cooked. Remove marrow bone. (Add more water if soup is too thick.) Add ditalini macaroni, cook for 10 to 12 minutes, stirring occasionally. Remove from stove and let stand 20 minutes. Warm soup before serving. Serves 4.

Bean Soup

MINESTRA DI FAGIOLI

- ½ pound dry red kidney beans, soaked overnight in cold water
- 1 onion
- 1 carrot
- 6 cups beef broth
- ¾ cup heavy cream
- yolk of one egg, beaten
- salt and pepper to taste

Cook beans, onion and carrot in small amount of salted water, for 3 hours. Drain. Put beans, onion and carrot through a fine sieve. Place in pan with broth. Let boil for 3 or 4 minutes. Add egg and cream, salt and pepper, stirring constantly. Remove from stove immediately. Soup can be served with croutons. Serves 6-8.

Cabbage and Rice Lombardy Style

VERZATA DI RISO ALLA LOMBARDA

- 1 cup rice
- 1 small new cabbage (about 3 pounds), cleaned and diced
- ⅓ cup salt pork, chopped to a pulp (bacon can be substituted)
- 2 tablespoons butter
- 3 large very ripe tomatoes, peeled and diced or one 10-ounce can peeled tomatoes, drained and diced
- 2 tablespoons parsley, finely chopped
- 1 clove garlic
- 1½ quarts beef or chicken broth
- ⅓ cup freshly grated Parmesan cheese
- salt and pepper to taste

Place salt pork and butter in large saucepan. Cook over medium flame for about 5 minutes, stirring occasionally. Add tomatoes, parsley and garlic. Simmer for 10 minutes. Remove garlic and add cabbage. Cover and simmer for 20 minutes. Add broth, salt and pepper to taste, cover and simmer for one hour. If necessary, add a little water. Add rice and simmer for 18 to 20 minutes more. Serve sprinkled with cheese. Serves 6-8.

Rice and Turnip Soup

RISO E RAPE

- 3 tablespoons butter
- 4 tablespoons salt pork, finely chopped or 4 slices bacon, finely chopped
- 2 pounds small white turnips, peeled and diced
- 1 teaspoon salt
- 2 tablespoons fresh parsley, chopped
- 2½ quarts chicken or beef broth, well seasoned
- 1 cup rice
- ⅛ teaspoon black pepper
- ½ cup grated Parmesan cheese

Rinse turnips in cold water and drain. Place butter, salt pork or bacon and turnips in large saucepan. Simmer for 5 minutes, stirring occasionally. Add salt and parsley and cook another minute. Add broth, cover and cook over low flame for about 20 minutes, or till turnips are tender. Add rice and pepper and cook for 15 to 18 minutes more, stirring occasionally. Correct seasoning. Skim part of fat from top. Serve sprinkled with Parmesan cheese. **Serves 6-8.**

Rice and Potato Soup

RISO E PATATE

- 3 tablespoons salt pork, finely chopped
- 3 tablespoons olive oil
- ½ onion, chopped fine
- 2 tablespoons fresh chopped parsley
- 1½ pounds potatoes, peeled and sliced very thin
- 2 quarts beef or chicken broth
- 1 cup rice
- salt and pepper to taste

Sauté salt pork, oil, onion and parsley in large saucepan. Do not allow onion to brown. Add potatoes and 1 cup broth, cover and simmer for 15 minutes. Add rest of broth, salt and pepper to taste. Add rice when broth starts to boil. Cook for 15 to 18 minutes, stirring occasionally. Skim part of fat from top. Serves 6-8.

Rice with Peas

"RISI E BISI"

Here is a delicious Venetian dish.

- 2 cups rice
- 4 tablespoons butter
- 2 slices bacon, chopped
- 1½ tablespoons parsley, chopped
- 1 medium onion, chopped
- 2 cups shelled fresh or frozen sweet peas
- 7 to 7½ cups beef or chicken broth
- ¾ cup grated Parmesan cheese

Sauté onion, parsley and bacon in butter until onion is soft and lightly golden. Add peas and 3 cups of broth, cover and simmer for 15 to 20 minutes if fresh peas are used, or about 5 minutes when using frozen peas. Add rice, cover and cook for 15 to 18 minutes, stirring occasionally. Add a cup of broth at a time when necessary. Season with salt and pepper to taste. When rice is done, all the broth in the pan should have been absorbed by the rice, which should be quite moist. Serve sprinkled with cheese and dotted with more butter. Serves 6.

Fish Chowder Lazio

ZUPPA DI PESCE ALLA LAZIO

- 1 pound whiting
- 1 one-pound lobster
- 1 pound cuttlefish
- 1 dozen baby clams
- 1 pound mullet
- 1 small onion, chopped
- 1 small carrot, diced
- 1 stalk of celery, diced
- 3 tablespoons parsley, chopped
- ½ cup olive oil
- 1 clove garlic, finely chopped
- ⅓ teaspoon crushed red pepper
- 3 anchovy fillets, chopped
- ¾ cup dry red wine
- 4 very ripe Italian egg tomatoes, peeled and diced
- 1 tablespoon tomato paste
- 6 pieces of toast cut in 4 pieces each
- salt and pepper

Have fish cleaned and save heads; they will be used to make a broth. Rinse fish in cold water and dice. Split lobster lengthwise and discard the stomach and intestinal canal which runs from the stomach to the end of tail. Place fish heads in saucepan together with onion, celery, carrot and 1 tablespoon parsley. Add 2 quarts of water and 1 teaspoon salt. Bring to a boil and boil uncovered for 30 minutes. Strain fish broth and set it aside. Wash clams carefully and place in small skillet with 4 tablespoons oil and 1 tablespoon parsley, sprinkle lightly with salt and pepper, cover and simmer for about 5 minutes or until clams open. Remove from stove and set aside. Mix garlic, 2 tablespoons parsley, anchovy, red pepper and wine. Place rest of oil in large saucepan. Add garlic mixture as soon as oil is warm. Simmer until wine has evaporated. Add tomatoes and tomato paste and simmer for 10 minutes, stirring occasionally, then add cuttlefish. Cover and simmer for 10 minutes, adding some of the fish broth when necessary. Add rest of fish broth and lobster, and cook for about 7 minutes. Remove clams from shells and add to soup together with rest of fish. Pour clam broth carefully to avoid the sand that might have sunk to bottom of the pan. Cook slowly for 10 minutes. Correct seasoning. Place toast at the bottom of a large tureen, add the soup and serve. Serves 6-8.

Fish Chowder Fano

ZUPPA DI PESCE ALLA FANO

- 5 pounds mixed fish in season, such as whiting, flounder, bass, etc., cleaned
- 1 clove garlic, minced
- 2 tablespoons carrot, minced
- ¼ cup celery, minced
- 1 bay leaf
- ⅓ cup olive oil
- 2 small scallions, minced
- ¼ cup parsley, minced
- 1 cup dry white wine
- ½ pound very ripe Italian egg tomatoes, peeled and diced, or 1 cup canned vegetable juice
- 1 cup water
- salt and pepper to taste

Sauté scallion and garlic in olive oil until tender, add tomatoes, carrot, celery, parsley and bay leaf. Simmer uncovered for 10 minutes, stirring occasionally, then add wine and simmer uncovered for 10 minutes more, add fish and water, and simmer uncovered for 15 minutes. Season to taste. Serves 4-6.

Fish Chowder Rimini

ZUPPA DI PESCE ALLA RIMINI

- ½ cup olive oil
- 1 onion, minced
- 1 small clove garlic, minced
- ⅓ cup parsley, chopped
- 2 pounds very ripe Italian egg tomatoes, peeled and diced
- 1 tablespoon tomato paste, diluted in ¾ cup water
- 12 pounds mixed fish in season (such as flounder, porgy, eels, bluefish, pike) cleaned
- ⅓ cup wine vinegar
- salt and pepper to taste

Sauté onion in oil until soft, then add tomatoes, tomato paste mixture, garlic and parsley. Simmer uncovered for 15 to 20 minutes, then add fish and let come to a boil. Add the vinegar and cook over low flame for 15 minutes. Season to taste. Serves 8-10.

Mussel Chowder

ZUPPA DI COZZE

- 4 pounds large mussels
- ½ cup olive oil
- 1 large clove garlic
- 4 tablespoons parsley, chopped
- ¾ cup dry white wine
- 3 tablespoons tomato paste diluted in 1 cup lukewarm water
- ¼ teaspoon crushed red pepper
- salt and pepper to taste

Scrub outsides of shells clean under running water. Sauté garlic in oil in large skillet or saucepan. Discard garlic when golden. Add tomato paste mixture and wine and cook uncovered over medium high flame for 10 or 15 minutes until about ¼ of liquid has evaporated. Add mussels, parsley, crushed red pepper, salt and pepper to taste, and cook over medium high flame, stirring occasionally, for 3 to 5 minutes, until all mussels are open. Serve with toasted and buttered Italian bread that has been rubbed with garlic. (This is optional.) Serves 6.

SAUCES

SALSE

Tomato Sauce Italian Style

SALSA DI POMODORI ALL'ITALIANA

- ⅓ cup olive oil
- 2 small cloves garlic
- ¼ pound fresh chopped pork
- 2 six-ounce cans tomato paste, diluted in 2½ cups warm water
- ½ tablespoon parsley, minced
- 2 leaves fresh sweet basil or ⅛ teaspoon dried basil
- salt and pepper to taste

Sauté garlic in oil. Discard when golden, then add pork and brown. Add rest of ingredients and simmer uncovered for one hour. Add a little water if sauce becomes too thick. Enough for 1 or 1½ pounds macaroni or rice.

Tomato Sauce Sicilian Style

SALSA DI POMODORI ALLA SICILIANA

- 1 cup peeled diced eggplant
- 2½ pounds very ripe Italian egg tomatoes
- ⅓ cup olive oil
- 1 clove garlic
- 1 sweet red pepper, minced
- 4 leaves fresh basil, minced or 4 anchovy fillets, minced
- salt and pepper to taste

Place tomatoes in *hot* water and let stand for 5 minutes. Drain, dice and pass through a sieve. Sauté garlic until golden. Remove garlic and discard. Add eggplant to oil and simmer for 5 minutes, stirring occasionally. Then add tomatoes, red pepper and basil and cook uncovered over low flame for 40 minutes or until sauce is thick. Add the anchovies and simmer for 5 minutes more. Season to taste. Enough for 1 pound macaroni or rice.

Tomato Sauce Neapolitan Style

SALSA DI POMODORI ALLA NAPOLETANA

- 3 tablespoons butter
- 2 tablespoons olive oil
- 2½ pounds very ripe Italian egg tomatoes
- 3 leaves fresh basil or ¼ teaspoon dried basil
- salt and pepper to taste

Place tomatoes in *hot* water and let stand for 5 minutes. Drain, dice and pass through a sieve. Place butter and oil in saucepan, together with tomatoes and basil. Cook uncovered over low flame for 45 minutes or until thick. Season to taste. Enough for one pound of macaroni or rice.

Meatless Tomato Sauce

SALSA DI POMODORI DI MAGRO

- ⅓ cup olive oil
- 1 clove garlic
- 2 six-ounce cans tomato paste
- 2 leaves fresh sweet basil, or ⅛ teaspoon dried basil
- 2 cups water
- ⅛ teaspoon oregano (optional)
- salt and pepper to taste

Sauté garlic in oil until golden. Discard garlic. Mix tomato paste with water and add to oil in saucepan, together with basil and oregano. Cook uncovered over low flame for 35 to 45 minutes, or until sauce is thick. Season to taste. Enough for 1 pound of macaroni or rice.

Pizzaiola Sauce

SALSA ALLA PIZZAIOLA

- 3 tablespoons olive oil
- 1 large clove garlic
- 1½ pounds very ripe egg-shaped tomatoes, peeled and diced or 3 cups canned Italian peeled tomatoes, diced
- ½ teaspoon salt
- ¼ teaspoon pepper
- ⅛ teaspoon oregano
- 1 teaspoon parsley, chopped fine

Sauté garlic in oil until golden. Do not brown. Discard garlic. Add tomatoes and rest of ingredients and cook uncovered over moderate flame for about 25 minutes, stirring occasionally. Taste for seasoning. Enough for 1 pound of macaroni or rice.

Mushroom Sauce

SALSA AI FUNGHI

- ½ pound sliced mushrooms
- ¼ cup onion, minced
- 1 tablespoon parsley, minced
- 1 tablespoon celery, minced
- 2 tablespoons carrots, minced
- ¼ cup butter or olive oil
- 1 cup tomato paste diluted in 1½ cups water
- salt and pepper to taste

Sauté onions, celery, parsley and carrots in butter or oil until onion is soft. Add tomato paste mixture and simmer uncovered for 25 minutes. Add mushrooms, season to taste and simmer for 10 to 15 minutes more. Enough for one pound of macaroni or rice.

Sauce Bolognese

RAGÙ ALLA BOLOGNESE

- 6 tablespoons butter
- ¼ cup salt meat, chopped to a pulp or 1 slice of prosciutto, finely diced
- 1 small onion, chopped very fine
- ¼ cup carrot, chopped fine
- ½ pound chopped sirloin of beef
- 1 strip of lemon peel about 2 inches long and 1 inch wide
- ⅛ teaspoon nutmeg
- 2 tablespoons tomato paste
- 2½ cups milk
- ¼ cup heavy cream
- salt and pepper to taste

Place butter and salt meat or prosciutto in saucepan. When butter has melted add onion and carrot. Stir. Add meat. Let meat brown, stirring occasionally, over medium flame. Add lemon peel and nutmeg. After a minute or so, add tomato paste and milk. Stir until paste is blended. Some people prefer beef broth to the milk, but there is no doubt that milk makes a superior sauce. Salt and pepper to taste. Cover and simmer slowly for one hour, stirring occasionally. Remove lemon peel. Add cream. Simmer 2 minutes more. Use as directed.

Green Sauce Genovese

PESTO ALLA GENOVESE

Having been born and living in a land always green, full of olive trees and laurels, the Ligurians have found a way of giving a green color even to their soups and spaghetti. They have "invented" *pesto*. This is a sauce suitable for any kind of macaroni, but it is quite indispensable for trenette (very much like fettuccelle, or thin egg noodles) and minestrone alla genovese (a vegetable soup). The housewives of Liguria collect the youngest leaves of basil and put them in a mortar together with fresh garlic, a pinch of salt and a mixture of grated Sardo (a cheese produced mostly in Sardinia, rather salty and piquant) and Parmesan cheese, and pound everything vigorously with a wooden pestle into a paste. Then some olive oil is blended in. At times the meat of a walnut or two is added to the mixture, or a few pine nuts; and some also add a little butter.

½ cup fresh basil leaves
4 cloves garlic
⅛ teaspoon salt
¼ cup grated Sardo cheese
¼ cup grated Parmesan cheese
1 walnut (optional)
3 tablespoons butter (optional)
1 cup olive oil

Place basil, garlic, walnut, cheese and salt in a mortar. Pound into a paste, then blend in butter and oil. Taste for seasoning. Enough for one pound of macaroni.

Mornay Sauce

SALSA MORNAY

4 tablespoons butter
1 heaping tablespoon flour
1½ cups milk
½ teaspoon salt
2 tablespoons grated Parmesan cheese
1 egg yolk
dash of white pepper
dash of nutmeg

Melt butter in small saucepan and add flour. Stir into smooth paste and add milk. Sir continually and cook over low flame for 10 minutes. Sauce should have the consistency of thick cream. Add salt, pepper and nutmeg. Stir. Remove from stove and stir in cheese and egg yolk rapidly. Makes about 1½ cups.

Thin White Sauce

SALSA BESCIAMELLA

- 2 tablespoons butter
- 2 tablespoons flour
- 1 cup milk (light cream may be substituted if a richer sauce is desired)
- ½ teaspoon salt
- pinch of white pepper

Place butter in small saucepan over low heat. Blend in flour when butter is melted, then add milk, salt and pepper and continue stirring over low heat until sauce comes to a boil. Sauce should have the consistency of heavy cream. To keep warm and to prevent film from forming on top, cover and place saucepan in pan of hot water. Makes one cup.

Heavy White Sauce

SALSA BESCIAMELLA DENSA

- 2 tablespoons butter
- 2 tablespoons flour
- 1 cup milk
- ½ teaspoon salt
- pinch of white pepper

Place butter in small saucepan over low heat. When butter is melted add flour and mix thoroughly into a smooth paste. Then add milk, salt and pepper and continue stirring, over low heat, until sauce comes to a boil. Simmer one minute more. Sauce should have the consistency of very thick cream. Makes one cup.

Pink Sauce

SALSA AURORA

- 1 recipe Thin White Sauce (page 35)
- 1 tablespoon ready-cooked plain tomato sauce
- 2 tablespoons butter

Blend tomato sauce with white sauce, remove from heat and stir in butter. Serve with hard-boiled eggs, cauliflower and asparagus. Makes about a cup.

Onion Sauce

SALSA ALLA CIPOLLA

1 medium onion, minced
2 tablespoons butter
1 recipe Heavy White Sauce (page 35)
2 tablespoons heavy cream
salt and pepper to taste

Place onion in small saucepan with one cup of water and let boil for 8 minutes. Drain and sauté onion gently in butter for one minute. Add to White Sauce and put through a sieve, mashing onion with the help of a spoon. Add heavy cream and warm sauce again. Serve with roast lamb or sweetbreads. Makes about one cup.

Horseradish Sauce

SALSA DI RAFANO

1 cup heavy cream, beaten stiff
1 tablespoon dry English mustard
1 tablespoon vinegar
1 teaspoon sugar
1/8 teaspoon Cayenne pepper
1½ tablespoon horseradish
salt to taste

Blend mustard with vinegar and gently fold into whipped cream together with rest of ingredients. Serve with boiled meat.

Sauce for Fish

SALSA PER PESCE

hard-boiled yolks of 3 eggs
6 anchovy fillets, minced
½ cup olive oil
juice of a small lemon
a pinch of white pepper

Place yolks, anchovies, ¼ cup oil, and pepper in an electric blender. Start blender and blend for one minute, add rest of ingredients gradually and blend for a few seconds more. If electric blender is not available, put yolks and anchovies through a sieve, add pepper and blend in oil and lemon juice gradually, beating with a spoon until smooth. To be used with fried fish fillets or broiled fish.

Mayonnaise

SALSA MAIONESE

- 2 egg yolks
- ½ teaspoon salt
- ¼ teaspoon white pepper
- 1 tablespoon white wine vinegar or 3 tablespoons lemon juice
- 1 cup olive oil
- 1 clove garlic (optional)

Place egg yolks in small mixing bowl. Add salt, pepper, two or three drops of vinegar or lemon juice and equal amount of oil. Beat vigorously with spoon or rotary egg beater or if you have an electric mixer, beat at mayonnaise speed. As soon as mayonnaise becomes firm, add a few more drops of oil and vinegar or lemon juice. Continue to beat and add (a few drops at a time) all the oil and vinegar or lemon juice. Add garlic and let stand for ½ hour. Discard garlic when ready to use. Makes about 1 cup.

Mayonnaise with Pickles

MAIONESE CON SOTT'ACETI

- 1 recipe Mayonnaise (see above)
- 1 tablespoon capers
- 2 tablespoons minced sour pickles
- ⅛ teaspoon dry mustard

Blend mustard with Mayonnaise. Drain capers and pickles well and add to Mayonnaise.

Mayonnaise with Gelatine

SALSA MAIONESE ALLA GELATINA

- 1 cup Mayonnaise (see above)
- 1 teaspoon unflavored gelatine softened in cold water
- 2 tablespoons boiling water

Dissolve gelatine in boiling water and add to Mayonnaise. Mix well with a spoon. This sauce is used for decorating fish, meats and vegetables in molds. It should be used immediately after the gelatine is added, as otherwise it will become too hard to use.

Mayonnaise with Cream

MAIONESE ALLA PANNA

1 recipe Mayonnaise (page 37)   3 heaping tablespoons whipped heavy cream

Blend ingredients together and serve with cold or hot asparagus.

Garlic Mayonnaise

MAIONESE ALL'AGLIO

1 recipe Mayonnaise (page 37)   1 large clove garlic put through a garlic press

Blend ingredients together and chill before using.

White Stock

FONDO BIANCO

1½ pounds veal bones
1 pound chicken wings and/or necks
1 onion, sliced
1 carrot
2 teaspoons salt
1 stalk celery
2 to 3 sprigs parsley
2 cloves

Place bones and chicken wings and/or necks in large saucepan with 3½ quarts cold water, bring to a boil and remove scum. Add rest of ingredients, cover and simmer for 3 hours. Remove all fat from top, strain through a sieve lined with a kitchen towel or a piece of clean cotton or linen cloth. Keep covered in refrigerator until ready to use. This is the basic ingredient of many sauces, soups or for any recipe where stock is indicated.

Brown Stock

FONDO BRUNO

2 pounds beef and veal bones
¼ pound pork rind
2 medium onions, sliced
2 carrots, diced
2 teaspoons salt
1 stalk celery
1 tablespoon parsley, chopped
pinch of black pepper

Place bones and rind in a baking dish, sprinkle with 3 tablespoons melted butter and let brown on all sides in 450° oven for about 25 minutes, turning them occasionally. Remove bones and pan juice to large saucepan, cover with 3½ quarts water. Add onions, carrots, celery, parsley, salt and pepper. Bring to a boil, remove scum, cover and simmer for 3 hours. Let cool and remove *all* fat from top, strain broth, cover and place in refrigerator until ready to use. It will keep for a week or 10 days. Makes about 2 quarts. This is the basic ingredient of many sauces, soups or for any recipe where stock is indicated.

Brown Chaufroid Sauce

SALSA CHAUFROID SCURA

- 1 tablespoon shortening or margarine
- 1 tablespoon flour
- 2 cups Brown Stock (see above)
- ½ teaspoon tomato paste
- 2 tablespoons dry Marsala, Port or Madeira wine

Melt margarine or shortening in saucepan, stir in flour and cook over low flame, stirring for about 2 to 3 minutes or until the mixture becomes light brown. Add Brown Stock and tomato paste, stirring until sauce comes to a boil. Cover and simmer for about one hour or until reduced by one half, without stirring. Be sure to skim off fat and scum from time to time. Strain through a fine sieve. Add wine, bring to a boil and boil uncovered for 5 minutes. Use as directed. Season to taste before using. Makes about 1 cup.

Wine Sauce for Fish

SALSA AL VINO BIANCO

Especially indicated for fillets of flounder or any other fish cooked in wine.

- 1 cup wine
- 1 small onion, sliced
- 3 egg yolks
- 1 teaspoon lemon juice
- 5 tablespoons butter

Bring to a boil one cup of the wine used in cooking the fish. Boil until all but ¼ of a cup has evaporated. Remove from stove and let stand for five minutes. Then place yolks in double boiler, over medium heat, add wine and lemon juice and mix until sauce thickens. Remove sauce from stove, blend in butter and serve, or keep warm in double boiler until ready to serve.

Maître d'hôtel Butter

BURRO ALLA MAÎTRE D'H

¼ pound butter
⅓ cup parsley, chopped
juice of half a lemon

Blend ingredients together, then melt butter over low flame. Use as directed. Good with broiled fish.

Housewife's Sauce

SALSA DELLA MASSAIA

5½ tablespoons butter
1 tablespoon flour
1 cup lukewarm water
¼ teaspoon salt
⅛ teaspoon white pepper
2 egg yolks
juice of one lemon

Melt 1½ tablespoons butter in small saucepan and gradually blend in flour. Add water, salt, pepper and egg yolks. Beat slowly with egg beater or mix with a wooden spoon until sauce comes to a boil. Remove from stove and add rest of butter. The amount of butter to be added is according to taste, from 4 tablespoons to ¼ of a pound. Add lemon juice just before serving. Makes about one cup. Use with cauliflower, fish, artichokes or broccoli.

Hunters' Sauce

SALSA DEI CACCIATORI

3 tablespoons butter
2 slices prosciutto, diced fine
1 medium-size onion, minced
1 cup dry white wine
⅛ teaspoon sage
⅛ teaspoon thyme
1 crumbled bay leaf
¼ cup broth or water
1 additional tablespoon butter blended with 1 tablespoon flour
¼ cup heavy cream, scalded
2 tablespoons chopped parsley
salt and pepper to taste

Sauté onion in 3 tablespoons butter together with prosciutto. Add wine, thyme, sage and bay leaf as soon as onion is soft. Cook over high flame until wine is reduced to half its original amount. Then add broth or water, butter and flour mixture and cook, stirring until sauce comes to a boil. Boil for 3 minutes, then remove from stove and add scalded heavy cream and parsley together with salt and pepper to taste. Especially indicated for game. Makes 1 cup.

Venetian Sauce

SALSA VENETA

1 recipe Housewife's Sauce (page 40)
2 ounces wine vinegar
3 ounces dry white wine
1 onion, minced
8 drops green vegetable coloring or 2 tablespoons cooked strained spinach

Place wine, vinegar and onion in saucepan, bring to a boil and cook until liquid has evaporated to ¾ of its original amount. Remove from stove, strain and add to Housewife's Sauce, together with vegetable coloring or strained spinach. Makes about 1¼ cups.

Caper Sauce

SALSA AI CAPPERI

1 recipe Housewife's Sauce (page 40)
2 tablespoons capers

Add capers to sauce when ready to use.

MACARONI, RICE AND CORN MEAL

PASTA, RISOTTI, POLENTA

⁋⁋

Sauces are the indispensable base of any good cuisine. They can make a dish great or very unsatisfactory.

Italian cuisine is famous for its many *pasta* dishes, but despite the fact that Americans consume yearly more than a billion pounds of *pasta* in all forms and shapes, more than 90% of the time the sauce is either a thin tomato soup, or tomato and chopped beef, or clams or mushrooms, or a so-called Italian tomato sauce with so many vegetables in it and in such a quantity that the result is more like a thick vegetable soup than a tomato sauce.

Tomato sauce in its many variations (with fish, meat or mushrooms, etc.) is only one chapter in sauces for *pasta*, although sauces with a tomato base are unquestionably the most universally popular. A word, therefore, should be said about the preparation of tomato sauces, either plain or those containing other ingredients. This seems called for because of the widespread misconceptions and misinformation about preparation and cooking time. When a recipe calls for Italian egg-shaped tomatoes, and they are not available (they are now being widely grown in the United States, especially in California, and are on the market all through the warm season), perfectly satisfactory sauces can be made from very ripe fresh ordinary tomatoes. Fresh tomatoes are always either peeled and diced or put through a sieve before using. Tomato paste, canned tomatoes or tomato purée may also be used either by themselves or in combination. The only drawback about using canned tomatoes alone is that they are frequently loosely packed and not quite ripe enough for a good red sauce. For those who especially favor tomato sauce made with fresh tomatoes and who also happen to have a freezer, the sauce can be prepared in great quantity during the months when fresh ripe egg-shaped tomatoes are available, and frozen in pint or half-pint containers. (As a matter of fact all of the tomato sauces in this book can be treated in the same way.) A pint of sauce is more than enough for 1 pound of *pasta*, as there should be enough to season, moisten and coat each strand or piece of *pasta*, but not so much that the bottom of the serving dish is a lake of sauce.

And *don't overcook!* It is very important, on the contrary, to forget anything you may have heard about the necessity, or even the desirability of cooking the sauce for hours and hours on end in order to arrive at an authentic Italian sauce! In my opinion this is a holdover from the ancient era of cooking on huge wood stoves, but it is certainly extremely bad practice in times when practically all cooking is done on high-speed gas or electric ranges. Such impossibly long cooking times as are often recommended not only discourage today's busy housewife, but also the overcooking merely destroys vitamins and very frequently renders the sauce dark, forbidding and bitter.

Every Italian town has its own way of cooking, therefore it is not at all surprising that Italians have accumulated innumerable ways of seasoning their *pasta*, most of which are completely unknown in this country. Their land is rich in fruit, vegetables, poultry, meat and game of every description; their seas, lakes and rivers abound in fish of every species. Consequently game, poultry, meat, shellfish, anchovies, tuna, cheeses, herbs, eggs, ham, peas, tuffles, mushrooms, heavy cream, etc., are used for making the great variety of sauces with which the Italians flavor their *pasta*.

There are a few simple rules that should be kept in mind when cooking *pasta*.

One: Not less than six quarts of water should be used to cook one pound of spaghetti, macaroni, or any other kind of *pasta*. Two tablespoons of salt should be added to the water. For best results a deep saucepan should be used. Long kinds of *pasta*, such as spaghetti, spaghettini, bucatini, vermicelli, linguine, etc., should not be broken. This applies to all kinds and shapes of *pasta*. In Bologna there is a saying, *Conti corti e tagliatelle lunghe* ("Short bills but long noodles"). Big bills are always unpleasant and short or broken noodles (or for that matter any other kind of broken *pasta*) are unpleasant to look at, and they give one the impression of eating badly served leftovers.

Second: Water must be boiling before the *pasta* is placed in the pan and should be kept boiling during the cooking process. The whole quantity of *pasta* has to be put into the pan at the same time. As in many cases the *pasta* will be longer than the pan, the *pasta* will have to be pushed down gently with a fork, or better, a wooden spoon. Stir and cover.

TYPES OF PASTA

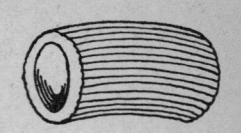

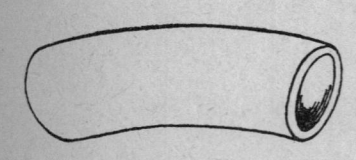

RIGATONI

OCCHI DI LUPO

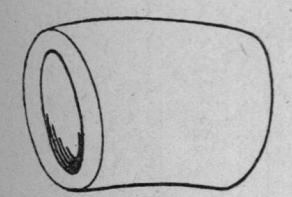

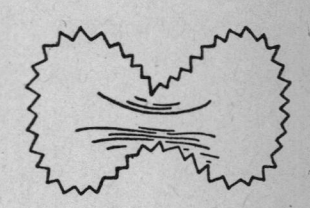

FARFALLE (EGG BOWS)

TUFOLI

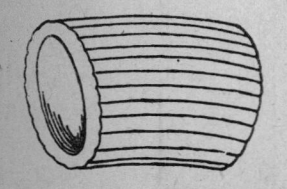

MOSTACCIOLI

TUFOLI RIGATI

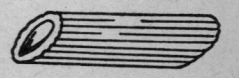

MOSTACCIOLI RIGATI

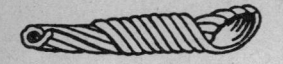

SPIEDINI	MARGHERITE
MEZZANI	MAFALDE
ZITI	TAGLIATELLE (WIDE EGG NOODLES)
CAVATELLI	(FINE EGG NOODLES)
FUSILLI	MACCARONCELLI (MACARONI)

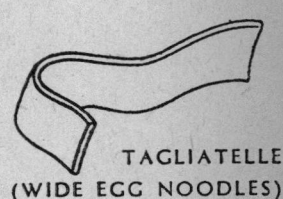

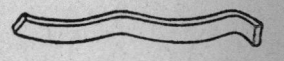

45

PERCIATELLI
(THIN MACARONI)

BUCATINI

SPAGHETTI

SPAGHETTINI
(THIN SPAGHETTI)

FETTUCCELLE

LINGUINE

MEDIUM WIDE EGG NOODLES

LASAGNE

TRIPOLINI
(SMALL EGG BOWS)

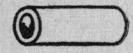

DITALI

DITALINI

ACINI DI PEPE
(PEPPER CORNS)

ALPHABET

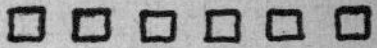

EGG BARLEY

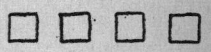

EGG FLAKES

EGG PASTINA

CANNELLONI OR MANICOTTI

In a few seconds the water will boil to overflowing. Remove cover and keep water boiling vigorously.

Third: Use a fork or a long wooden spoon to stir *pasta* frequently during cooking.

Fourth: DON'T OVERCOOK IT. Cooking time varies with the shape and thickness of the *pasta* and also with the kind of flour used by the manufacturer. For example, spaghettini should be cooked about 6 to 8 minutes, homemade medium or wide egg noodles about 4 minutes, while the store-bought lasagne require 12 to 15 minutes. The important thing to remember is to taste the *pasta* after it has been cooking for 4 minutes and keep on tasting it by fishing out a strand or two every couple of minutes until it is ready.

After a while, with the help of instructions on the box, you will know exactly the cooking time required for each kind and shape, to please your taste. Just remember that all *pasta* should be *al dente*, that is, firm to the bite.

Fifth: Drain *pasta* immediately. Some people believe that it should be rinsed with cold water to stop the cooking process. I strongly disagree with this theory. It is a fact that once *pasta* has been rinsed in cold water, it becomes cold and no amount of hot sauce will make it hot again, with the result that it is served practically stone-cold, instead of being served steaming hot. If you follow the next instruction, you will not have to worry about stopping the cooking process.

Sixth: Serve immediately. The ideal way to serve *pasta asciutta* is to mix it with the sauce and the cheese in the pan in which it has been cooked, then place it on a hot oval platter, sprinkle with cheese and dot with butter flakes.

Pasta is made of a mixture of flour and water, except in its more delicate forms where eggs are used instead of water, as in noodles, pastina, capellini, etc., and all the homemade dough used for ravioli, cappelletti, cannelloni, etc.

Italian cuisine offers literally hundreds of recipes for the innumerable varieties of *pasta*, both *asciutta* and for soups. It would be impossible here for me to give every recipe, as that would make a book in itself, but I will give some of the classic Italian recipes, such as Ravioli, Cappelletti, Lasagne, Gnocchi, Fettuccine (homemade egg noodles), Tagliatelle, Pasta e Lenticchie (lentil soup), Pasta e Fagioli (bean soup), Minestrone, etc. At the same time, I will give some unusual recipes, and some that are much more common over here than in Italy, such as Chicken Tetrazzini, Spaghetti with Meat Balls, etc.

As I mentioned before, *pasta*, or macaroni or spaghetti, as it is called here, comes in a great variety of shapes and forms.

Some are more suitable to one recipe than to another, but at the same time a great many are interchangeable.

Homemade Wide Egg Noodles

FETTUCCINE ALL'UOVO

4 cups sifted flour	3 tablespoons water
4 large eggs	1½ teaspoons salt

Sift flour onto clean board. Make a hole in middle of flour and put in eggs, water and salt. Beat eggs with fork, slowly mixing about one half of the flour with it. Mix in rest of flour by hand, and knead until dough is smooth (about 10 minutes). Cut dough in 3 pieces. Roll out each piece on floured board till paper-thin. Fold sheets of dough into rolls, and cut crosswise into strips about ½" to ⅔" wide, using a very sharp long knife. Toss noodles gently with fingers to unfold them. Spread them on floured board, and let stand, covered with a towel, for not longer than one hour. Cook noodles in 8 quarts boiling salted water for about 4 minutes, stirring frequently. Exact cooking time depends on the thickness of the noodles. Be sure to taste noodles after 3 minutes. Drain and use as directed or with any favorite sauce.

Homemade Medium Egg Noodles

TAGLIATELLE ALL'UOVO

Follow recipe for Wide Egg Noodles (see above). Cut rolled sheets of dough into strips about ⅓-inch wide.

Majestic Egg Noodles al Triplo Burro

MAESTOSE FETTUCCINE AL TRIPLO BURRO

This is the name given to this famous dish prepared by the King of Fettuccine at the Alfredo alla Scrofa Restaurant in Rome. They are served with the now famous solid gold fork and spoon given as a gift to Alfredo by Mary Pickford and Douglas Fairbanks.

1 recipe Homemade Wide Egg Noodles (page 49)	2 cups grated Parmesan cheese
1¼ cup whipped sweet butter	pinch freshly ground black pepper

Season egg noodles with butter and cheese, mixing well. Serves 6.

Homemade Egg Noodles Bologna Style

TAGLIATELLE CON RAGÙ ALLA BOLOGNESE

1 recipe Homemade Wide Egg Noodles (page 49)	½ cup freshly grated Parmesan cheese
1 recipe Sauce Bolognese (page 33)	

Mix noodles and sauce together. Serve immediately with Parmesan cheese. One pound store-bought egg noodles may be substituted. Serves 6.

Egg Noodles Rugantino

TAGLIATELLE ALLA RUGANTINO

1 pound wide or medium egg noodles	1 cup grated Parmesan cheese
½ recipe Mushrooms Trifolati (page 133)	6 tablespoons butter

Cook noodles in plenty of boiling salted water for 4 to 5 minutes or until tender, stirring frequently. Drain and season with mushrooms, butter and Parmesan. Serves 4.

(*Recipe from Ristorante Rugantino, Rome*)

Green Egg Noodles Bologna Style

TAGLIATELLE VERDI ALLA BOLOGNESE

3½ cups sifted flour	1 recipe Sauce Bolognese (page 33)
2 eggs at room temperature	
1 cup cooked puréed spinach	1 cup grated Parmesan cheese
1½ teaspoons salt	

Sift flour onto clean board. Make a hole in middle of flour and in it put eggs, spinach and salt. Beat eggs and spinach with fork, slowly mixing half of flour with it. Mix in rest of flour by hand. Knead until dough is smooth, about 10 minutes, adding more flour if necessary. Roll the dough into a ball and let stand for 15 minutes. Cut dough in four pieces. Roll out each piece on floured board until paper-thin. Allow sheets of dough to dry on floured board for 20 minutes. Fold each sheet into a roll. Cut crosswise into strips about ½ inch wide. Toss noodles gently with fingers to unfold them. Spread on floured board and let stand for not more than one hour. Cook noodles in 8 quarts boiling salted water for 2 to 3 minutes, stirring frequently. One pound of store-bought green noodles may be substituted. Drain, mix with sauce and serve with cheese. Serves 6.

Homemade Cannelloni or Manicotti

2 cups sifted flour
2 large eggs
1½ tablespoons water
¾ teaspoon salt

Place flour on pastry board, make a hole in the center and in it put eggs, water and salt. Beat eggs with fork, slowly mixing in half of the flour. Mix in rest of flour by hand. Knead until dough is smooth, about 10 minutes. Cut dough in half and roll each piece on floured board until paper-thin. Cut sheets of dough in 3-inch squares. Cook 6 at a time in 4 quarts of boiling salted water for 5 minutes. Remove from pan one at a time with perforated spoon and place unfolded on damp towels. Continue operation until all squares are cooked. Fill as directed. Makes about 2½ dozen.

Cannelloni Stuffing

RIPIENI PER CANNELLONI

MEATLESS STUFFING:

1½ cup grated Parmesan cheese
1¾ cup ricotta cheese
about 4 tablespoons Heavy White Sauce (page 35)
⅛ teaspoon nutmeg
1 egg, beaten
salt and pepper to taste

Blend all ingredients and use as directed on page 52.

SAUSAGE AND RICOTTA STUFFING:

2 cups ricotta cheese	5 tablespoons grated Parmesan cheese
4 fresh sweet Italian pork sausages (without seeds)	1 egg, beaten
	salt and pepper to taste

Prick sausages with fork, place in small skillet, add enough water to cover and simmer for half an hour or until all water has evaporated. Brown sausages on all sides in their own fat. Remove skin and mince. Add rest of ingredients. Mix well and use as directed on page 52.

Cannelloni alla Nerone

½ recipe for Homemade Cannelloni (page 51)	¾ cup grated Parmesan cheese
2-3 chicken livers, sautéed in butter	4 tablespoons butter
	2 tablespoons flour
breast of large chicken, sautéed in butter	½ cup heavy cream
	1½ cups milk
5 slices prosciutto or 4 slices cooked ham	⅓ teaspoon salt
	⅛ teaspoon white pepper

Put chicken breast, prosciutto and chicken livers through food grinder. Melt butter in small saucepan, blend in flour, add milk and heavy cream gradually, stirring until it reaches boiling point. Reduce heat; cook for 3 minutes longer. Add seasoning and blend. Taste for seasoning. Sauce should have the consistency of heavy cream. Place over hot water and cover tightly to prevent film from forming. Add ½ cup cheese to chicken mixture, and 5 to 6 tablespoons of sauce, blending well. Correct seasoning. Usually the prosciutto has enough salt to take care of the seasoning. Spread about 1½ tablespoons of chicken mixture on half of each square, allowing ½" margin. Starting from the spread end of the squares, roll tightly. Make a layer of the stuffed cannelloni in a large, well-buttered baking dish. Sprinkle with remaining ¼ cup cheese and pour sauce over all. If necessary, two layers instead of one can be made, in which case, make a layer of cannelloni, sprinkle with half of the cheese, half of the sauce, then one more layer of cannelloni, cheese and sauce. Bake uncovered at 375° for 20 minutes. Serve hot. Serves 6-8.

Cannelloni may be prepared and filled in advance and kept

between sheets of waxed paper, in the refrigerator, until ready to cook.

(*Recipe from Ristorante Rugantino, Rome*)

Manicotti all'Etrusca

- 1 recipe Homemade Manicotti (page 51)
- 6 tablespoons butter
- 2 tablespoons flour
- 1 cup light cream
- 1 cup milk
- ⅓ teaspoon salt
- 1 egg yolk
- ½ pound fresh mushrooms, sliced fine
- ½ cup grated Parmesan cheese
- 2 cups cooked chicken, chopped

Melt 4 tablespoons butter in small saucepan, blend in flour, add milk and cream gradually, stirring until sauce starts to boil. Reduce heat; cook for 3 minutes longer. Add salt and white pepper to taste. Remove from fire and stir in egg yolk. Place over hot water and cover tightly to prevent film from forming. Sauté mushrooms in 2 tablespoons butter over medium fire for 3 minutes, stirring occasionally. Mix mushrooms, chicken and 5 to 6 tablespoons of sauce, blending well. Season to taste. Spread about 1½ tablespoons of chicken mixture on half of each square allowing ½″ margin. Starting from the spread part of the squares roll tightly. Make a layer of the stuffed manicotti in a large well-buttered baking dish. Sprinkle with cheese and pour sauce over all. If necessary make 2 layers instead of one, in which case make one layer of manicotti, sprinkle with half of the cheese, half of the sauce, then another layer of manicotti placed crosswise, and remaining cheese and sauce. Bake at 375° for 20 minutes. Serve immediately. Serves 6-8.

Manicotti may be prepared and filled in advance and kept between sheets of waxed paper, in the refrigerator, until ready to cook.

Homemade Lasagne

LASAGNE FATTE IN CASA

- 2 cups sifted flour
- 2 large eggs
- 2 tablespoons water
- ½ teaspoon salt

Sift flour on clean board. Make depression in middle of flour and put in it the eggs, water and salt. Beat eggs with fork, slowly mixing about one half of the flour with it. Mix in rest of flour by hand. Knead until dough is smooth (about 10 minutes). Cut dough in two pieces. Roll each piece on floured board until paper-thin. Let sheets of dough dry for about 10 minutes. Fold sheets into rolls. Cut crosswise into strips about 2 inches wide using a very sharp knife. Unfold them one by one and cut each strip into 3 or 4 pieces, so that each strip measures about 2" x 6". Cook a few at a time in large pot of boiling salted water for 5 minutes, draining with a flat skimmer. Place cooked lasagne, completely unfolded, on table top or large platter. Use as directed.

Once dough is ready to be rolled into sheets, it can be kept in refrigerator wrapped in buttered tinfoil, for 24 hours. When ready to be used, let stand at room temperature for ½ hour, still in the wrapping, and proceed as above.

Old Fashioned Neopolitan Lasagne

LASAGNE NAPOLETANE ALL'ANTICA

- 1 recipe Homemade Lasagne (page 53)
- 2 slices of bacon, minced
- 4 tablespoons butter
- 1 clove garlic
- ½ onion, minced
- 2 tablespoons finely chopped carrot
- 1 tablespoon finely chopped celery
- 1 teaspoon chopped parsley
- ½ pound chopped beef
- 2 Italian pork sausages (hot or sweet) with casing removed
- ¼ teaspoon marjoram
- 2 cups fresh or canned peeled Italian egg tomatoes, diced
- ½ cup tomato paste diluted in 1⅓ cups water
- ½ cup dry white wine
- ½ pound ricotta cheese
- ¼ teaspoon salt
- 1 egg, beaten
- ½ cup grated Parmesan cheese
- ½ small mozzarella cheese, diced
- salt and pepper to taste

Place bacon, butter, garlic, onion, carrot and celery in saucepan and sauté gently for 4 to 5 minutes. Discard garlic and add beef and sausage, marjoram and parsley and simmer, stirring occasionally, until meat is browned. Add wine and cook until wine has evaporated. Add peeled tomatoes and tomato paste mixture. Simmer uncovered for 30 minutes. Season to taste and cook 10 to 15 minutes more, or until sauce is thick. Mix ricotta cheese, egg, Parmesan cheese, a dash of pepper and ¼ teaspoon salt into a smooth paste. Butter a square or rectangular baking dish. Cover the bottom with sauce, then make a layer of lasagne, then one of the cheese mixture. Dot with mozzarella cheese and cover all with plenty of sauce. Repeat until lasagne are all used, ending with sauce. Dot with butter and a few cubes of mozzarella and bake in 375° oven for 30 minutes. Serves 4-6.

Ravioli Italian Style

RAVIOLI O AGNOLOTTI ALL'ITALIANA

DOUGH:
- 3½ cups sifted flour
- 3 egg yokes
- ½ tablespoon salt
- ⅔ cup water

STUFFING:
- ⅔ cup cooked ham, ground or ½ cup prosciutto, ground
- 1 cup cooked chicken breast, ground
- 1 cup veal, ground (about ¼ pound), previously sautéed in olive oil
- ¼ teaspoon nutmeg
- 2 egg yolks
- ½ tablespoon salt
- ¼ teaspoon pepper
- 1 tablespoon melted butter
- 1 tablespoon grated Parmesan cheese

SAUCE:
- 1 cup tomato paste diluted in 2 cups water or: 1 cup frozen concentrated tomato juice and 2 cups water
- 5 large ripe tomatoes, peeled and diced
- 3 tablespoons olive oil
- 1 clove garlic
- 5 tablespoons butter
- 3 leaves fresh sweet basil or ½ tablespoon fresh parsley, chopped
- ¼ teaspoon crushed red pepper
- 1 cup grated Parmesan cheese
- 6 quarts beef or chicken broth or consommé, salted to taste
- salt and pepper to taste

Place meats for stuffing in mixing bowl and add egg yolks, butter, cheese and seasoning. Mix into a smooth paste. Place in refrigerator till ready to use.

Place flour on board. Make depression in center and place egg yolks, water and salt in it. With fork gradually beat eggs and water with flour till about half the flour is used. Add remaining flour and knead into a smooth firm paste (about 10 minutes). If dough is too soft add more flour. Cut dough in four and roll out on floured board into four very thin sheets. Place stuffing on one sheet of dough with a teaspoon at intervals of about 1½ inches. When first sheet is covered with mounds of stuffing cover it with a second sheet of dough. Press around each mold with fingers, then cut ravioli into 2-inch squares with pastry cutter. Make sure that edges of ravioli are firmly closed as otherwise stuffing will come out in the cooking. Place ravioli on lightly floured towel, leaving space between each. Sprinkle with flour and let stand for 30 minutes. Turn ravioli after half an hour. While ravioli are drying prepare sauce.

(Ravioli can be prepared and filled in advance and kept between sheets of waxed paper in the refrigerator, until ready to cook.)

Place oil, tomatoes, tomato paste or juice, water and garlic in saucepan. Simmer for 25 minutes over medium flame, stirring occasionally, or till sauce is reduced ⅓ its original amount. Remove from stove. Strain through a fine sieve and place in clean saucepan with butter, parsley, basil, red pepper and salt and pepper to taste. Simmer till sauce is reduced ½ its original amount.

Place ravioli, 15 at a time, in boiling broth and let cook for 7 to 10 minutes, stirring occasionally. Remove with strainer and place in large heated bowl. Sprinkle with 1½ tablespoons cheese and 3 or 4 tablespoons sauce. Repeat till all ravioli are cooked, placing each cooked batch on top of ravioli in bowl. Serve ravioli in individual dishes. Serve rest of sauce and cheese in separate dishes along with ravioli. Serves 8.

Ravioli can also be cooked in plain salted water.

Dumplings Italian Style

GNOCCHI ALL'ITALIANA

2½ cups boiled potatoes, mashed	1 recipe Tomato Sauce Italian Style (page 31)
2 eggs, lightly beaten	1 cup grated Parmesan cheese
½ teaspoon salt	
2¼ cups flour	

Place potatoes, eggs, and salt in mixing bowl and mix thoroughly. Add 1½ cups flour, mixing well. Place dough on floured board and add rest of flour. Knead dough for 3 or 4 minutes. If dough becomes too sticky, sprinkle board with more flour. Cut dough into six pieces. Roll dough into long sausage-like strips and cut into pieces ⅔-inch long. Sprinkle dumplings with flour. Have ready a large pan with 8 quarts of boiling water to which 2 tablespoons of salt have been added. Place one third of dumplings in boiling water and remove with strainer when they rise to top. Place in hot serving dish and repeat operation until all dumplings are cooked. (Keep water boiling.) Add sauce to dumplings and ⅔ of the cheese, mixing well. Sprinkle rest of cheese on top. Serves 4-6.

Linguine in Egg Sauce No. 1

LINGUINE STRASCINATE NO. 1

1 pound linguine	1 cup grated Romano cheese
4 sweet Italian or breakfast pork sausages	grated peel of one lemon
½ cup salt pork, finely diced	¼ teaspoon pepper
3 eggs at room temperature	3 tablespoons butter

Cook linguine in boiling salted water for 8 to 10 minutes. While linguine are cooking, prepare sauce. Remove pork sausage from casing and roll in balls the size of a dime. Fry sausage balls and salt pork until light brown, about five minutes over medium flame. Beat eggs together with pepper and lemon peel. Taste linguine for salt. Drain and replace in hot pot. Add eggs, cheese, hot salt pork and sausages with the drippings and mix well. The egg mixture will attach itself to the linguine and will be cooked by their heat, so care should be taken that these are not allowed to cool before the egg mixture is added. If after thorough mixing the eggs are still raw, cook the mixture over very low flame for a minute or so, stirring constantly. Add butter and serve immediately. Serves 6.

Linguine in Egg Sauce No. 2

LINGUINE STRASCINATE NO. 2

1 pound linguine	1 cup grated Romano cheese
8 slices bacon, diced	¼ teaspoon pepper
3 eggs at room temperature, slightly beaten	4 tablespoons butter

Cook linguine in boiling salted water for 8 to 10 minutes. Fry bacon in small skillet until crisp, about five minutes over low flame. Taste linguine for salt. Drain and return to hot pot. Add eggs, cheese, pepper, HOT bacon and bacon fat, and mix well. Place in hot serving dish and top with slices of butter. If eggs are still raw follow directions for Linguine in Egg Sauce No. 1. Serves 6.

Linguine with Ricotta Cheese Roman Style

LINGUINE CON LA RICOTTA ALLA ROMANA

- 1 pound linguine
- ½ pound ricotta cheese
- ¼ pound whipped sweet butter
- ½ cup grated Parmesan or Romano cheese
- salt and pepper to taste

Cook linguine in boiling salted water, stirring often, for 8 to 10 minutes or to desired tenderness. In the meantime, place ricotta cheese and butter in skillet and simmer, stirring constantly for 7 to 8 minutes. Drain linguine, combine with ricotta mixture, and sprinkle with Parmesan cheese and pepper. Serves 4-6.

Spaghetti Carbonara

SPAGHETTI ALLA CARBONARA

- 1 pound spaghetti
- 6 slices bacon, diced fine
- 2 tablespoons olive oil
- ⅓ cup dry white wine
- 3 eggs at room temperature, slightly beaten with
- ⅓ cup grated Parmesan cheese
- ⅓ cup grated Romano cheese
- freshly ground black pepper

Cook spaghetti in boiling salted water for 7 to 10 minutes. Meanwhile place oil and bacon in small skillet and sauté until bacon is crisp. Then add wine and cook over medium flame until wine has evaporated. Taste spaghetti for salt, drain and return to hot saucepan. Add to it the eggs and cheese mixture, plenty of black pepper and very HOT bacon fat, mixing well. The egg mixture should attach itself to the spaghetti and be cooked by its heat so care should be taken that it is not allowed to cool before the addition of the egg mixture. If, after thorough mixing, the eggs still look raw, place the saucepan over a low flame for a minute or so, stirring constantly. Place on hot serving dish and serve immediately. Serves 4-6.

Here is a recipe from one of the most famous restaurants in Naples, Grande Ristorante Transatlantico in Borgo Marinaro a Santa Lucia. The restaurant is owned by Comm. Luigi Marinella & Sons and it is known not only for its cuisine, but also for its well-stocked cellar and for its large veranda on the sea, where one can enjoy the breath-taking view of the Gulf of Naples while eating.

Spaghetti Transatlantico

- 1 pound spaghetti
- ¼ cup olive oil
- 1 large clove garlic
- 1½ pounds fresh very ripe peeled Italian egg tomatoes or 1½ pound can of peeled tomatoes (preferably imported from Italy) together with 1 cup canned vegetable juice
- 2 tablespoons olive oil
- 1 dozen small shrimps, shelled and deveined
- 1 small cuttlefish, cleaned and diced (optional)
- ½ dozen mussels, rinsed thoroughly in cold water
- ½ dozen Little Neck clams, rinsed thoroughly in cold water
- ½ teaspoon salt
- ⅛ teaspoon pepper
- 2 tablespoons minced parsley or ⅛ teaspoon dried parsley

Sauté garlic in ¼ cup olive oil until golden but not brown. Discard garlic. Add fresh tomatoes or canned tomatoes with vegetable juice and simmer uncovered for 30 minutes. Place 2 tablespoons oil in another skillet, together with mussels and clams. Simmer until shells open. Remove clams and mussels from shells and add to tomato sauce along with shrimps, cuttlefish, parsley, salt and pepper. Simmer for 10 to 15 minutes. In the meantime, cook spaghetti in boiling salted water for 7 to 10 minutes, stirring often. Drain. Mix with sauce and serve. No cheese is needed. Serves 4.

Spaghetti with Meat Balls

SPAGHETTI CON POLPETTINE

- ½ recipe Meat Patties Maddalena (page 90)
- 1 pound spaghetti
- ¼ cup olive oil
- 1 clove garlic
- 1 cup tomato paste diluted in 2 cups water
- ¼ teaspoon dried basil or 2 large leaves fresh basil
- ½ cup canned vegetable juice cocktail
- ½ cup grated Parmesan cheese
- salt and pepper to taste

Shape meat into balls the size of a walnut instead of patties. Have meat balls cooked. Sauté garlic in oil and discard when golden. Add tomato paste mixture, basil, vegetable juice and bring to a boil. Simmer uncovered for 35 to 40 minutes or until sauce has the right consistency. Season to taste, add meat balls and simmer for 7 to 10 minutes. In the meantime cook spaghetti in large pot of boiling salted water for 7 to 10 minutes or to desired tenderness. Drain. Mix spaghetti with ⅔ of sauce and cheese. Place meat balls in center, pour rest of sauce over all and sprinkle with remaining cheese. Dot with butter and serve. Serves 4-6.

Spaghetti all'Amatriciana

- 1 pound spaghetti
- 3 tablespoons chopped onion
- ½ clove garlic
- 2 tablespoons olive oil
- ½ cup chopped salt meat
- 1½ pounds very ripe Italian egg tomatoes, peeled and diced
- ½ cup grated Parmesan cheese
- ½ cup grated Romano cheese
- salt and pepper to taste

This is a dish from Abruzzo. The cuisine of this Italian region is known for its simple, healthful and at the same time appetizing dishes. A few years ago, Romans took over this dish and now it has become the specialty of many Roman *trattorie*. The traditional recipe calls for Pecorino cheese but as many people find it much too sharp, I have used a combination of Romano and Parmesan cheeses.

Place onion, garlic, oil and salt meat in saucepan. Sauté gently until onion is golden. Remove and discard garlic. Add tomatoes, salt and pepper and simmer for 30 minutes, stirring occasionally. Cook spaghetti in boiling salted water for 10 minutes. Drain. Season with sauce and cheese. Dot with butter and serve. Serves 4.

Spaghetti and Truffles Umbria Style

SPAGHETTI CON TARTUFI ALL'USO D'UMBRIA

- 1 pound spaghetti
- ⅓ cup olive oil
- 1 large clove garlic
- 6 fillets of anchovies chopped and mashed into a paste
- 1 cup tomato paste, diluted in 2 cups lukewarm water
- 2 canned white truffles, the size of a walnut, minced
- salt and pepper to taste

Sauté garlic in oil until golden. Discard garlic and add anchovies and tomato paste mixture. Simmer for 30 minutes, season to taste and simmer 15 minutes more. Meanwhile cook spaghetti in boiling salted water, for 7 to 10 minutes or to desired tenderness, stirring often. Drain spaghetti, season with sauce and serve sprinkled with truffles. Serves 4.

(The original recipe calls for fresh black truffles, but as they are not available in this country, I have substituted white canned truffles because they retain more of their original flavor.)

Spaghetti and Peas

SPAGHETTI CON PISELLI

- 1 pound spaghetti
- ⅓ cup salt pork, chopped to a pulp
- 2 tablespoons olive oil
- 2 slices of onion, finely chopped
- 1 clove garlic
- ½ tablespoon chopped parsley
- 1 tablespoon celery, finely minced.
- 2 cups peeled ripe fresh or canned tomatoes, diced
- 1 tablespoon tomato paste mixed in 1 cup water
- 1 cup fresh or frozen sweet peas
- salt and pepper to taste

Sauté salt pork, olive oil, onion, garlic, parsley and celery over low flame for 5 minutes. Remove garlic and add tomatoes, water and tomato paste. Simmer for 10 minutes. Add peas and salt and pepper. Cook slowly for 30 minutes. Cook spaghetti in boiling salted water for 10 minutes, stirring occasionally. Drain and mix with sauce. Serves 6.

Spaghetti in Tuna Sauce No. 1

SPAGHETTI AL TONNO NO. 1

- 1 pound spaghetti
- ½ cup chopped tuna fish, canned in olive oil
- 5 tablespoons butter
- ⅓ cup olive oil
- ¼ cup chopped parsley

Place the butter, oil, tuna and parsley in small saucepan. Simmer very slowly for 3 or 4 minutes. Add 3 tablespoons water and simmer, without boiling, for 10 minutes more. In the meantime, cook spaghetti in boiling salted water for 10 minutes, stirring occasionally. Drain. Mix with sauce and serve immediately. Serves 6.

Spaghetti with Tuna Sauce No. 2

SPAGHETTI AL TONNO NO. 2

- 1 pound spaghetti
- ⅓ cup olive oil
- 1 clove garlic
- ½ cup tomato paste
- 2 cups water
- ½ cup tuna fish, chopped (preferably canned in olive oil)
- 3 fillets of anchovies, chopped fine
- salt and pepper to taste

Sauté garlic in oil until golden. Discard garlic. Mix tomato paste with water and add to oil. Simmer for 45 minutes. Add anchovies and tuna, salt and pepper. Simmer 10 minutes more. Cook spaghetti in boiling salted water for 10 minutes, stirring occasionally. Drain. Add sauce and serve. Serves 4-6.

Spaghettini with Anchovy Sauce

SPAGHETTINI ALLE ACCIUGHE

½ pound spaghettini (thin spaghetti)	2 small ripe tomatoes, peeled and diced
½ cup olive oil	5 anchovy fillets (canned in olive oil), finely chopped
2 small cloves of garlic	salt and pepper to taste

Brown garlic in oil. Discard garlic when golden. Add tomatoes and simmer for about 10 minutes. Add anchovies and simmer another 2 or 3 minutes. Taste for seasoning.

Cook spaghettini in 4 quarts of boiling salted water for 6 to 7 minutes, stirring occasionally. Drain and mix with sauce. This dish does not require cheese and is very easy and quick to make. Serves 2-4.

Bucatini with Kidney

BUCATINI CON ROGNONE

1 pound bucatini macaroni	2 small onions, chopped
1 small veal kidney	2 tablespoons parsley
¼ pound butter	salt and pepper

Remove fat from kidney, dice and wash in salt water. Place in shallow pan with onion and butter, salt and pepper. Sauté about 10 minutes, or until tender. Meanwhile, boil bucatini macaroni in boiling salted water for 10 minutes, drain and mix with kidney sauce. Sprinkle with parsley and serve. Serves 4-6.

Vermicelli with Clams Transatlantico

VERMICELLI CON LE VONGOLE ALLA TRANSATLANTICO

Here is another recipe from Grande Ristorante Transatlantico in Naples.

1 pound vermicelli	½ cup olive oil
2 pounds Little Neck clams	4 tablespoons chopped parsley
2 cloves garlic	salt and pepper to taste

Brush clams carefully and place in bowl of cold water for one hour. Drain. Place vermicelli in large pot of boiling salted water and cook, stirring often, for 7 to 10 minutes or until of desired tenderness. (Remember not to overcook.) As soon as you start cooking the vermicelli, sauté garlic in oil, discarding when golden. Add clams, cover and cook over medium flame, stirring occasionally, until clams open, about 5 minutes. Add parsley and ¼ teaspoon pepper and simmer for 3 minutes more. Drain vermicelli and place in hot serving dish. Quickly remove clams from sauce and strain sauce through a piece of linen to prevent any sand from getting into the food. Add to vermicelli, mixing well, and top with clams in their shells. No cheese is required. If you feel that the vermicelli are too dry for your taste, add a little butter before adding clams. Serves 4.

Macaroni Pizzaiola

OCCHI DI LUPO ALLA PIZZAIOLA

| 1 pound occhi di lupo (or any other kind of macaroni) | ¾ cup grated Parmesan cheese (optional) |
| 1 recipe Pizzaiola Sauce (page 32) | |

Place macaroni in boiling salted water and cook, stirring often with wooden spoon, for 12 minutes or until tender but still firm. Drain. Mix with sauce and cheese. Serves 4.

Egg Noodle Pie Bologna Style

PASTICCIO DI TAGLIATELLE ALLA BOLOGNESE

1 recipe Homemade Egg Noodles (page 50) or Green Egg Noodles Bologna Style (page 50)	mix or the equivalent in homemade unsweetened pie crust
2 ten-ounce packages pie crust	1 egg
	milk

Make your own pie crust pastry or follow directions on packages, substituting the egg for part of the water. Line a

3-quart baking dish or casserole with ¾ of the pastry. Place Noodles in casserole. Role out rest of pastry and slash it in 2 or 3 places to allow steam to escape while baking, then cover casserole with it, flute edges and brush lightly with milk. Bake in 375° oven for 35 minutes or until crust is lightly golden. Serve cut in wedges, after removing from casserole, or if desired serve directly from casserole. This is a dish especially indicated for company. It can be served as a main dish, or as a first course. Serves 6-8. Bucatini with Kidney (page 62) and Chicken Tetrazzini (page 65) can be served the same way.

Egg Noodle Casserole

PASTICCIO DI FETTUCCINE

- 1 pound wide egg noodles
- 3 eggs, lightly beaten
- 1½ cups grated Parmesan cheese
- ½ cup Swiss cheese, mozzarella, or any mild white cheese, diced
- ¼ pound butter
- ½ cup light cream
- 1 sweetbread, diced
- 4 chicken livers, coarsely diced
- ¼ pound sliced mushrooms
- 3 tablespoons butter
- ¼ cup dry Marsala wine, or any dry red wine
- bread crumbs

Cook noodles in plenty of boiling salted water until tender, but still quite firm. In the meantime, place 3 tablespoons butter, sweetbread, chicken livers and mushrooms in skillet and sauté just long enough to brown the meat. Season to taste with salt and pepper and add wine. Simmer for 5 minutes more, stirring occasionally. Drain noodles, place in a bowl and mix with the butter, grated and diced cheese, mushroom and liver mixture, cream and eggs. Sprinkle a 3-quart greased casserole with bread crumbs, fill it with noodles, sprinkle top with more bread crumbs, and place in 300° oven for 20 to 25 minutes. Remove from oven and let stand for five minutes. Unmold on serving platter or serve directly from casserole. Serves 6-8.

Egg Noodle Timbale

TIMBALLO DI FETTUCCINE

- 1 pound wide egg noodles
- ½ cup imported Italian Pecorino cheese, grated
- ½ cup ricotta cheese
- ½ cup mozzarella cheese, diced
- 1 tablespoon bread crumbs
- 1 cup tomato paste, dissolved in 2 cups warm water
- ⅓ cup olive oil
- 1 clove garlic
- 2 Italian sweet pork sausages, diced
- 2 leaves sweet basil or ¼ teaspoon dried basil
- ½ tablespoon chopped parsley
- salt and pepper to taste

Sauté garlic in oil until golden, then remove. Add tomato paste, sausages, basil and parsley, salt and pepper. Simmer for 30 to 45 minutes. Cook egg noodles in boiling salted water, stirring occasionally, for 5 to 7 minutes. Drain. Put into a large mixing bowl, add cheese, tomato sauce (leaving ⅓ cup aside) and diced sausages. Mix well and pour into baking dish which has been sprinkled with bread crumbs. Top with rest of sauce, and bake in moderate oven for 20 to 25 minutes. Serves 4-6.

Chicken Tetrazzini

SPAGHETTI TETRAZZINI

- ¼ pound sliced mushrooms
- 1 cup cooked chicken, diced
- 3 tablespoons butter
- ½ teaspoon salt
- ⅛ teaspoon pepper
- ¼ cup dry white wine
- 1 pound spaghetti
- 1 cup grated Parmesan cheese
- 2 recipes Mornay Sauce (page 34)

Sauté mushrooms and chicken in butter for 2 minutes, stirring occasionally. Add wine, salt and pepper and cook over medium-high flame for 5 minutes or until wine has evaporated. In the meantime, cook spaghetti in salted water for 10 minutes, drain and mix with rest of ingredients. Place in large buttered baking dish or individual casseroles, and bake in 350° oven for 20 minutes. Serves 6-8.

Macaroni and Cheese Casserole

PASTICCIO DI MACCHERONI

- 2 cups uncooked elbow macaroni
- 1 recipe Mornay Sauce (page 34)
- 1½ cups grated Parmesan or Swiss cheese
- white pepper to taste

Cook elbow macaroni in boiling salted water for about 10 minutes, or until just tender, but still quite firm. Drain. Mix with sauce, cheese and pepper. Turn into buttered casserole, dot with butter and bake at 350° for 30 minutes. Serves 4.

Squab and Macaroni Casserole

PASTICCIO DI MACCHERONI E PICCIONI

- 2 one-pound squabs, each cut in 4 pieces
- 3 chicken livers, diced
- 4 tablespoons butter
- 2 slices prosciutto, diced fine (very lean bacon may be substituted)
- 1 small onion, minced
- ¼ cup carrots, minced
- 3 tablespoons celery, minced
- ⅓ cup dry white wine
- 1 pound mezzani or any small macaroni
- ¼ cup grated Parmesan cheese
- 1 recipe Mornay Sauce (page 43)
- salt and pepper

Gently sauté onion, carrot, celery and prosciutto in butter, until onion is soft. Add squabs and brown. Add wine and let cook uncovered until wine has evaporated. Add one cup water, salt and pepper and cover. Simmer for 20 minutes, add chicken livers and simmer 10 minutes more, or until squabs are tender. Cook macaroni in boiling salted water for about 10 minutes or to desired tenderness. Drain. Bone squabs and dice meat, and add to macaroni together with squab gravy, previously strained, ¾ of the Mornay Sauce, and the Parmesan cheese. Mix well and place in well-buttered casserole, pour rest of sauce over all and bake at 350° for 20 minutes. Serves 6.

Macaroni Pie

PASTICCIO DI MACCHERONI

- 2 ten-ounce packages pie crust mix or the equivalent in homemade unsweetened pie crust
- 1 egg
- 1 pound rigatoni or any other kind of macaroni
- 1 recipe Neapolitan Tomato Sauce (page 32) or your favorite tomato sauce
- 1½ cups grated Parmesan cheese
- 3 tablespoons butter
- milk

Make a pie crust according to directions on packages, or your own, substituting the egg for part of the water. Line a 3-quart baking dish or casserole with ¾ of the pastry. In the meantime cook macaroni in boiling salted water until tender. Drain and season with tomato sauce, cheese and butter. Place this mixture in lined baking dish or casserole. Be sure that the macaroni has enough sauce, but at the same time there should not be too much of it or the bottom and sides of crust will not be as crisp as they should be. Roll out rest of pastry and slash it in 2 or 3 places to allow steam to escape while baking. (Instead of slashing crust, you may cut out the center with a small fancy-shaped cookie cutter.) Then cover casserole with it, flute edges and brush lightly with milk. Bake in 375° oven for 35 minutes or until crust is lightly golden. Serve cut in wedges. Serves 6-8.

RICE

Rice with Sage

RISOTTO IN CAGNONE

- 1 pound rice
- ¼ pound butter
- 1 clove garlic
- ½ teaspoon sage
- ½ cup grated Parmesan cheese

Cook rice in boiling salted water for 15 to 18 minutes. Two or three minutes before rice is done, gently sauté garlic and sage in butter, being careful not to let butter become brown. Discard garlic as soon as it becomes lightly golden. Drain rice, place in serving dish, pour hot butter over it and mix well. Sprinkle with cheese and serve. Serves 4.

Green Rice

RISO VERDE

1 recipe Rice with Sage (see above)
2 tablespoons cooked strained spinach

Blend spinach with rice and serve. Especially indicated to serve with roast turkey or capon.

Rice with Mushrooms

RISOTTO CON FUNGHI

1 pound rice
1 pound mushrooms, sliced
2 tablespoons olive oil
¼ pound whipped sweet butter
1 clove garlic
2 tablespoons onion, minced
½ cup grated Parmesan cheese

Cook rice in boiling salted water for 15 to 18 minutes. About 5 minutes before rice is cooked, gently sauté garlic and onion in oil and half of the butter, until onion is soft but not brown. Discard garlic. Add mushrooms, sprinkle with salt and pepper and cook over medium flame, stirring frequently, for about 4 minutes. Drain rice, place in hot serving dish, add mushrooms, rest of butter and cheese. Serves 4-6.

Rice alla Milanese

RISOTTO ALLA MILANESE

Risotto alla Milanese is a very simple dish to prepare and at the same time it is a very delicious one. Very few people outside Milan know how to make it well. One is frequently served the so-called Risotto alla Milanese with fundamentally only a vague resemblance to the traditional Risotto Ambrosiano. Here is the recipe used by the Giannino Restaurant in Milan, given to me by the owner, Mr. Cesare Bindi.

2 cups rice
1 small onion, chopped very fine
⅓ cup of raw beef marrow, diced fine
¼ pound whipped sweet butter
8 cups beef broth
⅛ teaspoon powdered saffron
1 cup freshly grated Parmesan cheese
salt to taste

Place onion in a piece of wet cheesecloth and squeeze out some of the juice. Place onion in deep saucepan with 3 tablespoons butter and the diced marrow. Cook very slowly for 2 to 4 minutes taking care that the onion does not become brown. Add the rice. Stir constantly with a wooden spoon. After a minute or so, add a cup of hot broth. Continue adding hot broth as needed, stirring occasionally. Cook for 10 minutes and add saffron. Rice should be cooked over medium high flame. Continue adding broth and stirring until rice is cooked (about 5 to 8 more minutes). Correct seasoning. By this time all of the broth in the pan should have been absorbed by the rice; at the same time rice should not be too dry. Place rice on hot serving dish with rest of the butter and the Parmesan cheese. Mix well and serve immediately. Serves 4-6.

Rice Country Style

RISOTTO PAESANO

- 2 cups rice
- 2 pounds shell beans or ½ cup red kidney beans soaked overnight
- 4 tablespoons butter
- 3 slices bacon, diced
- 2 tablespoons olive oil
- 1 small onion, minced
- 2 medium potatoes, peeled and diced
- ½ cup carrots, diced
- 1½ cups zucchini, diced
- ⅓ cup celery, diced
- 2 cups cabbage, diced
- ¼ cup grated Parmesan cheese
- salt and pepper to taste

Shell beans and place in saucepan with 3 quarts of slightly salted water. Bring to a boil, cover and cook for one hour or until tender. Then place butter, bacon, oil and onion in large saucepan and sauté gently for five minutes. Add potatoes, carrots, zucchini, celery and cabbage. Simmer uncovered 3 to 4 minutes, stirring occasionally. Add two cups of warm water and simmer uncovered until three quarters of the liquid has evaporated. Add rice and cook for 2 minutes, stirring occasionally, over low flame. Drain beans and add to rice together with two cups of bean broth. Keep rest of bean broth hot. Cook rice over medium flame for 15 to 18 minutes, stirring occasionally, and continue adding bean broth as needed (about 6 to 7 cups). When rice is tender, season with salt and pepper to taste. Add cheese and serve. Serves 6.

Rice Finanziera

RISOTTO ALLA FINANZIERA

- 2 cups rice
- 2 tablespoons onion, chopped fine
- 4 tablespoons butter
- 5 to 6 cups beef broth

SAUCE:

- 4 tablespoons beef marrow
- 4 tablespoons butter
- 2 tablespoons onion, chopped fine
- 8 chicken livers, diced
- 1 slice of lemon peel about 2 inches long and 1 inch wide
- ¼ cup dry Marsala wine or other dry wine
- ½ cup Parmesan cheese
- salt and pepper to taste

Place marrow, butter and 2 tablespoons onion in small saucepan. Simmer slowly for 5 minutes. Add chicken livers and lemon peel. Simmer 3 minutes more. Add wine, salt and pepper to taste, and simmer 10 minutes. Remove lemon peel. While sauce is cooking, sauté onion in butter. Add rice, stir, cover and simmer for 2 or 3 minutes; add one cup of broth and continue adding a cup of broth at a time when necessary till rice is cooked (about 15 to 18 minutes). Correct seasoning. Add sauce and one half of the cheese to rice. Place in serving dish, sprinkle with rest of cheese and dot with butter. Serves 4-6.

Risotto Fagiano

RISOTTO ALLA FAGIANO

- 2 cups rice
- 1 medium onion, minced
- ¼ pound butter
- 6 cups hot chicken or beef broth or water
- breast of a small chicken
- ¼ cup dry white wine
- 1 cup fresh or frozen peas, cooked in salted water until tender
- ½ cup grated Parmesan cheese
- 1 white truffle, the size of a large walnut, sliced paper-thin
- salt and pepper to taste

Gently sauté onion until soft (leaving aside 2 tablespoons of it) in 4 tablespoons butter. Add rice and simmer for 8 minutes, stirring often. Add 1½ cups of broth or water; continue to add as needed, stirring occasionally, and cook for 15 to 18 minutes, seasoning to taste. While rice is cooking, brown chicken breast in 2 tablespoons butter, add wine, lower flame and let it cook uncovered for 12 to 15 minutes turning occasionally. Also sauté until soft, 2 tablespoons onion in rest of butter, add to it the peas and let simmer for a few minutes, stirring occasionally. Remove chicken from stove, bone and dice it and add to rice together with peas, mixing well. Remove to hot serving dish, sprinkle with Parmesan and sliced truffle. Serves 4-6.

(*Recipe from Ristorante Fagiano & Taverna Fagianetta, Rome*)

Rice and Kidney Casserole

RISO CON ROGNONCINI TRIFOLATI

- 1½ cups rice
- 4 tablespoons butter
- 4 tablespoons olive oil
- 1 small onion, minced
- 2 tablespoons leek, minced
- 1 tablespoon chopped parsley
- 3 small veal kidneys, diced, or 6 lamb kidneys, diced
- 4 small zucchini, diced
- ¼ cup dry white wine
- ⅓ cup beef broth
- ¼ cup grated Parmesan cheese

Cook rice in boiling salted water for 10 minutes. Drain. While rice is cooking, sauté onion, leek and parsley in butter and oil. Do not allow onion to become brown. Add kidney, stir and cook over medium flame for 3 minutes, stirring occasionally. Add zucchini, stir and cook over medium-high flame for 10 minutes. Add rice, wine and broth and mix well. Add salt and pepper to taste. Remove rice to a casserole and bake in 375° oven for 30 minutes. Serve sprinkled with cheese and dotted with butter. Serves 4-6.

Lamb kidneys should stand in salted water for at least 2 hours before using. Some people prefer lamb to veal kidneys as the former make a juicier dish.

Rice Casserole Genoa Style

RISO ALLA GENOVESE

- 2 cups rice
- 4 tablespoons butter
- 4 fresh sweet Italian sausages with casings removed, minced, or: ¼ pound fresh pork, chopped
- ½ onion, minced
- the raw hearts of 2 fresh artichokes, diced
- 1 cup fresh or frozen peas
- ½ pound mushrooms, sliced
- 3 cups beef or chicken broth
- ⅓ cup grated Parmesan cheese
- 1 teaspoon fresh parsley, chopped, or ⅛ teaspoon dried parsley
- 1 tablespoon bread crumbs
- 3 tablespoons melted butter
- salt and pepper to taste

Gently sauté sausages or chopped pork and onion in 4 tablespoons butter until meat is brown. Add artichokes, peas, parsley and mushrooms. Cover and simmer for 5 minutes. Add broth, salt and pepper, stir and cover, simmering for 30 minutes. Taste for salt and pepper. Cook rice in salted water for 7 minutes, drain and add to cooked ingredients. Mix well and add two tablespoons of cheese. Place in buttered casserole and bake in 375° oven for 15 minutes. Remove from oven, sprinkle with rest of cheese, bread crumbs and melted butter. Return to oven for 15 minutes more. Serves 4-6.

Rice and Shrimp Adriatic Style

RISOTTO CON SCAMPI ALL'ADRIATICA

- 2 cups rice
- 1 pound fresh small shrimps
- ¼ cup olive oil
- 4 tablespoons onion, chopped fine
- 2 tablespoons carrot, chopped fine
- 1 tablespoon celery, minced
- 1 clove garlic
- 1 cup dry white wine
- 5 cups hot water
- 6 tablespoons butter
- 1 teaspoon salt
- ⅓ cup grated Parmesan cheese
- 3 tablespoons butter
- salt and pepper to taste

Shell and devein shrimps. Do not discard shells. Rinse shrimps and shells separately in cold water. Slowly sauté carrot, celery, garlic and two tablespoons onion in olive oil. Remove garlic when golden. Add wine and shells and simmer for 10 minutes. Add water and 1 teaspoon salt, cover and simmer for 30 minutes. Sauté rest of onion in 6 tablespoons butter till lightly golden. Add shrimps and simmer for 5 minutes. Add rice. Cook uncovered, stirring occasionally, for 3 or 4 minutes. Strain broth of shells, skim off fat and add 2 cups of broth to rice. Rice should be cooked over medium flame. Continue adding hot broth as needed, stirring occasionally. Cook rice 15 to 18 minutes. Correct seasoning. Rice should have absorbed all the broth in the pan, but at the same time it should not be too dry. Serve immediately, sprinkled with cheese and dotted with butter. Serves 6.

CORN MEAL

Soft Polenta

POLENTA TENERA

2 quarts water
2 cups yellow corn meal
1 tablespoon salt

Place water and salt in large saucepan, bring to a boil and gradually pour corn meal into water, stirring constantly with a wooden spoon to prevent lumping. Cook over medium flame, stirring constantly for about 30 minutes or until of the consistency of mashed potatoes.

Thick Polenta

POLENTA DURA

1 recipe Soft Polenta (see above)

Cook corn meal 25 minutes more, or until it forms a crust at the bottom and sides of the pan.

Polenta Casserole

POLENTA AL FORNO

1 recipe Thick Polenta (see above)
3 cups cooked turkey, diced
1 pound mushrooms, sliced
3 tablespoons butter
½ cup grated Parmesan cheese
1 recipe Tomato Sauce Italian Style (page 31)

Sauté mushrooms in butter for 5 minutes. Then place corn meal in a large buttered baking dish, level off top with a spoon, and cover with turkey, mushrooms, sauce and cheese. Sprinkle with freshly ground black pepper and bake in 350° oven for 45 minutes. Serves 6.

Polenta Ring with Chicken Livers

ANELLO DI POLENTA CON FEGATINI

- 1 recipe Thick Polenta (page 73)
- 1 pound mushrooms, sliced
- 1½ pounds chicken livers, coarsely diced
- 4 tablespoons butter
- 3 slices lean bacon, diced
- ¼ cup dry white wine
- ¼ teaspoon sage
- salt and pepper to taste

Place polenta in a well-buttered 2-quart ring mold, and keep warm by placing ring in a larger pan with hot water until ready to serve. Then place bacon in a skillet, and sauté until crisp. Add butter, livers and mushrooms. Sauté, stirring often, over medium flame just long enough to brown livers (about one or two minutes). Season to taste and add sage and wine. Lower flame and cook for 2 or 3 minutes more. Remove polenta from ring to a round platter, place mushrooms and livers in the center and pour pan juice over polenta. Serves 6-8.

Polenta with Sausage

POLENTA PASTICCIATA CON SALSICCIA

- 1 recipe Soft Polenta (page 73)
- 6 tablespoons butter
- ½ pound sweet or hot Italian sausage with casings removed, diced
- ¼ teaspoon sage
- 1 cup tomato paste diluted in 2 cups beef broth or water
- ½ cup grated Parmesan cheese
- salt and pepper to taste

Gently sauté sausage in butter for 10 minutes, stirring occasionally. Add sage, tomato paste mixture, salt and pepper and simmer uncovered for 30 to 40 minutes, until sauce has reached right consistency. Taste for seasoning and place polenta on large hot platter. Using a tablespoon greased on the outside, make depressions in polenta, pour sauce over all and sprinkle with cheese. Serves 4.

EGG DISHES

UOVA

Frog Legs Omelet

FRITTATA DI RANE

- 8 eggs, slightly beaten
- 6 pair frog legs, boned and diced
- 8 tablespoons olive oil
- salt and pepper

Sauté frog legs in 4 tablespoons of oil for about 8 minutes over low heat. Drain off oil and add legs to eggs, salt and pepper. Place rest of oil in clean skillet and cook egg mixture over low flame for 3 or 4 minutes. Holding a dish over top of skillet, turn skillet over, then slide omelet back into pan with cooked side up. Continue cooking another 2 or 3 minutes. Serves 4.

Mushroom Omelet

FRITTATA DI FUNGHI

- 6 eggs
- 1/4 pound mushrooms, sliced
- 2 tablespoons grated Parmesan cheese
- 1/4 teaspoon nutmeg
- 6 tablespoons olive oil
- 1/2 teaspoon salt
- 1/4 teaspoon pepper

Sauté mushrooms in 2 tablespoons olive oil, over low flame for 5 minutes. Drain. Add salt, pepper and nutmeg to eggs and beat. Put remainder of oil in clean frying pan and cook egg mixture in it, over low flame, for 4 or 5 minutes. Cover with drained mushrooms. Fold omelet and cook another minute. Sprinkle with Parmesan cheese and serve immediately. Serves 4.

Spinach Omelet

FRITTATA DI SPINACI

½ pound spinach
8 eggs, beaten
8 tablespoons olive oil
salt and pepper

Cook spinach in salted water until tender (about 15 minutes). Drain. Sauté in 3 tablespoons olive oil, stirring often, for about 3 minutes. Place spinach, eggs, salt and pepper in a bowl and mix well. Pour rest of oil into clean frying pan and cook egg mixture over medium heat 2 to 3 minutes. Hold a dish upside down over skillet, turn skillet over, then slide omelet back into the pan with the cooked side up and cook for 2 or 3 minutes more. Serves 4.

Onion Omelet

FRITTATA DI CIPOLLE

2 medium-size onions, sliced thin
10 well-beaten eggs
8 tablespoons olive oil
salt and pepper

Sauté onions in 3 tablespoons of oil for 6 to 8 minutes, over low heat. Drain off oil and add onions to eggs, salt and pepper. Place rest of oil in clean skillet and cook egg mixture over low heat for 3 to 4 minutes. Holding a dish over top of skillet, turn skillet over, then slide omelet back in pan with cooked side up. Cook another 3 to 4 minutes. Serves 6.

Potato Omelet No. 1

FRITTATA DI PATATE NO. 1

7 large potatoes, boiled in skins and mashed
7 egg yolks
3 egg whites, beaten stiff
1 pinch of nutmeg
⅓ cup grated Parmesan cheese
5 tablespoons olive oil
1 tablespoon fresh parsley, chopped
salt and pepper

Mix mashed potatoes, egg yolks, parsley, cheese, nutmeg, salt and pepper and finally fold in egg whites. Place olive oil in 9-inch skillet. When hot, add the potato mixture. Level top with spoon. Cook over low flame for about 6 to 8 minutes on each side. Serves 6-8.

Potato Omelet No. 2

FRITTATA DI PATATE NO. 2

7 large potatoes, boiled in skins and mashed	3 tablespoons prepared tomato sauce
5 eggs, beaten	5 tablespoons olive oil
1 large onion, chopped	salt and pepper

Mix mashed potatoes, eggs, tomato sauce and salt and pepper. Sauté onion in oil. Do not allow to brown. Remove onion (leaving oil in skillet) and add to potato mixture. Mix well. Place potatoes in skillet with oil, over high flame, reduce heat to low, and cook about 6 to 8 minutes on each side. Serves 6-8.

Peas and Eggs

PISELLI CON UOVA

3 tablespoons olive oil	1 teaspoon salt
4 slices lean bacon, diced	½ teaspoon pepper
2 boxes frozen sweet peas	4 large eggs

Place oil and bacon in 8-inch skillet and simmer for 5 minutes. Add peas, salt and pepper. Simmer uncovered for 30 minutes, stirring occasionally. Add a little hot water if necessary. Level top with a spoon and break each egg on top of peas. Cover and let cook for 4 to 6 minutes. Eggs should look poached. Serves 4.

Scrambled Eggs with Sausage

UOVA STRAPAZZATE CON LA SALSICCIA

2 fresh Italian sweet sausages	8 eggs, beaten
¼ cup olive oil or butter	salt and pepper to taste

Break each sausage in 4 to 5 pieces and sauté gently in oil, turning occasionally, for 6 minutes. Add eggs and cook over low flame for about 3 minutes, stirring occasionally. Serves 4.

Eggs Florentine

UOVA ALLA FIORENTINA

- 6 lightly poached eggs
- 1 recipe Spinach in Butter (page 130)
- ½ recipe Mornay Sauce (page 34)
- 3 tablespoons grated Parmesan cheese
- 1 tablespoon bread crumbs
- pepper to taste

Place spinach in a buttered baking dish. Level top with a spoon and arrange eggs on top. Pour Mornay Sauce over all and sprinkle with cheese and bread crumbs. Bake in 350° oven for 15 minutes. Serves 3-6.

FISH

PESCI

ʃʃʃ

Baked Fillets of Flounder

FILETTI DI PESCE PASSERA GRATINATI

8 fillets of flounder
½ cup olive oil
1 tablespoon wine vinegar
⅓ teaspoon oregano
salt and pepper

Mix oil, vinegar, oregano, salt and pepper. Place fish fillets in single layer in greased baking dish. Pour oil mixture over all and bake in 375° oven for 20 minutes. Serves 4.

Broiled Flounder

PESCE PASSERA AI FERRI

4 flounders, cleaned, about 1 pound each
flour
olive oil
8 tablespoons butter
3 tablespoons parsley, minced
2 lemons cut in wedges

Roll fish in flour, then brush with oil, using a pastry brush, and sprinkle with salt and pepper. Broil for 10 minutes each side. Mix butter, parsley and the juice of half a lemon in small saucepan, over very low flame. Allow butter to melt, then pour over fish and serve with wedges of lemon. Serves 4.

Flounder, as many other fish, is delicious broiled on charcoal. Try it. With a cool bottle of Orvieto and a good salad it will be a perfect summer meal.

Fillet of Flounder with Mushrooms

FILETTI DI PESCE PASSARA AI FUNGHI

2 pounds fillet of flounder	4 tablespoons butter
1 cup milk	2 tablespoons grated Parmesan cheese (optional)
½ pound white seedless grapes	½ cup heavy cream
½ pound sliced mushrooms	salt and pepper to taste
1 tablespoon flour	

Sauté mushrooms in 3 tablespoons butter for 3 to 4 minutes, stirring occasionally. Season to taste. Poach fillets in milk, by pouring milk in large skillet; when boiling add fish, salt and pepper to taste, and simmer for 5 to 10 minutes, depending on thickness of fillets. Remove fish. Cream butter and flour and stir into the milk left in skillet. Add cheese and cream and continue stirring until it becomes as thick as medium white sauce. Arrange fish in buttered baking dish in layers with grapes and mushrooms, cover with sauce and bake at 400° for 10 to 12 minutes. Serves 4-6.

Mackerel Fillets Venetian Style

FILETTI DI SGOMBRO ALLA VENETA

4 mackerel fillets	1½ cups dry white wine
½ teaspoon salt	about ¾ cup Venetian Sauce (page 41)

Place fillets, wine and salt in saucepan, bring to a boil, cover and simmer for about 10 minutes. Drain fillets, place in individual plates or serving dish and pour sauce over fish. Serves 4.

Baked Whiting in Green Sauce

MERLANGO GRATINATO AL VERDE

2 whitings, about one pound each	7 tablespoons olive oil
	bread crumbs
4 tablespoons parsley, finely minced	1 lemon, cut in wedges
	salt and pepper to taste

Mix parsley, salt, pepper and 6 tablespoons olive oil. Place whiting in greased baking dish, pour oil mixture over them, sprinkle lightly with bread crumbs and rest of oil. Bake in

375° oven for 25 minutes. Remove from oven and serve with lemon wedges. Serves 2.

Fillets of Bass Massaia Style

PESCE PERSICO ALLA MASSAIA

- 1½ pounds bass fillets
- 1 tablespoon salt
- 1 bay leaf
- 1 tablespoon wine vinegar
- ⅓ teaspoon thyme
- 1 cup Heavy White Sauce (page 35)
- ⅓ cup heavy cream at room temperature
- 3 tablespoons melted butter
- 3 hard-boiled eggs, finely diced
- ½ cup parsley, finely minced

Bring to a boil 2 quarts of water with 1 tablespoon salt, bay leaf, vinegar and thyme. Boil for 5 minutes and add fillets. Cover and cook over low flame for about 10 minutes. Add heavy cream and butter to white sauce. Drain fillets. Place on serving dish, top with white sauce and sprinkle with eggs and parsley. Serves 4.

Cuttlefish Veneziana

SEPPIE ALLA VENEZIANA

- 2 pounds very small cuttlefish
- ⅓ cup olive oil
- 2 cloves garlic
- ½ cup dry white wine
- salt and pepper to taste

Cuttlefish is best when very small and should be cooked whole. Sauté garlic in oil until golden, then discard garlic and add fish. Cook uncovered over medium heat stirring occasionally, until all moisture has evaporated, then add wine, salt and pepper to taste, and continue cooking for 10 to 15 minutes more. Serve with Soft Polenta (page 73). Serves 4.

Cuttlefish in Tomato Sauce

SEPPIE AL POMIDORO

- 2 pounds small cuttlefish, cleaned
- ⅓ cup olive oil
- 2 tablespoons onion, minced
- 1 clove garlic
- 3 tablespoons tomato paste diluted in ½ cup water
- ½ cup dry white wine
- ⅛ teaspoon crushed red pepper
- salt and pepper to taste

Gently sauté garlic and onion in olive oil until golden. Discard garlic, add tomato mixture and simmer uncovered for 10 minutes. Add fish, wine, salt and pepper, and crushed red pepper. Simmer uncovered for 15 to 20 minutes. Serve hot. Serves 4. Serve with a tossed green salad.

Fillets of Sole Oltremare

SOGLIOLE D'OLTREMARE

8 small fillets of sole	1 dozen mussels, shelled
flour	1 tablespoon butter
1 large egg, beaten	½ lemon
4 tablespoons butter	2 tablespoons parsley, chopped
1 dozen very small shrimps, shelled and cleaned	salt and pepper to taste

Season fillets slightly with salt and pepper, roll in flour and dip in egg. Place 2 at a time in 4 tablespoons hot butter and sauté until golden on both sides (use medium high flame so as not to burn the butter). Remove fillets to hot dish and keep warm. Place shrimps and mussels in skillet in which fillets were cooked, together with 1 tablespoon butter, and cook over medium high flame for 5 minutes. Sprinkle with lemon juice and parsley, reduce flame and simmer 2 minutes more. Cover fillets with shrimps and mussels and serve. Serves 4.

(Recipe from Ristorante D'Angelo, Naples)

Fillet of Sole Messalina

FILETTI DI SOGLIOLA ALLA MESSALINA

2 pounds fillet of sole	tomatoes, peeled and diced
½ pound mushrooms, sliced	or 1½ cups hardpack canned
¾ cup good dry white wine	tomatoes put through a sieve
1 tablespoon tomato paste	4 tablespoons butter, melted
½ pound very ripe Italian egg	salt and pepper to taste

Place mushrooms in bottom of large buttered baking dish. Fold each fillet in two and place in single layer on top of mushrooms. Sprinkle with salt and pepper and pour wine over all. Bake in 375° oven for 20 to 25 minutes. Drain liquid from baking pan without disturbing the fish (keep fish warm) and place in saucepan with tomato paste. Bring to a boil and cook until liquid is reduced by three-fourths. Add fresh or canned tomatoes and cook uncovered over medium flame for 15 to 20 minutes or until sauce is thick. Remove from stove and add butter. Arrange fillets on serving platter or individual plates, place mushrooms on top of fillets, and pour sauce over all. Serves 4.

One of the oldest hotels in Venice is the Albergo Cavaletto & Doge Orseolo. It has been in business since 1308 and is today one of the loveliest spots in Venice. At one time, part of the building was an hospice of the Ursulines. It was given to this Order by the Doge Orseolo and afterwards became a part of the hotel. All through the centuries it has been a favorite with writers, musicians, painters and sculptors; it has given its name to the *calle*, the Basin, the bridge and the arch that leads from Piazza San Marco to the hotel. At present, it is more of a family hotel with all the charm and comforts of home. Its restaurant, one of the best in Italy, has for its chef the well-known Domenico di Sciullo who was kind enough to give me the recipes of some of its famous dishes. Here is one of them:

Shrimps di Sciullo

SCAMPI ALLA DI SCIULLO

2 pounds large shrimps
flour
2 large eggs, beaten
¼ pound butter

2 cups sliced mushrooms, sautéed in butter for 3 to 4 minutes
¼ cup dry white wine
salt and pepper

Shell and devein shrimps. Rinse in cold water and drain. Sprinkle lightly with salt and pepper, roll in flour and dip in beaten egg. Melt butter in large skillet. Add shrimps and sauté over medium flame, turning often, until shrimps are golden. Add mushrooms, sprinkle with wine and cook over medium high flame for 2 minutes or until most of wine has evaporated. Serves 4.

Grilled Shrimps

SCAMPI ALLA GRIGLIA

2 pounds large shrimps	2 tablespoons parsley, finely chopped
about ½ cup olive oil	
¼ teaspoon pepper	4 tablespoons butter
½ teaspoon salt	juice of large lemon

Shell and devein shrimps. Rinse in cold water. Mix oil, salt, pepper and parsley. Dip shrimps in this mixture. Broil at 500° about 2 inches from flame for 2 minutes on each side. Remove to a baking dish, sprinkle with 4 tablespoons of the oil mixture and bake in 450° oven for 10 minutes. Remove shrimps to hot serving dish, or individual plates, and keep warm. Add the butter and lemon juice to baking dish and return to oven for 2 or 3 minutes, removing as soon as butter is hot. Pour over shrimps. Serve with fried potatoes. Serves 4.

Cod Vicentina

BACCALÀ ALLA VICENTINA

2 pounds salt cod, cut in 4-inch squares and soaked for 24 hours	2 cloves garlic, finely chopped
	1 small onion, chopped
6 tablespoons grated Parmesan cheese	4 anchovies, chopped
	3 tablespoons parsley, chopped
¼ cup olive oil	½ cup dry white wine
4 tablespoons butter	1½ cups milk

Place cod, in single layer, in large well-buttered baking dish. Sprinkle with Parmesan cheese.

Brown garlic and onion in oil. Remove garlic, add anchovies, parsley and wine. Simmer for 5 minutes. Add 1 tablespoon butter and the milk. Bring slowly to boiling point. Pour this sauce over cod. Dot with remaining butter and bake in moderate oven until the cod has absorbed the sauce. Serve with polenta. Serves 6.

Cod Benedettina

BACCALÀ ALLA BENEDETTINA

1½ pounds boneless salt cod, cut in serving pieces and soaked for 24 hours
2 cups hot mashed potatoes
¼ cup olive oil
1 cup heavy cream, whipped very stiff
3 tablespoons butter

Boil cod in a small amount of water for 15 minutes. Remove skin. Mash cod into a smooth paste. Add mashed potatoes. Add olive oil slowly. Stir well. Add whipped cream and mix thoroughly. Pour into well-buttered baking dish. Dot with butter and bake in moderate oven for 20 minutes. Serves 6.

This dish can also be served as a fish pie, by placing cod mixture in uncooked pie crust and then baking in a moderate oven for about 20 to 30 minutes or till crust is done.

Cod Biscaglia

BACCALÀ BISCAGLIA

2 pounds salt cod, cut in pieces about 3 by 4 inches and soaked in water for 24 hours
flour
olive oil, as needed (about 2 cups)
2 pounds fresh peeled tomatoes, diced
2 cloves garlic
⅓ cup parsley, chopped
salt and pepper to taste

Dip cod in flour and sauté in olive oil until golden on both sides. Place on serving dish and keep warm. Brown garlic in 4 tablespoons of oil in which the cod was cooked. Remove garlic. Add pepper, salt, and tomatoes and simmer slowly for about 20 minutes. The sauce should be thick. Pour over cod and sprinkle with parsley. Serves 6.

Cod Mistral

MERLUZZO ALLA MISTRAL

4 slices of fresh cod about ½ inch thick, dipped in flour
½ cup olive oil
1 pound ripe peeled tomatoes, diced
1 clove garlic
1 tablespoon fresh parsley, chopped
½ cup dry white wine
½ pound sliced mushrooms
3 tablespoons bread crumbs
2 tablespoons butter
salt and pepper to taste

Lightly sauté cod in oil till both sides are golden. Remove cod from skillet and place it in large baking dish, the bottom of which has been sprinkled with half of the bread crumbs. Add tomatoes to oil left in the skillet, together with garlic, salt and pepper and parsley. Simmer for 10 minutes. Remove garlic and add wine and mushrooms. Simmer till half of the wine has evaporated. Add sauce to cod, after having removed part of the oil with a spoon. Sprinkle with bread crumbs and dot with butter. Bake in moderate oven for 15 to 25 minutes. Serves 4.

Fillets of Cod Florentine

FILETTI DI MERLUZZO ALLA FIORENTINA

- 8 small fillets of fresh cod
- 2 pounds fresh or frozen spinach, cooked in salted water and sautéed in butter
- 1½ cups dry white wine
- ⅓ cup grated Parmesan cheese
- 1 cup Mornay Sauce (page 34)
- salt and pepper

Make a single layer of the fillets in a large skillet. Sprinkle lightly with salt and pepper and add wine. Simmer for 10 minutes. Remove fillets from skillet. Place spinach in baking dish about 9 inches wide, and top with fillets. Cover with Mornay Sauce and sprinkle with Parmesan cheese. Place in 350° oven for about 15 to 20 minutes. Serves 4-6.

Tunafish Patties Nizzarda

POLPETTE DI TONNO ALLA NIZZARDA

- 14-ounce can tuna fish
- 2 cups mashed potatoes
- ¼ cup grated Parmesan cheese
- 3 eggs, well beaten
- 4 tablespoons parsley, chopped
- 1 clove garlic, chopped very fine
- ½ teaspoon salt
- ¼ teaspoon pepper
- ½ cup bread crumbs
- 2 cups olive oil

Mash tuna thoroughly and mix to a smooth paste with potatoes, cheese, eggs, parsley, garlic and seasoning. Shape into flat cakes, ½ inch thick and 2 inches in diameter. Dip in bread crumbs and fry in hot oil until golden. Serve hot or cold. Serves 6.

Lobster Fra Diavolo

ARAGOSTA FRA' DIAVOLO

- 2 live lobsters, about 1½ pounds each
- ½ cup olive oil
- 1 clove garlic, finely chopped
- ½ small onion, chopped
- 1 pound fresh peeled tomatoes, chopped
- 2 tablespoons tomato paste dissolved in 2 tablespoons water
- ⅔ cup white wine
- ½ teaspoon red pepper
- 4 teaspoons parsley, chopped
- 1 teaspoon oregano
- salt and pepper

Wash lobsters. Chop off claws and cut lobsters into three pieces each. Crack claws with flat side of knife. Heat oil in large skillet until very hot. Add lobsters and cook over high heat for 3 to 4 minutes. Add garlic. Then with one minute intervals of cooking between them, add salt, pepper and onion. When lobsters are red, add tomatoes and paste. After 2 to 3 minutes add wine, parsley, oregano and red pepper. Stir. The fire should be hot and the whole cooking process should not take more than 15 minutes. Serves 2-4.

Eels Marinara

ANGUILLE IN UMIDO ALLA MARINARA

- 2 pounds fresh eels, cleaned and cut into 3-inch pieces
- ⅓ cup olive oil
- 1 small onion, minced
- 2 cloves garlic
- 1 small piece of lemon peel, about 2x1 inch
- ⅛ teaspoon sage
- 2 tablespoons tomato paste diluted in ½ cup water
- ½ cup dry white wine
- salt and pepper to taste

Place oil in saucepan together with onion, garlic, lemon peel and sage. Sauté gently until garlic is golden. Discard garlic. Add eels and cook over low flame for 4 to 5 minutes, turning occasionally. Add tomato paste mixture and wine. Simmer uncovered for 10 minutes. Season to taste and simmer uncovered for 10 minutes more. Almost all moisture should be gone. Serves 2-4.

Molded Salmon

SPUMA DI SALMONE

- 1 pound canned salmon
- 6 tablespoons butter, at room temperature
- ¾ cup heavy cream, beaten stiff
- 1 envelope unflavored gelatine
- ¼ cup cold water
- ½ cup boiling water
- ¼ teaspoon salt
- salt and pepper to taste

Mix drained salmon and butter into a smooth paste. Add salt and pepper to taste and put through a sieve. Blend with cream. Dissolve gelatine in ¼ cup cold water. Add boiling water, ¼ teaspoon salt and stir until gelatine is dissolved. Place in refrigerator for a few minutes until thoroughly chilled and slightly thickened, then pour a thin layer on bottom of mold and place in refrigerator until set. Now coat the sides of mold with a thin layer of gelatine, about ¼ inch thick. This is done by pouring enough gelatine on one side only of the mold and placing it in the refrigerator until set. When mold is completely coated with gelatine, place salmon mixture in mold, level top with spoon and chill for not less than 3 hours. Serves 4-6. It can be prepared the day before, if desired.

MEAT

CARNE

//

BEEF

Short Ribs Italian Style

COSTE ALL'ITALIANA

- 3 pounds lean short ribs of beef
- 3 tablespoons butter
- ⅓ cup chopped salt pork
- ¼ cup cognac
- 1¼ cups beef broth
- juice of one large lemon
- salt and pepper to taste

Place butter, salt meat and short ribs in saucepan. Cook over medium-high flame until meat is browned on all sides. Add cognac and broth, salt and pepper and cook 10 minutes more. Remove meat with its gravy to a casserole, cover and bake in oven at 400° for 1½ to 2 hours, depending upon thickness, basting occasionally. Remove meat to hot platter. Skim off fat from cooking gravy. Place gravy in small saucepan and cook over high flame for 5 minutes. Remove from stove, add lemon juice and pour over meat. Serve with Potato Croquettes (page 144). Serves 6.

Beef Stew

STUFATO DI MANZO AL VINO BIANCO

- 2 pounds boneless neck, flank or chuck of beef, cut for stew
- 1 teaspoon salt
- ½ teaspoon pepper
- dash crushed red pepper
- ⅛ teaspoon nutmeg
- ¼ teaspoon thyme
- 1 small laurel leaf
- 1 tablespoon celery, chopped
- 3 small cloves of garlic
- 2 cups dry white wine
- 1 large onion, sliced fine
- ¼ cup salt pork, chopped fine
- 3 slices bacon, chopped fine
- 1 tablespoon olive oil

Place meat in large bowl with salt, pepper, crushed red pepper, nutmeg, thyme, laurel, celery, 1 clove garlic and wine. Cover and let marinate overnight. Sauté rest of garlic and onion with salt pork, bacon and oil over very low flame for 5 minutes. Discard garlic. Drain meat and add to pan. Simmer uncovered, stirring occasionally, for 3 or 4 minutes. Brown meat over moderately high flame. Strain marinade and add to meat. Cover and simmer slowly for 2 to 2½ hours. If necessary, add a little beef broth or water to the meat. Correct seasoning. Serves 4-6.

Beef Stew Romana

STUFATINO ALLA ROMANA

- 2 pounds lean chuck or any lean and boneless beef
- 1½ teaspoons lard
- 4 slices minced bacon
- 1 clove garlic
- ⅓ teaspoon marjoram
- ¾ cup dry red or white wine
- 2 tablespoons tomato paste diluted in ½ cup lukewarm water
- ¼ cup minced onion
- salt and pepper to taste

Have meat cut in thin strips or diced as for stew. Place onion, garlic, lard and bacon in saucepan and sauté gently until onion is tender. Discard garlic. Add meat, sprinkle with salt, pepper and marjoram, and brown on all sides. Add wine and cook over medium flame until wine has evaporated; pour in diluted tomato paste and simmer uncovered for 10 minutes. Add enough warm water to cover meat. Cover saucepan tightly and simmer for about 2 hours or until meat is tender. Add more water during cooking if necessary. Serves 4-6.

Meat Patties Maddalena

POLPETTINE DI MANZO E SALSICCIA MADDALENA

- 1 pound chopped beef
- 1 pound sweet Italian sausages, with casing removed
- 1 large clove of garlic, minced (optional)
- 4 tablespoons parsley, chopped
- 1 teaspoon salt
- ¼ teaspoon pepper
- 6 slices white bread, soaked in milk and pressed dry
- 2 small eggs, beaten
- 1 cup olive oil
- bread crumbs

Mix beef, sausages, garlic, parsley, salt and pepper, soaked bread and eggs into a smooth paste. Shape into patties about

1½ inches wide. Roll in bread crumbs and fry a few at a time in hot oil, over medium-high flame, until brown on both sides (about 5 to 7 minutes). Serves 6.

Meat Patties

POLPETTE DI CARNE COTTA

This is a good way to use leftover cooked meat:

- 3 cups cooked beef, or pork, or veal, chopped
- 2 slices prosciutto, minced fine or 3 slices bacon, minced fine
- 4 tablespoons grated Parmesan cheese
- 4 slices bread soaked in milk and squeezed dry
- 2 eggs, beaten
- ½ teaspoon allspice
- 2 tablespoons parsley, chopped
- 1 cup olive oil
- bread crumbs
- salt and pepper to taste

Mix chopped meat, prosciutto or bacon, Parmesan cheese, soaked bread, eggs, allspice, salt and pepper and parsley into a smooth mixture. Shape into patties 2 inches wide. Roll in bread crumbs and fry a few at a time in hot oil until golden brown on both sides. Serves 4.

Meat Loaf

POLPETTONE

- 1 pound chopped veal or beef
- 1 pound chopped lean pork
- 4 slices bread soaked in milk and squeezed dry
- 1 onion, chopped fine
- 1½ tablespoons butter
- 2 eggs, lightly beaten
- 1 teaspoon salt
- ½ teaspoon allspice
- ¼ teaspoon pepper
- 2 to 3 slices bacon
- bread crumbs

Sauté onion in butter until soft. Add to bread, beef and pork, together with salt, pepper, allspice and eggs, mixing well. Butter a loaf pan, sprinkle it with bread crumbs and fill it with meat mixture. Level top with a spoon, sprinkle with bread crumbs and place bacon on top, or if desired, substitute flakes of butter for bacon. Bake in 350° oven for 1½ hours. Serves 6.

Here is a rare and delicious dish very simple to prepare. It can be cooked in a chafing dish, but is better cooked in a skillet over a high flame. The recipe was given to me by Cavalier Angelo Pozzi, owner of two of the best restaurants in Italy, the Caffè Ristorante Savini and the Tantalo. Cavalier Pozzi himself cooked my Beef Woronoff, which was indeed a great honor. (This dish is always prepared at the table, but seldom by Cavalier Pozzi.)

I inquired about the origin of the name. Smiling, this charming gentleman and great chef explained that he had facetiously called it Woronoff because it had magic powers of keeping a man young. The Russian Woronoff kept men young with monkey glands; but he felt that his dish could accomplish the same thing in a much more pleasant way. His eyes were filled with mirth when he told me I would be surprised at the number of middle-aged men AND women who made Beef Woronoff their favorite dish at the Savini and the Tantalo. After a taste of Cavalier Pozzi's specialty, I think you will agree with me that once you have had the opportunity of eating such an exquisite delicacy, you will go on eating it and loving it, whether or not it really possesses the power of prolonging one's youth span.

Beef Fillet Woronoff

FILETTO ALLA WORONOFF

SAUCE:
2½ teaspoons cognac
2½ teaspoons Worcestershire sauce
½ teaspoon prepared mustard

Combine above ingredients and mix well.

4 slices of fillet of beef, one inch thick
8 tablespoons butter
¼ teaspoon rosemary
salt and pepper to taste

Place half the butter in skillet. Add rosemary and fillets of beef when butter is slightly brown. Cook over high flame for 2 to 3 minutes on each side. Season with salt and pepper on both sides. Add the rest of the butter and the sauce and cook one minute more, turning meat once. Remove meat to hot serving dish or individual plates. Keep warm. Cook sauce over high flame, stirring constantly, one minute more or until sauce becomes clear. If desired, strain sauce to remove rosemary. Pour over meat and serve immediately. Serves 4.

The sauce can be made in great quantity and kept for months, in small bottles, especially if stored in a cool place. Can be used with chopped steak or any broiled meat.

Beef Fillet Chateaubriand

FILETTO ALLA CHATEAUBRIAND

6 slices beef fillet, about 1 inch thick	3 tablespoons parsley, chopped
¼ pound butter	juice of 1 lemon
	salt and pepper

Put half the butter in large skillet over high flame. Cook beef, with salt and pepper, 2 minutes on each side (rare), or 4 minutes each side (medium). Remove meat to hot plate. Place parsley and rest of butter in saucepan and cook over low flame until butter melts. Add lemon juice, mix and pour over beef. Serve immediately. Serves 6.

Fillet of Beef Arlesiana

MEDAGLIONI ALLA ARLESIANA

6 slices fillet of beef, about ⅔ inch thick	1½ cups olive oil
6 slices medium-size, unpeeled eggplant, ½ inch thick	1 clove garlic
	4 ripe tomatoes, peeled and chopped
½ cup flour	3 tablespoons parsley, chopped
1 large egg, beaten	salt and pepper to taste

Dip eggplant slices in flour and egg. Fry in oil until golden. Remove to warm dish. Sauté garlic until brown in 4 tablespoons of oil used for frying eggplant. Remove garlic. Add tomatoes and cook over medium flame for 10 minutes. Season to taste. Sprinkle fillets with salt and pepper and broil in hot oven, 1 inch from flame, for 2 minutes on each side (rare). Place eggplant in large heated serving dish. Top each slice with a fillet. Pour sauce over all and sprinkle with parsley. Serves 6.

Fillet of Beef Carignano

MEDAGLIONI ALLA CARIGNANO

- 6 slices fillet of beef, cut about ¾ inch thick
- ½ cup cognac
- ½ cup heavy cream
- ¼ teaspoon paprika
- ¼ pound butter
- 6 slices bread, cut to shape of fillet
- 1 teaspoon salt
- ½ teaspoon black pepper

Marinate fillets for ½ hour in cognac, salt and pepper. Dry on towel. Sauté in butter until cooked as preferred. While fillets are cooking, sauté bread in butter in another pan. Place fried bread on hot serving dish and put a fillet on each slice. In pan used for cooking fillets place the cognac marinade and the heavy cream. Cook over medium-high flame for 5 minutes, stirring constantly. Correct seasoning. Add paprika. Pour over fillets and serve immediately. Serves 6.

Fillet of Beef Rossini

TOURNEDOS ALLA ROSSINI

- 4 slices fillet of beef, cut about ⅔ inch thick
- 4 slices liver pâté
- ¼ cup flour
- 1 small truffle, cut in four
- ½ cup Madeira wine
- ¼ pound butter
- 4 slices toast
- salt and pepper to taste

Marinate liver pâté and truffle in Madeira for 1½ hours. Remove pâté, dip in flour and fry in butter. Keep warm. Sprinkle fillet slices with salt and pepper and sauté in butter over high flame (2 minutes each side for rare, 3 minutes each side for medium). Place slices of toast in serving dish. Top each with a slice of fillet and a slice of truffle. Sprinkle with a little of the Madeira used for marinating the pâté and put dish in 400° oven for 2 minutes. Remove from oven. Top each fillet with a slice of pâté. Pour over all a sauce made by adding the remaining Madeira marinade to the pan in which fillets were cooked, simmering for 3 minutes. Serves 4.

Steak with Caper Sauce

BISTECCA ALLA SALSA DI CAPPERI

- 4 pounds porterhouse or sirloin steak about ⅔ inch thick
- 1 large lemon
- 2 medium onions, chopped
- 3 tablespoons capers
- ½ cup olive oil
- ½ teaspoon paprika
- salt and pepper

Sprinkle steak with salt, pepper and paprika. Place onions and oil in large skillet. Cook very slowly for about five minutes. Add steak to onions and brown meat on both sides over high flame, reduce flame and add capers, cook to taste. Before serving sprinkle steak with lemon juice, or serve surrounded with lemon wedges. Serves 6.

Beefsteak Florentine No. 1

BISTECCA ALLA FIORENTINA NO. 1

- 3 pounds sirloin or porterhouse steak, about 1 inch thick
- ¼ teaspoon nutmeg
- ⅔ teaspoon salt
- ½ teaspoon freshly ground black pepper
- ⅔ cup olive oil

Sprinkle meat with nutmeg, salt and pepper. Place meat in large, deep dish and cover with oil. Marinate for ½ hour. Remove meat from dish and cook on a grill over hot coals 2 minutes each side (rare) or 4 minutes each side (medium). I recommend this procedure wherever possible, but steak is also very good when broiled in an oven at about 500°, one inch from flame. Cooking time is the same. Serves 4.

Beefsteak Florentine No. 2

BISTECCA ALLA FIORENTINA NO. 2

- 4 pounds porterhouse or sirloin steak, about 2 inches thick
- salt and pepper to taste

Broil steak on charcoal fire approximately 3 inches from flame for about 4 minutes on each side for rare, 8 minutes each side for medium rare. Sprinkle each side with salt and pepper one minute before turning. Serves 4.

This method of broiling steak, now used by everyone, actually originated in Florence.

Pot Roast Lombardy Style

MANZO ALLA LOMBARDA

- 3 pounds shank, plate, rump or round of beef
- 4 slices bacon, minced
- 1 carrot
- ½ stock celery
- 1 onion
- ¼ cup parsley, minced
- a piece of lemon peel about 2 inches long and one inch wide
- 1 cup red wine
- ½ cup stock or water
- salt and pepper

Place bacon in a heavy pan and cook over low flame until bacon is soft, and has expelled most of its fat. Add meat and brown on all sides. Add rest of ingredients, cover and simmer for 1¾ hours for rump or round, and 2 hours for plate or shank. Add more stock or water if necessary during cooking. Serves 6.

Beef Certosina

MANZO ALLA CERTOSINA

- 3 pounds eye round
- 2 slices bacon, minced
- 2 tablespoons butter
- 2 tablespoons olive oil
- ½ teaspoon nutmeg
- 6 anchovy fillets, minced
- ⅓ cup minced parsley
- 1 cup stock or water
- salt and pepper

Place bacon, butter and oil in a heavy pan together with beef. Brown meat on all sides, then add rest of ingredients, cover and simmer for about 1¾ hours or until tender. Add more stock or water if necessary during cooking. Serve sliced with pan gravy, skimmed of fat. Serves 6.

Roast Beef Italian Style

MANZO ARROSTO ALL'ITALIANA

- 5 pounds eye round or top sirloin, tied with string and with no fat around it
- 1 large clove garlic
- ½ cup olive oil
- ⅓ cup cognac
- salt and pepper

Rub beef with garlic, salt and pepper. Place in baking pan and pour oil and cognac over it. Sprinkle with salt and pepper. Roast in 350° oven for 1 hour and 20 minutes for rare, about 1 hour and 45 minutes for medium rare, basting occasionally. Serve with its gravy. Serves 8-10.

VEAL

Veal Cutlets Milanese

COTOLETTE DI VITELLO ALLA MILANESE

1 pound veal cutlets, sliced very thin	1 cup bread crumbs
2 eggs, slightly beaten with ½ teaspoon salt	⅔ cup butter

Dip cutlets in beaten egg and roll in bread crumbs. If any egg mixture is left, repeat operation. Fry cutlets, a few at a time, in hot butter, over medium flame, on both sides until golden. Serve immediately garnished with lemon wedges. Serves 4.

If desired, especially when entertaining, cutlets can be prepared for cooking, wrapped in waxed paper and placed in refrigerator for no more than four hours before cooking.

Saltimbocca Roman Style

SALTIMBOCCA ALLA ROMANA

8 very thin slices of veal, each about 4 by 5 inches	8 slices prosciutto
½ teaspoon sage	¼ pound butter
	pepper to taste

Sprinkle each slice of veal with pepper and sage. (Do not use salt as the salt in the prosciutto will be enough to flavor meat.) Cover with a slice of prosciutto. Secure with toothpick or skewer. Sauté gently in butter for 5 to 6 minutes on each side. (This recipe can be ideally prepared in a chafing dish.) Serve with mixed green salad and Mushrooms Trifolati (page 133). Serves 4.

Fifty years ago, Giovanni Bindi left Pisa with his wife, a young son, three small daughters and very little capital. They moved to Milan, or to be more precise, to what was then the suburbs of Milan. With their small capital, Giovanni Bindi opened a wine shop, Giannino, which eventually became a small restaurant, with Signora Virginia Bindi doing all of the cooking.

Simple, cheerful, clean cooking it was, that of a good Tuscan housewife, who believed in serving her customers the same nourishing food she so carefully chose for her own family. Giannino's customers were workmen, and they ate their meals on the big marble-top table.

But soon the news of Virginia Bindi's cooking got around, and customers began to come in from the center of town. Who was the first one to arrive in a brougham? Nobody seems to remember, but the time had come to lay a couple of small tables with table cloths and napkins.

Giannino's grew; the tables were too few and, for lack of space, use had to be made of the old courtyard. Sometimes, in the summer, tables partly blocked the carriageway through the court; and whenever a cart had to go through, the customers cheerfully picked up their tables and carried them out on the sidewalk, where they would go on with their meal. If anything, this novel inconvenience added to the popularity of the place.

With the years even more room was needed, and now Giannino has taken over the whole building. Giovanni and Virginia Bindi have passed on, but Cesare, as manager, and Ilde, his sister, supervising the cooking, are following in the footsteps of their parents, who never forgot that they had found their first friends among the laborers. Their greatest pride, in the 55 years of the restaurant's existence, is the distribution of food every afternoon to the poor of the district, started many years ago by the founders of Giannino; and the free Christmas meal, when the restaurant welcomes as many poor people as there are seats, and its staff serves them a complete dinner, including wine. Each year Giannino becomes better known, not only for its celebrated cuisine, but also for the beauty of the restaurant itself.

The place was bombed during the last war, and was redecorated by the architect Palumbo with such discreet originality that the atmosphere of the original Giannino is retained. One of the most interesting features is the ultramodern kitchen, with a huge glassed-in arch that gives onto the master dining room, so that the preparation of all food is in plain view of the customers.

Giannino's setting changes with the season. In winter there are additional dining rooms, intimate and cheerful, with large fireplaces, and through the rest of the year the garden is a triumph of all the best flowers and fruits of Italy. On the restaurant's fiftieth anniversary, Cesare Bindi offered an award of half a million lire in commemoration of his father, to the best sculptor or painter from Milan, to be chosen among those whose exhibitions in that year, 1948, had had the most success. A painting of Mario Sironi was chosen from the 18 entries and it now hangs at Giannino's.

Here is a recipe from this famous restaurant in Milan, which is among the best in Europe:

Veal Valdostana

VALDOSTANA DI VITELLO

- 8 veal cutlets, cut and pounded thin
- 4 slices prosciutto
- 4 tablespoons cream cheese
- 1 small black truffle, sliced fine
- flour
- 5 tablespoons butter
- ¼ cup dry white wine
- salt and pepper to taste

Between two slices of veal place one slice of prosciutto, 1 tablespoon cheese and some truffle. Sprinkle lightly with salt and pepper. Seal edges of meat by beating edges hard with dull side of kitchen knife. Dip lightly in flour and sauté in butter until both sides are golden, about 10 minutes. Add wine, cover and simmer for 10 to 15 minutes. Serves 4.

Veal Scaloppine with Marsala

SCALOPPINE DI VITELLO AL MARSALA

- 1 pound veal scaloppine
- ⅓ cup flour
- 6 tablespoons butter
- ¼ cup imported dry Marsala wine
- salt and pepper

Roll veal scaloppine in flour. Sauté in butter in large skillet, for 2 to 3 minutes each side. Sprinkle with salt and pepper and add Marsala. Simmer for 2 minutes more. Serves 4.

Veal Scaloppine Pizzaiola

SCALOPPINE DI VITELLO ALLA PIZZAIOLA

- 2 pounds veal cutlets, cut very thin
- 6 tablespoons olive oil
- ½ recipe Pizzaiola Sauce (page 32)
- salt and pepper to taste

Sprinkle veal lightly on both sides with salt and pepper. Place oil and veal in large skillet and sauté gently for 7 to 10 minutes, turning often. Serve in large dish or individual dishes, topped with sauce. Serves 4-6.

Rolled Veal with Anchovies

INVOLTINI DI VITELLO ALLE ACCIUGHE

- 2 pounds veal cutlets, pounded flat
- ½ cup diced Swiss cheese
- 1 anchovy fillet for each cutlet
- ⅓ pound butter
- ⅓ cup dry white wine
- 2 tablespoons parsley, chopped fine
- salt and pepper to taste

Place a few pieces of cheese and one anchovy fillet on top of each cutlet. Sprinkle lightly with pepper. Roll and tie with thread. Place in skillet with butter, sprinkle lightly with salt and cook for 10 minutes, turning meat occasionally. Add wine, cover and cook 10 minutes more. Remove threads. Serve with sauce sprinkled with parsley. Serves 6.

Rolled Veal with Tomato Sauce

INVOLTINI DI VETELLO AL POMIDORO

- 1 pound veal cutlets pounded flat
- 4 large slices prosciutto
- 6 tablespoons butter
- 1 tablespoon flour
- 3 tablespoons olive oil
- 1 clove garlic
- 1 tablespoon carrot, minced
- 1 tablespoon onion, minced
- 4 tablespoons Italian tomato paste diluted in 1¼ cups lukewarm water
- ¼ pound diced mushrooms
- 1 tablespoon chopped parsley
- salt and pepper to taste

Gently sauté garlic, carrot and onion in olive oil. Discard garlic when golden. Add tomato paste, salt and pepper to taste and simmer for 30 minutes. Remove all fat from prosciutto. Chop fat and add to sauce, together with parsley and mushrooms. Simmer 10 minutes. Blend 2 tablespoons butter with flour and add to sauce. Simmer 10 minutes more, stirring occasionally. Cut prosciutto slices to correspond to the number of slices of veal. Place a piece of prosciutto on top of each veal cutlet, and cover each cutlet with tomato sauce. Roll cutlets and secure with skewers or toothpicks. Place meat in a skillet with rest of butter and sauté over very low fire for 20 minutes, turning meat occasionally. Add rest of sauce, cover and simmer 20 minutes more. Serve with its sauce. Serves 2-4.

Veal Birds Delizia

IMBOTTINI DELIZIA

- 1 pound veal cutlets, pounded flat, about 4 by 5 inches
- 2 tablespoons cream cheese
- ¼ cup ham, minced
- 1 tablespoon white truffle, minced
- 2 tablespoons celery, chopped fine
- 5 tablespoons butter
- ⅓ cup port wine
- ¼ teaspoon flour
- salt and pepper

Make a mixture of the cheese, ham, truffles and celery. Sprinkle meat lightly with salt and pepper. Place some of the truffle mixture in the center of each slice of veal. Roll each slice individually and tie with strong thread. Melt 4 tablespoons butter in skillet. Add meat and ¼ cup wine and cook over medium flame for 8 to 10 minutes, turning occasionally. Remove meat to hot serving platter. Add flour and remaining butter and wine to skillet. Cook over medium-high flame for a minute or so, until sauce thickens. Pour over meat and serve. Serves 2-4.

(*Recipe from Ristorante Cavaletto e Doge Orseolo, Venice*)

Stuffed Shoulder of Veal

SPALLA DI VITELLA RIPIENA

- 4 pounds shoulder of veal, boned
- ½ pound chopped pork
- 6 tablespoons grated Parmesan, or 3 tablespoons grated Pecorino cheese
- 1 teaspoon salt
- ½ teaspoon black pepper
- ⅛ teaspoon cinnamon
- ¼ teaspoon nutmeg
- 1½ tablespoons parsley, chopped
- 2 eggs, well beaten
- 2 slices white bread
- ½ cup milk
- ⅓ cup olive oil
- 2 cloves garlic
- 5 slices bacon
- ½ cup white Chianti wine

Soak bread in milk till thoroughly wet. Remove from milk and squeeze dry. Place bread in mixing bowl with cheese, pork, salt and pepper, cinnamon, nutmeg and parsley. Mix well and add eggs. Stuff veal with this mixture. Roll veal and cover with bacon strips. Tie meat with string and sprinkle with additional salt and pepper. Place oil and garlic in large pan over low flame. Discard garlic when golden. Add meat and sear over high flame for about 10 minutes turning meat often. Lower flame and cook for 1 hour. Add wine and simmer 45 minutes more. Serves 8.

Veal Shoulder with Mustard Sauce

SPALLA DI VITELLO AL SENAPE

- 3 pounds shoulder of veal, boned
- 1 carrot, finely diced
- 1 large onion, sliced thin
- ½ teaspoon thyme
- 1 tablespoon chopped parsley
- 2 bay leaves
- ⅓ cup wine vinegar
- 1½ cups dry white wine
- 4 tablespoons butter
- ½ tablespoon prepared mustard
- 1 teaspoon salt
- ½ teaspoon pepper
- ⅓ cup olive oil

Make a marinade of wine, vinegar, carrot, onion, thyme, parsley, bay leaves, salt and pepper and allow veal to stand in this for at least 5 hours. Remove veal. Spread with a mixture of the butter and mustard. Roll veal and tie with string. Sear in oil, over high flame, until all sides are lightly browned. Cover and simmer for 1½ hours over low flame. Remove veal and keep in warm place. To juices left in pot add the marinade and cook over high flame until the mixture is reduced by one half. Strain and serve as gravy, with meat. Serves 6.

Veal Shoulder Carabiniera

SPALLA DI VITELLO ALLA CARABINIERA

- 4 pounds shoulder of veal, boned
- 4 slices very lean bacon
- ¼ cup olive oil
- 5 tablespoons butter
- salt and pepper to taste

Season meat with salt and pepper, then place bacon strips across meat an inch or so apart. Roll meat tightly and tie with string. Place butter and oil in large saucepan or Dutch oven together with meat. Brown on all sides, cover and simmer for 1¾ hours, or until tender, turning meat occasionally and basting with pan gravy. Add a little water if necessary during cooking. Remove meat to hot platter, slice and serve with pan gravy. Serves 6. Serve with Peas Roman Style (page 129) and Potato Croquettes (page 144).

Jellied Veal

CIMA DI VITELLO

- 1½ pounds boneless veal stomach, cut in one piece
- ⅓ pound leg or shoulder of veal, chopped
- ⅓ pound leg or shoulder of veal, diced
- ¼ pound cooked ham, cut in one slice and diced
- ¼ pound beef tongue, diced
- 1 dozen pistachio nuts, shelled and coarsely chopped
- ¼ pound butter
- ¼ cup celery, diced
- 1 carrot, diced
- 1 small onion, sliced
- peel of lemon, about 2 inches long and 1 inch wide
- 1 envelope unflavored gelatine
- ½ cup dry white wine
- 1 cup hot water
- salt and pepper to taste

Make a mixture of chopped and diced veal, ham, tongue, pistachio nuts, salt and pepper and put aside. Make a pocket or sack of the veal by sewing edges together, leaving one side open. Fill pocket with veal mixture and sew edges together. Season meat, then place butter, vegetables and lemon peel in large saucepan together with the meat. Brown meat on all sides, cover and simmer 2 hours, adding a little white dry wine, broth or water if necessary. Turn meat occasionally. Remove from pan and let cool. Soften gelatine in wine, then add hot water and mix until thoroughly blended. Let stand until thick but still runny. Place meat on a chilled platter, and cover with gelatine, being sure that all sides are coated. Place in refrigerator a few minutes before serving. Veal should be served chilled, but not too cold. Serve in ½ inch slices. Serves 6-8.

Veal Stew Casalinga

SPEZZATINO DI VITELLA ALLA CASALINGA

- 2 pounds stewing veal, cut into serving pieces
- 1 clove garlic
- 7 tablespoons olive oil
- 4 fresh tomatoes, peeled and cut in small pieces
- 1 onion, chopped
- 1 cup fresh or frozen sweet peas
- 3 large potatoes, diced
- 1 stalk celery, chopped
- 1 large carrot, diced
- salt and pepper to taste

Sauté garlic in a small pan in 3 tablespoons oil till lightly brown. Discard garlic. Add tomatoes, ½ teaspoon salt and ¼ teaspoon pepper. Sauté onions in rest of oil in deep saucepan. Add meat and cover. Simmer for 15 minutes. Add rest of ingredients. If necessary, add some water. Stir occasionally. Correct seasoning after simmering for one more hour. Serves 6.

Veal Stew with Tomato Sauce

SPEZZATINO DI VITELLO AL POMIDORO

- 2 pounds veal rump cut into 1½ inch cubes
- ⅓ cup olive oil
- 1 large clove garlic
- 1 teaspoon salt
- ⅛ teaspoon pepper
- 1 bay leaf, crumbled
- 1 tablespoon fresh parsley, minced or ⅛ teaspoon dried parsley
- ¾ cup dry white wine
- 5 ripe Italian egg tomatoes, peeled and diced or 2 tablespoons tomato paste diluted in 1¼ cups of water

Sauté garlic in oil until golden. Do not brown. Discard garlic. Add meat and brown on all sides. Add salt, pepper, bay leaf and parsley. Cook a minute or so and add wine. Cook over medium-high flame until wine has evaporated. Add tomatoes or tomato paste mixture. Cover and simmer for about 1½ hours. Add a little water during cooking if necessary. Serves 4.

Veal Stew with Peas

SPEZZATO DI VITELLO CON PISELLI

- 2 pounds veal rump, cut into 1½ inch cubes
- 5 tablespoons butter
- 3 slices of bacon, finely diced
- 1 medium onion, minced
- ⅓ cup dry white wine
- 2 tablespoons tomato paste diluted in 1 cup beef or chicken broth or water
- 2 boxes frozen peas or 1½ pounds fresh peas or 1-pound can of peas, drained
- 1 teaspoon salt
- ⅛ teaspoon pepper

Sauté onion in butter and bacon until soft. Do not brown. Add meat and brown on all sides. Add wine. Cook uncovered over medium-high flame until wine has evaporated. Add tomato paste mixture, salt and pepper, cover and simmer for about one hour, adding a little broth or water if meat gets too dry. Add peas and simmer for 15 minutes or until peas are tender. When using canned peas cook meat for about 1 hour and 20 minutes, add peas and simmer for 5 minutes. Serves 6.

Tripe Toscana

TRIPPA IN UMIDO ALLA TOSCANA

2 pounds precooked veal tripe, cut into one-inch squares*	2 cups beef broth
	½ cup freshly grated Parmesan cheese
5 tablespoons butter	4 tablespoons butter
1 tablespoon tomato paste	salt and pepper to taste

* Tripe can be bought precooked at many butcher shops.

Rinse tripe in cold water several times. Place tripe in large saucepan with cold water and 1 tablespoon salt. Cover and simmer for one hour. Drain and let cool. Place tripe and 5 tablespoons butter in saucepan. Simmer uncovered for 8 to 10 minutes, stirring occasionally. Add tomato paste dissolved in ½ cup broth. Cover and simmer for 30 minutes. Add rest of broth, salt and pepper to taste and simmer 1½ hours. Serve sprinkled with cheese and dotted with butter. Serves 4.

Tripe Roman Style

TRIPPA ALLA ROMANA

2 pounds precooked veal tripe, thoroughly washed and cut in 2-inch squares	½ cup tomato paste diluted in ½ cup water
1 small onion	1-pound can Italian peeled tomatoes
1 clove garlic	½ cup grated Parmesan cheese
1 tablespoon fresh parsley, chopped	5 tablespoons olive oil
	1 tablespoon salt
2 leaves fresh basil or ⅛ teaspoon dried basil	½ teaspoon pepper
	½ teaspoon salt
1 stalk celery	1 clove

Simmer tripe for 2 hours in 6 quarts of water to which have been added 1 tablespoon salt, onion, clove, celery and parsley. Drain tripe, removing clove, onion, celery and parsley.

Brown garlic in oil and remove. Add tomato paste, peeled tomatoes, basil, salt and pepper to taste. Simmer for 15 minutes. Add tripe. Simmer for 45 minutes. If sauce becomes too dry add a little water. Serve sprinkled with Parmesan cheese. Serves 6.

Creamed Veal Kidneys

ROGNONE DI VITELLO ALLA PANNA

2 veal kidneys	1 tablespoon Cognac
4 tablespoons olive oil	½ cup heavy cream
1 tablespoon chopped onions	1 tablespoon lemon juice
¼ pound mushrooms, sliced	salt and pepper

Remove fat from kidneys. Rinse in cold water and dice. Sauté onion in olive oil until golden. Add kidneys and simmer for 6 to 8 minutes. Remove kidneys from skillet. To the juice in the skillet add cream, lemon juice and Cognac. Cook, stirring frequently, until sauce is reduced to half its original amount. Add mushrooms and simmer for 2 minutes. Add sauce to kidneys. Serves 2-4.

Veal Kidney Madeira

ROGNONE DI VITELLO AL MADERA

2 veal kidneys	3 tablespoons parsley, chopped
½ pound fresh mushrooms, sliced	⅓ cup Madeira wine
⅓ cup olive oil	salt and pepper

Remove fat from kidneys and rinse in cold water. Cut into thin slices. Sauté in very hot oil over high flame, using large skillet, for 2 to 3 minutes. Reduce flame and add mushrooms, Madeira, 1 tablespoon parsley, salt and pepper. Simmer slowly for 8 minutes (do not bring to a boil). Remove from pan and sprinkle with rest of parsley. Serves 2-4.

Calf Liver with Wine Sauce

FEGATO AL VINO

⅓ cup olive oil	about ⅔ inch thick and cut in about 1½-inch squares
2 large onions, sliced very fine	
1 pound calf liver, sliced	⅓ cup dry red wine
	salt and pepper to taste

Place oil and onion in small skillet and simmer for 5 to 10 minutes, or till onions are cooked. Add liver. Cook over high flame for 2 minutes, stirring. Add wine, salt and pepper. Cook 3 to 4 minutes more, over medium-high flame, stirring. Serves 4.

Calf Liver with Sage Sauce

FEGATO DI VITELLO ALLA SALVIA

1 pound calf liver, sliced thin and dipped in flour	½ cup butter
2 eggs, beaten with ½ teaspoon salt	½ teaspoon sage

Dip liver in egg mixture and fry in hot butter until golden on both sides. Place liver on hot serving dish. Add sage to butter and simmer, stirring occasionally, for 2 minutes. Add to liver and serve. Serves 4.

Calf Liver Genoa Style

FEGATO DI VITELLO ALLA GENOVESE

1 pound calf liver, sliced very thin	½ cup dry white wine
2 tablespoons butter	2 tablespoons wine vinegar
2 tablespoons olive oil	⅓ cup beef broth
½ small onion, chopped fine	3 tablespoons bread crumbs
2 tablespoons parsley, chopped	2 tablespoons grated Parmesan cheese
1 clove garlic	salt and pepper to taste

Sauté butter, oil, onion, parsley and garlic until onion is soft. Discard garlic. Add liver, wine, vinegar and broth. Top with bread crumbs and cook over medium flame for about 8 to 10 minutes. Remove liver, and cook sauce for 4 to 5 minutes more; add salt and pepper to taste. Add liver. Sprinkle with cheese, simmer a minute or two more and serve. Serves 4.

Calf Liver Italian Style

FEGATO DI VITELLO ALL'ITALIANA

- 1 pound calf liver, sliced thin, dipped in flour
- ½ cup butter
- 2 slices prosciutto, chopped fine
- ½ small onion, minced
- ½ teaspoon sage
- 3 tablespoons parsley, chopped
- 1 tablespoon flour or cornstarch
- ½ cup chicken or beef broth
- ¼ cup dry Marsala wine
- salt and pepper to taste

Fry liver in hot butter until golden on both sides. Remove liver to hot platter. To the butter in skillet add prosciutto, onion, sage and parsley. Sauté for 3 or 4 minutes or until onion is tender but not brown. Stir in flour, and add broth, Marsala wine, salt and pepper. Simmer for 10 to 12 minutes. Add liver and simmer just long enough to warm up the liver. Serve immediately with lemon wedges. Serves 4.

Veal Shanks Milanese

OSSIBUCHI ALLA MILANESE

Here is another recipe given me by Cavalier Angelo Pozzi, owner of two of the very best and most famous restaurants in Milan: the Caffè Ristorante Savini and the Tantalo. At Cavalier Pozzi's restaurants a special kind of needle is provided to extract the marrow from the bone. The needle is jokingly called the Tax Collector.

- 3 whole shanks of veal, sawed into 3-inch pieces and rolled in flour
- ⅔ cup olive oil
- 1 onion, sliced thin
- 1 bay leaf
- 2 small carrots, diced
- 1 stalk of celery, diced
- ½ cup dry white wine
- 2 pounds very ripe tomatoes, peeled and diced or same amount of peeled canned tomatoes
- 1 teaspoon tomato paste
- 1½ tablespoons fresh chopped parsley
- 1 clove of garlic, chopped
- 1 tablespoon lemon peel, grated
- salt and pepper to taste

Brown veal shanks in ½ cup olive oil, in large skillet, over medium flame, on both sides, for 10 minutes. Place rest of oil in saucepan with onion, bay leaf, carrots and celery. Sauté over medium flame for 5 minutes. Add wine and simmer till all wine has evaporated. Add shanks, tomatoes and paste, cover and simmer 1½ hours. If necessary, add a small amount of wine or water during cooking. Remove shanks from saucepan. Strain sauce. Place sauce back in pan together with parsley, garlic, lemon peel and shanks. Simmer for 5 minutes more and serve. Serves 6-8.

LAMB

Spring Lamb in Egg Sauce

ABBACCHIO IN BRODETTO

4 pounds shoulder of spring lamb, diced as for stew	⅓ cup dry white wine
4 tablespoons lard, olive oil or butter	2 eggs
	juice of a large lemon
1 clove garlic	1 bay leaf
1 tablespoon flour	salt and pepper to taste
	parsley (optional)

Sauté garlic in lard, oil or butter until golden. Discard garlic. Add meat and brown. Sprinkle meat with flour, and cook over medium heat for 2 to 3 minutes more, stirring occasionally. Add wine and bay leaf, and cook uncovered until wine has evaporated. Add 1½ cups hot water, cover tightly and cook over low flame for 40 minutes, season to taste and cook for 20 minutes more or until meat is tender, adding more water if necessary. When meat is done there should be not more than a few tablespoons of pan gravy. Beat eggs with lemon juice, add to meat, stirring well. Remove from fire immediately. Serves 6-8.

Breaded Spring Lamb Chops

COTOLETTE DI AGNELLO PANATE

2 pounds very lean loin lamb chops, cut ¼ inch thick	¼ teaspoon pepper
	bread crumbs
2 eggs	1 cup olive oil
½ teaspoon salt	1 large lemon cut in wedges

Dip chops in eggs lightly beaten with salt and pepper and then roll in bread crumbs. Fry in hot oil over medium-high flame until chops are light brown on each side. Remove to hot serving dish, and serve with lemon wedges. Serves 4-6.

Spring Lamb Cacciatora

SPEZZATINO DI ABBACCHIO ALLA CACCIATORA

- 4 pounds diced shoulder or leg of spring lamb
- 2½ tablespoons lard or ⅓ cup olive oil
- 1 small clove of garlic, minced
- ½ teaspoon rosemary
- ⅛ teaspoon sage
- 1 heaping teaspoon flour
- ½ cup wine vinegar
- ½ cup water
- 4 anchovy fillets, chopped
- salt and pepper to taste

Brown meat in lard or oil, add garlic, rosemary and sage. Stir and sauté gently for a minute or two. Stir in flour and pour in vinegar and water, stirring well. Cover tightly and cook over medium-high flame for 45 minutes. Add anchovy fillets, salt and pepper to taste and cook a few minutes more, or until meat is tender. Add a little water during cooking if necessary. Serves 6-8.

Leg of Lamb with Marsala

COSCIA DI MONTONE AL MARSALA

- 1 small leg of lamb, about 5 to 6 pounds, lean
- 1 clove garlic
- 1½ teaspoons rosemary
- 1 tablespoon butter
- ½ cup olive oil
- ½ cup dry Marsala wine
- salt and pepper

Rub lamb with salt and pepper. Cut a slit in each side and insert half a clove of garlic, ¼ of the rosemary, salt and pepper. Place in roasting pan with butter. Pour oil over meat and sprinkle with rest of rosemary. Place in hot oven, about 400°, and cook for 10 minutes. Reduce heat to 325° and roast for 2½ hours, basting occasionally with Marsala. Slice very thin. Serves 6.

Spring Lamb Roast with New Potatoes

ARROSTO DI AGNELLO CON PATATINE

- 1 leg of baby lamb, about 4 to 5 pounds
- 1 large clove of garlic
- 1 teaspoon salt
- ½ teaspoon black pepper, freshly ground
- ½ teaspoon rosemary
- ½ cup olive oil
- ½ cup red wine
- 3 pounds small new potatoes, peeled, and cut in half

Rub half a clove of garlic on lamb. With a sharp knife cut 2 small incisions on each side of leg and insert the rest of the garlic, one half of the salt, pepper and rosemary. Sprinkle both sides with rest of salt, pepper and rosemary. Place meat on baking pan and pour oil over it. Place in oven at 400° for 10 minutes, lower flame to 325° and cook for one hour. Place potatoes around meat, sprinkle with salt and pepper and, if desired, some rosemary. Cook for 30 minutes basting occasionally. Add wine and cook for 30 minutes more. Serves 4-6.

Roast Baby Lamb

AGNELLO ARROSTO

- 1 baby lamb about 8-10 pounds, ready to cook
- 1 large clove garlic
- 1 teaspoon rosemary
- ⅓ cup olive oil or ⅓ cup butter or bacon strips
- salt
- freshly ground black pepper

Rub lamb with garlic, sprinkle inside and out with salt and pepper. Divide garlic in four. Make a slit in each shoulder and leg and insert a pinch of pepper, rosemary and garlic. Rub with butter or oil and cook in 325° oven, turning occasionally, for 3½ hours. Use wine for basting during cooking. If lamb is cooked on a spit, wrap it in bacon strips instead of using butter or oil and brush (using a pastry brush) with wine. Serve on oval platter with a large bunch of watercress at both ends. Serves 6-8.

PORK

Pork Chops Neapolitan Style

COSTOLETTE DI MAIALE ALLA NAPOLETANA

- 4 large lean pork chops about one inch thick
- 4 large red, yellow or green peppers
- ½ pound whole button mushrooms
- 3 tablespoons olive oil
- 1 clove garlic
- 1 tablespoon tomato paste, diluted in ½ cup water
- ½ cup vegetable-juice cocktail or tomato juice
- salt and pepper to taste

Place peppers directly on top of gas burner over medium

flame. Turn often. Remove peppers when skin has become black and has a burned look. Remove burned skin under running cold water. Remove stems and seeds and cut peppers into one-inch strips. Rinse and let drain. Sauté garlic in oil in a skillet. Do not brown. Discard garlic. Add chops, sprinkle with salt and pepper, and brown on both sides. Remove chops. Place tomato paste mixture and vegetable juice in casserole, add peppers, mushrooms and chops, sprinkling each layer with salt and pepper. Bake in 350° oven for 30 minutes. Serves 4.

Pork Chops Modena Style

COSTOLETTE DI MAIALE ALLA MODENESE

- 8 large pork chops, about 1 inch thick
- ½ teaspoon rosemary
- ½ teaspoon sage
- ½ clove garlic, chopped
- 1 cup water
- ½ cup dry white wine
- salt and pepper

Mix rosemary, sage, garlic, salt and pepper. Rub chops with this mixture. Place chops in large greased skillet, add water and cover. Simmer until all water has evaporated (about 45 minutes). Remove cover and brown chops in their own fat. Add wine and cook for a minute or so, turning chops occasionally. Wine should be almost evaporated. Serves 4.

Roast Pork Fiorentina

ARROSTO DI MAIALE ALLA FIORENTINA

- 4 pounds lean loin of pork
- 2 cloves garlic, cut in half
- 4 to 6 cloves
- ½ teaspoon rosemary
- ⅔ cup water
- salt and pepper to taste

Make 4 small slits in meat and insert garlic, rosemary and a small pinch of salt and pepper. Make a series of shallow cuts across the fat side to mark into squares. Insert cloves in each square and roast in 400° oven in a pan containing the water, for 1¾ hours. Serve hot with sautéed turnip greens, or cold with artichoke hearts and mushrooms in olive oil. Any other vegetable can be substituted. Serves 4.

Loin of Pork Bologna Style

MAIALE AL LATTE ALLA BOLOGNESE

4 pounds lean pork loin, boned
6 tablespoons butter
about 1 quart milk
1 small white canned truffle (optional)
salt and pepper

Sprinkle pork with salt and pepper and let stand in refrigerator for about 8 hours. Place butter and pork in saucepan and brown meat on all sides (do not allow butter to burn). Add milk, cover and simmer 1½ hours. Remove meat, slice and serve with its sauce, to which may be added a diced white truffle. Sauce should be of the consistency of cream; if too thin, let boil uncovered for a few minutes. Serves 6.

Loin of Pork in Red Wine

MAIALE AL VINO ROSSO

5 pounds loin of pork
1 clove garlic
1 cup Barolo wine, or any good full-bodied red wine
½ cup tomato paste diluted in 1 cup of water
salt and pepper

Rub loin with garlic, salt and pepper, place in a large saucepan and let brown in its own fat. Pour wine over it, cover and simmer until wine has evaporated, turning meat once or twice. Add tomato paste mixture, cover and simmer for 1½ hours or until meat is tender, turning meat occasionally. Season sauce to taste. Serve with or without its sauce. (This sauce will be a treat when used with macaroni.) Serves 6-8.

Pork Sausage with Grapes

SALSICCIA CON L'UVA

8 sweet Italian sausages
2 cups white grapes
2 tablespoons butter

Puncture sausages with a needle and place in skillet with butter. Sauté gently for 10 minutes, turning occasionally. Add grapes and simmer for 15 minutes more. Serves 4.

POULTRY

POLLAME

⸺⸺⸺⸺⸺⸺⸺⸺⸺⸺⸺⸺⸺⸺⸺⸺⸺⸺⸺⸺⸺

Ristorante Rugantino in Rome, located in Trastevere (literally, beyond the Tiber), the old section of the city on the same bank as Castel Sant'Angelo and the Vatican, is to my mind among the best in Italy. It is not as well known as some of the other restaurants in the same neighborhood, which have become very popular with both the tourists and the international set because they are frequented by movie stars, playwrights, etc. For this very reason, Rugantino's prices are still moderate, and the whole restaurant retains the atmosphere of Trastevere and offers along with the best Roman and Italian cooking its own *Specialità della Casa*.

This picturesque restaurant takes its name from a famous *Maschera* of Trastevere. *Maschera* is the seventeenth and eighteenth century word for a character portrayed in a masque. The walls of the restaurant have murals representing Rugantino and his lady love, Nina, against the background of Roman ruins of the eighteenth century.

In warm weather one can enjoy lunch or dinner on the terrace in front of the restaurant, taking in at the same time a beautiful view of the Piazza Sonnino, with its flower vendors and small fruit stands. This is the heart of Trastevere, Rome's oldest residential section; and in its still largely medieval streets live people who are considered the real and the most typical Romans. Of powerful frame, their eyes and hair are dark, their complexions slightly bronzed. Their glance is lively and penetrating and their speech agreeable and eloquent. A new apartment building and the latest cars and motor scooters scurrying through the *piazza* to and from the Ponte Garibaldi—one of the main bridges crossing the Tiber—form a strange but pleasant contrast to the ancient church of San Crisogono just across the square, with its frescoes of the eighth, tenth and eleventh centuries. And just a few feet away is the Palazzetto degli Anguillara, the oldest medieval building in Rome, now restored in the style of the thirteenth century. Here is one of Rugantino's most famous dishes:

Chicken Diesola

POLLO ALLA DIESOLA

1 chicken of about 3 pounds
¼ pound butter
1 cup dry Champagne (a good dry white wine may be substituted)
salt and pepper

Have the chicken cleaned and split in half, and have the butcher flatten it. Sprinkle with salt and pepper and rub with a couple tablespoons melted butter. Place rest of butter in large iron skillet and let it melt. In it place the chicken, flat, cover tightly and cook over medium-high flame for 5 minutes. Turn chicken, cover and cook 5 minutes more over medium-high flame. Then lower flame and cook for 10 minutes. Add champagne or wine and cook uncovered over medium-high flame until wine has evaporated. Serves 2.

Chicken and Peppers Roman Style

POLLO CON PEPERONI ALLA ROMANA

⅓ cup olive oil
½ onion, chopped
1 clove garlic
1 3 to 3½ pound chicken
1 pound peeled ripe Italian egg tomatoes or 2 cups canned peeled Italian tomatoes
1 pound green peppers, cleaned and cut lengthwise into 2-inch slices
salt and pepper

Gently sauté garlic and onion in oil until garlic is golden. Discard garlic. Add chicken and brown on all sides. Add tomatoes, peppers, salt and pepper. Cover and simmer for 35 minutes, or until chicken is tender. If necessary, cook uncovered for last 10 to 15 minutes to reduce excessive moisture. Serves 4.

Chicken Cacciatora

SPEZZATINO DI POLLO ALLA CACCIATORA

2 small chickens about 3 pounds each, cut in serving pieces
½ cup olive oil
1 clove garlic
½ tablespoon rosemary
1¼ teaspoons salt
¼ teaspoon pepper
6 anchovy fillets, chopped
⅔ cup wine vinegar
1 cup red Chianti or other dry red wine
3 tablespoons tomato paste
⅓ cup chicken broth or water

Cook chicken, garlic and oil in skillet over a high flame for about 5 minutes, turning constantly. Remove garlic. Mix salt, pepper, rosemary, anchovies, vinegar and wine together. Add to chicken and simmer uncovered until liquid is reduced one third, about 10 minutes. Dissolve tomato paste in chicken broth or water and pour over chicken. Simmer covered for 20 minutes. Serve with green salad and Barolo wine. Serves 6-8.

Chicken Cacciatora Maddalena

POLLO ALLA CACCIATORA MADDALENA

- 1 chicken of about 3 pounds, cut into serving pieces
- ⅓ cup olive oil
- 1 small onion, minced
- 1 tablespoon chopped parsley
- 1 tablespoon celery, chopped
- 1 clove of garlic, minced
- 2 small bay leaves
- ¼ teaspoon rosemary
- ¾ cup dry white wine
- 2 tablespoons wine vinegar
- salt and pepper

Place in skillet the onion, parsley, celery, garlic and oil. Sauté gently until onion is golden. Add chicken. Sprinkle with salt and pepper and brown on all sides. Add bay leaves, rosemary, wine and vinegar. Cover and simmer for 35 to 45 minutes. Add a little water if necessary. Serves 2-4.

Chicken Priscilla

POLLO ALLA PRISCILLA

- 1 chicken, about 4 pounds, cut into serving pieces
- 1 clove garlic
- 3 tablespoons butter
- 3 tablespoons olive oil
- 1 cup dry white wine
- juice of 1½ lemons
- 3 large eggs, beaten
- salt and pepper

Sauté garlic in oil and butter. Remove garlic and add chicken, salt and pepper. Cover and simmer for 10 minutes. Add wine and simmer covered for 25 minutes. (Add more wine if necessary, to keep chicken moist.) Remove from stove, add lemon juice and stir. Add eggs and stir constantly. Place over low heat and stir about ½ minute. Remove immediately. Serves 4.

Chicken Marengo

POLLO ALLA MARENGO

- 1 frying chicken, 4 pounds, cut into serving pieces
- ¼ cup olive oil
- 5 tablespoons butter
- ⅓ teaspoon nutmeg
- 1 tablespoon flour
- ⅔ cup dry white wine
- juice of one lemon
- ⅓ cup parsley, chopped
- 1 lemon
- salt and pepper

Wash and dry chicken well. Place oil and butter in pot. Add chicken, nutmeg, salt and pepper. Simmer covered for 25 minutes. Remove chicken and add flour, lemon juice and wine to pot, blending carefully. Return chicken to pot and cook slowly for ten minutes, stirring constantly. Place chicken on serving platter. Sprinkle with the juice of one lemon and garnish with parsley. Serve gravy separately. Serves 4.

Chicken with Cream

POLLO ALLA PANNA

- 1 chicken, about 4 pounds, cut into serving pieces
- 2 medium onions, finely sliced
- 5 tablespoons butter
- ½ cup heavy cream
- 1 cup Thin White Sauce (page 35)
- 1 tablespoon tomato paste
- ¼ teaspoon curry powder
- ½ teaspoon paprika
- juice of one lemon
- 2 black truffles, sliced
- ½ pound sliced mushrooms
- 1 teaspoon salt
- ¼ teaspoon pepper

Cook onions in slightly salted boiling water for 8 to 10 minutes. Drain and let dry. Place onions and butter in pan, over medium flame for 2 minutes. Add chicken, salt and pepper and top with heavy cream. Stir and cover. Simmer for 20 minutes, stirring occasionally. Remove chicken from pan and keep in warm place. Add White Sauce and tomato paste to the pan. Let boil for about 2 minutes, stirring. Remove from fire and put through a sieve. Return sauce to pan and add curry, paprika and lemon juice. Stir. Add chicken, truffles and mushrooms. Simmer uncovered over very low flame for about 10 to 15 minutes. Serves 4.

Chicken Finanziera Style

POLLO ALLA FINANZIERA

- 1 chicken, about 4 or 5 pounds, cut into serving pieces
- 2 or 3 chicken livers
- 6 tablespoons olive oil
- 3 tablespoons celery, chopped
- 2 tablespoons parsley, chopped
- 2 leaves fresh sweet basil
- 1 small onion, sliced fine
- 1 carrot, diced
- 1 tablespoon flour
- ¼ cup chicken stock
- ½ cup dry red wine
- ¼ pound sliced mushrooms
- 3 cockscombs, diced, if available
- ½ cup dry Marsala wine
- salt and pepper

Place oil, celery, parsley, basil, onion and carrot in casserole and cook over low flame for 5 minutes. Add chicken and simmer for 15 minutes. Remove chicken and strain sauce. Put sauce back in casserole and add flour, blending well. Slowly add chicken stock and wine, stir and bring to a boil. Replace chicken, add salt and pepper and cook over low flame for 20 minutes. Remove chicken and place in hot serving dish. To sauce in casserole add mushrooms, livers, cockscombs, Marsala wine. Simmer for 6 to 8 minutes and pour over chicken. Serves 4-6.

Chicken Ghiottona

POLLO ALLA GHIOTTONA

- 1 3-pound chicken, cut into serving pieces
- 6 tablespoons butter
- 1 cup dry white wine
- 1 cup milk
- 1 cup tomato juice or vegetable-juice cocktail
- salt and pepper to taste

Place all ingredients in saucepan or skillet and simmer uncovered for 30 to 35 minutes, stirring occasionally. Taste for seasoning. Serves 4.

Chicken or Turkey Rolls

PANETTI DI POLLO O TACCHINO

Here is a good way to serve leftovers. This can be served as a hot entrée, allowing one per person, or as a main dish, in which case the minimum is 2 per person.

2 cups cooked chicken or turkey, chopped
½ cup Heavy White Sauce (page 35)
¼ cup heavy cream
1 tablespoon celery, minced
2 eggs, lightly beaten
½ cup Onion Sauce (page 36)
salt and pepper to taste

Mix into a smooth paste the chicken or turkey, White Sauce (make very heavy), cream, celery, eggs, and salt and pepper. Fill buttered muffin pans ¾ full with chicken mixture. Place in shallow pan with about ½ inch of water. Bake in oven at 400° for 20 minutes. Remove from pans, top with Onion Sauce and serve. Makes 6 rolls.

Fried Chicken and Mushrooms Tuscany Style

FRITTO ALLA TOSCANA DI POLLO E FUNGHI

2 broilers about 3 pounds each, cut in pieces
flour
2 pounds mushrooms
juice of a large lemon
½ recipe Batter No. 1 (page 159)
2 lemons cut in wedges
2 cups olive oil

Remove stems from mushrooms and rinse them together with mushrooms in water containing lemon juice. Season chicken with salt and pepper, roll in flour and fry in hot oil until each piece is tender and light brown. Remove to brown paper and keep warm. Drain mushrooms and stems, dip in Batter and fry in hot oil until golden on each side. Continue operation until all mushrooms are cooked, then place them in the center of a large round platter, arrange chicken all around and decorate with lemon wedges. Lemon should be used on mushrooms and, if desired, on chicken. Serves 6.

Squabs on the Spit Maria Luisa

PICCIONCINI ALLA MARIA LUISA

4 squabs, cleaned
about 12 slices of bacon
½ teaspoon rosemary
salt and pepper to taste

Clean birds well and dry thoroughly. Season birds inside and out with salt and pepper and rub inside with rosemary. Skewer a few slices of bacon across each squab. Tie legs of each bird together and truss wings close to the body. Insert spit and cook at high heat in electric rotisserie for about 30 minutes. Can be oven-roasted. Remove bacon before serving. Serves 4.

Squabs and Rice Maria Luisa

PICCIONCINI CON RISOTTO ALLA MARIA LUISA

1 recipe Squabs Maria Luisa (see above)
1 recipe Rice with Sage (page 67)

Split the birds down back and serve on top of rice. Serves 4.

Roast Duck

ANITRA ARROSTO

1 5-pound duck ready to cook
4 slices of bacon
¼ teaspoon sage
⅓ cup dry Marsala or port wine
1 tablespoon brandy or Cognac (optional)
salt and pepper

Wash and singe duck. Rub inside with ¼ teaspoon salt and sage. Place one finely diced slice of bacon inside the bird and sprinkle outside of duck with salt and pepper. Place in roasting pan and cover bird's breast with bacon slices. Roast uncovered at 450° for 40 minutes, basting occasionally with wine and brandy and with pan juice. Duck will be on the rare side, as it should be. Cook longer if preferred well done. Serves 4.

Duck Niçoise

ANITRA ALLA NIZZARDA

1 lean duck, about 4 pounds, cut into serving pieces
¼ cup olive oil or 4 tablespoons butter
1 small clove garlic
1 tablespoon fresh parsley, chopped
1 teaspoon poultry seasoning
1 bay leaf
½ teaspoon powdered thyme
1½ teaspoons salt
½ teaspoon pepper
1 can (1 pound) Italian peeled tomatoes, diced
1 cup dry white wine
⅓ cup Cognac
12 jumbo green olives, pitted and sliced
½ pound mushrooms, sliced

Remove as much fat as possible from duck. Sauté garlic in oil or butter in large saucepan until golden. Remove garlic. Place duck in pan and cook over high flame, uncovered, for about 10 minutes, stirring occasionally. Add parsley, poultry seasoning, bay leaf, thyme, salt, pepper and tomatoes. Cover and simmer over low flame for about 35 minutes. Add Cognac and wine. Continue simmering, uncovered, for about 30 minutes. Add mushrooms and olives. Stir and simmer for 30 minutes more. Skim fat from sauce before serving. Serve sauce separately. Serves 4.

Duck Fillets alla Dino

FILETTI DI ANITRA ALLA DINO

Roast Duck for 6 (page 120)
3 ounces purée de foie gras with truffles
2 tablespoons whipped sweet butter
1 recipe Brown Chaufroid Sauce (page 39)

Remove skin from breast of birds. Slice each breast into fillets about ½ inch thick, and as uniform as possible. Arrange on serving platter. Mix purée de foie gras and the butter into a smooth paste, and cover each fillet with some of the mixture. Cover fillets with sauce, and place in refrigerator for at least one hour. Serves 4-6. Remove remaining meat from birds and reserve it for other use.

Stuffed Turkey Lombardy Style

TACCHINO RIPIENO ALLA LOMBARDA

- 1 8- to 10-pound turkey
- ½ pound chopped beef
- 6 Italian sweet sausages, with skin removed or ½ pound chopped pork
- 2 eggs, lightly beaten
- ⅓ cup grated Parmesan cheese
- 2 teaspoons salt
- ¼ teaspoon pepper
- ⅛ teaspoon nutmeg
- ½ teaspoon poultry seasoning
- 1 dozen dried prunes, pitted and diced
- 1 cooking apple, peeled and diced
- 1 dozen chestnuts
- 3 slices bacon, finely diced
- ⅓ cup dry white wine
- ⅓ cup olive oil
- 4 slices bacon
- ¼ teaspoon rosemary
- about ¾ cup dry white wine

Rinse chestnuts in cold water. Peel and cook in lightly salted water until tender, about 20 to 25 minutes. Drain, remove inner skin and dice. Place in large mixing bowl. Dice turkey heart, liver and gizzard, and add to chestnuts. Add beef, sausages or pork, eggs, Parmesan cheese, salt, pepper, nutmeg, poultry seasoning, prunes, apple and diced bacon. Mix thoroughly. Blend in ⅓ cup wine. Stuff turkey loosely and sew up or skewer. Place turkey in roasting pan, sprinkle with oil, rosemary and lightly with salt and pepper. Place bacon strips across the breast, cover turkey with tin foil and roast at 325° for about 3½ hours. Baste frequently with pan drippings and ¾ cup wine. Serves 8-10.

In the Piazza Colonna, under the famous Portici di Vejo is perhaps the most famous and recherché restaurant in Rome, Grande Ristorante Fagiano & Taverna Fagianetta. The place is about 150 years old, and for years has been the rendezvous of the diplomatic corps and high society.

During the day, it is pleasant to take meals on the ground floor and gaze through the huge windows upon the famous Antonina column erected under Marcus Aurelius in 180 B.C.

At night, it is more appropriate to go down a flight of marble stairs to the Taverna Fagianetta, where one is welcomed by a bronze Bacchus from his small niche: *Vita, vinum est.* This is the Pompeian dining room where the furniture, the bas-reliefs, the floors and the frescoes on the walls and the ceiling bring to mind the pomp and gaiety of the Roman empire.

To the right is the Tuscan dining room, displaying in its furniture and décor the beauty and refinement of the Tuscan Renaissance. To the left is the *Abruzzese* dining room, dedicated to that region of Italy by the owner as an homage to his native province. All the beauty and charm of Abruzzo is represented in the paintings and ceramics, the many-colored fishing boats of the Adriatic and the popular costumes. And then there is the Roman dining room, *la sala dell'allegria*, where one can dine in the company of the most famous eaters of history, portrayed in a panel by Coppedé: Falstaff, Pantagruel, Carducci, Conte Ugolino, etc.

Here the pleasure of an environment of real distinction is not spoiled, as sometimes happens, by mediocre cuisine. The food served in these surroundings is a gourmet's delight, as may be demonstrated by the following recipe:

Fillets of Turkey Bolognese

FILETTI DI TACCHINO ALLA BOLOGNESE

breast of a 6- to 8-pound turkey, uncooked
bread crumbs
1 large egg beaten with ¼ teaspoon salt
⅛ teaspoon pepper
¾ cup olive oil
1 small mozzarella cheese, sliced fine
⅓ pound prosciutto or Canadian bacon, finely sliced
3 tablespoons ready-cooked tomato sauce (optional)

Have your butcher cut the turkey breast into fillets, about ⅓ inch thick. Dip fillets into egg, then into bread crumbs, and fry a few at a time in hot oil until golden on both sides. Arrange fillets in a single layer in large, well-buttered baking dish. Cut prosciutto or bacon the same size as the fillets, and place a slice on top of each fillet, then cover with a slice of mozzarella cheese. Place in 350° oven for 20 minutes. Have tomato sauce warm. Serve fillets topped with a drop of tomato sauce in the center of each. Serves 4-6.

Turkey Casserole alla Scarlatta

PETTO DI TACCHINO ALLA SCARLATTA

breast of a 6- to 8-pound turkey, uncooked
1 large egg
¼ teaspoon salt
⅛ teaspoon pepper
bread crumbs
¾ cup olive oil
2 pounds fresh or frozen broccoli, cooked in salted water until tender but still firm
4 ounces cooked tongue, sliced very thin or coarsely chopped
1 recipe Mornay Sauce (page 34)

Have your butcher cut the turkey breast into fillets, about ⅓ inch thick. Dip fillets into egg beaten with salt and pepper, then roll in bread crumbs. Fry a few at a time in hot oil until golden on both sides. Arrange drained broccoli at bottom of a large well-buttered baking dish or casserole, cover with a layer of turkey fillets and then with slices of tongue, or sprinkle with chopped tongue. Pour Mornay Sauce over all and cook in 350° oven for 20 minutes. Serves 4-6.

If desired, breaded veal cutlets (you will need about 1½ pounds) can be used instead of turkey fillets.

Truffled Roast Capon

CAPPONE TARTUFFATO

- 1 capon of about 5 pounds, ready to cook
- 2 canned white truffles the size of a walnut, sliced
- ½ cup dry Marsala wine (dry port or sherry may be substituted)
- 4 tablespoons butter, melted
- salt and pepper
- ½ teaspoon poultry seasoning

Insert half of the sliced truffles under the skin of the breast, then rub capon with pepper and poultry seasoning. Place rest of truffles inside the capon and truss it. Wrap well in aluminum foil and place in refrigerator for 24 hours. This will allow the capon to absorb much of the aroma of the truffles. Brush bird with melted butter and place on rack of shallow pan. Pour rest of butter over bird, cover with aluminum foil or with a cloth dipped in melted butter or oil, and roast in 300° oven for 2½ hours. Season with salt when half done and baste often with wine and pan gravy. Remove foil or cloth and cook 30 minutes more or until lightly brown. Serves 4-6.

Pheasant Norcia Style

FAGIANO ALLA NORCESE

Norcia is perhaps the largest producer of first-quality truffles in Italy. As a matter of fact, her truffles are so highly regarded that about half of each yearly crop goes from Norcia to France where they are then put on the market as a produce of the Perigord, where the best truffles in the world are found.

- 2 young pheasants, plucked and cleaned
- ½ cup white truffles, minced
- 1 recipe Chicken Liver Spread (page 14)
- ½ cup Grappa liqueur
- 1 pound bacon
- salt and pepper to taste

Choose birds that have hung not more than four days. Stuff with truffles, wrap in foil and place in refrigerator, or any cool place, for 24 hours. Unwrap birds, remove truffles and mix them with Chicken Liver Spread. Rub birds with salt and pepper and stuff with chicken liver mixture. Sew the openings and wrap each bird with bacon slices or a thin sheet of larding pork; tie with string. Truss and wrap in foil separately again, being sure that they are completely sealed inside the foil. Place in uncovered roasting pan in 450° oven for 30 minutes. Remove from oven, unwrap foil and return to roasting pan together with fat or juice that was enclosed in the foil, and cook for 10 to 15 minutes more, turning and basting birds every five minutes.

Birds are done when the juice that runs out when they are lifted and held tail down is clear and without a pink tinge. Remove from oven, carve and reshape the birds on a heated platter.

Pour about two-thirds of fat from roasting pan into small saucepan, add Grappa, blending well. Bring to a boil and boil for five minutes, serve in gravy boat or pour over birds. Serves 4-6.

Birds can also be cooked on a spit, in which case insert birds on the spit after trussing and then wrap with foil. This method of wrapping the birds is quite old; it facilitates the penetration of the truffle aroma and at the same time keeps the bird well-greased during cooking.

Rabbit Buongustaio

CONIGLIO DEL BUONGUSTAIO

- 1 rabbit, cut in serving pieces
- 1 cup dry Marsala wine
- ½ small onion, minced
- ¼ teaspoon thyme
- 1 bay leaf
- 2 tablespoons butter
- 2 very lean slices of bacon, minced
- ¼ cup celery, minced
- ¼ cup carrot, minced
- ¼ cup wine vinegar
- ½ cup dry white wine
- 1 teaspoon flour
- salt and pepper

Place rabbit in bowl, add to it the minced onion, thyme, bay leaf and Marsala, cover and marinate overnight. Then place butter and bacon in skillet, together with the drained rabbit. Brown meat on all sides, add carrot and celery, sprinkle with salt and pepper and add to it ¼ of the marinade. Cover and simmer for 45 minutes, or until meat is tender, adding more of the marinade whenever necessary. Remove meat to hot plate and keep warm. Add vinegar and white wine to sauce left in skillet, bring to a boil, and boil uncovered for five minutes. Skim fat with a spoon, put mixture through a sieve, and return to skillet. Blend in flour and cook, stirring until sauce comes to a boil. Pour over rabbit and serve. Serves 4.

Rabbit Leghorn Style

CONIGLIO ALLA LIVORNESE

1 rabbit cut in serving pieces	2 tablespoons olive oil
3 tablespoons onion, minced	1 cup tomato purée
1 clove garlic, minced	6 anchovy fillets, minced
1/3 cup parsley, minced	1 teaspoon salt
3 tablespoons butter	1/8 teaspoon pepper

Place oil, butter, onion, garlic, parsley and rabbit in saucepan and sauté, stirring occasionally, until meat has browned on all sides. Add tomato purée, minced anchovies, salt and pepper, stirring well. Cover and simmer for twenty minutes. Remove rabbit to casserole, adding a little stock, wine or water to sauce if it has become too thick. Cover and bake in 350° oven for 1½ hours or until meat is tender. Serves 4.

VEGETABLES

LEGUMI

ฯฯฯ

Sautéed String Beans

FAGIOLINI IN PADELLA

1 pound fresh string beans	2 cloves garlic
6 tablespoons olive oil	salt and pepper

Clean beans and slice in half. Cook covered in salted water until tender (about 30 minutes). Drain. Place garlic and oil in skillet. Remove garlic when golden. Add beans. Sprinkle with pepper and cook over low flame 5 minutes, stirring frequently. Serves 4.

String Beans Italian Style

FAGIOLINI ALL'ITALIANA

2 pounds fresh string beans	1 cup beef or chicken broth
½ cup dry salt fat back or salt pork, diced fine	⅓ cup parsley, minced
½ pound ripe Italian egg tomatoes, peeled and diced	salt and pepper

Place string beans and fat back or salt pork in large, low saucepan or skillet, with tomatoes, salt, pepper and broth. Cover and simmer for one hour and 20 minutes. If necessary, cook uncovered 5 minutes or until excessive moisture has evaporated. Sprinkle with parsley. Serves 6.

String Beans with Tomato Sauce

FAGIOLINI AL POMIDORO

- 2 pounds fresh string beans, cut in 2-inch pieces
- ½ cup olive oil
- 1 clove garlic
- 1 pound ripe tomatoes, peeled and diced or 1 pound canned peeled tomatoes, diced
- 2 tablespoons tomato paste diluted in ½ cup lukewarm water
- salt and pepper

Sauté garlic in oil until golden. Discard garlic. Add beans, salt and pepper and cook over low flame for about 5 minutes, stirring occasionally. Add tomatoes, paste and water. Cover and continue to simmer until beans are tender, about 30 to 40 minutes. If mixture becomes too dry during cooking, add water. Serves 6-8.

String Bean Casserole

TIMBALLO DI FAGIOLINI

- ½ pound chopped sirloin
- ⅓ cup olive oil
- 1 pound chicken livers cut in half
- ¼ pound butter
- 1 pound mushrooms, sliced
- 1⅓ cups Mornay Sauce (page 34)
- 2 boxes frozen cut string beans, cooked uncovered in salted water for about 20 minutes
- bread crumbs
- salt and pepper to taste

Add ½ teaspoon salt and ⅛ teaspoon black pepper to sirloin. Roll meat into balls the size of nickels and brown in oil. Remove from skillet and add to Mornay Sauce. Sauté chicken livers in 2½ tablespoons butter and add to sauce. Sauté mushrooms in 3 tablespoons butter for about 5 minutes and add to sauce. Sauté drained string beans in butter for 3 minutes, stirring occasionally. Add to ingredients in sauce. Mix gently and taste for seasoning. Place mixture in buttered baking dish, even top with spoon and sprinkle with bread crumbs. Bake in 400° oven for about 20 minutes. Serves 6-8.

String Bean Soufflé

SOUFFLÉ DI FAGIOLINI

1 box frozen cut string beans	½ teaspoon salt
5 tablespoons butter	1 egg yolk
1 tablespoon flour	2 egg whites beaten stiff with
1 cup milk	½ teaspoon salt
3 tablespoons grated Parmesan cheese	

Place string beans in 2 quarts boiling water with 1 tablespoon salt. Cook uncovered for 20 to 25 minutes or until tender. In the meantime place half of the butter in small saucepan. When butter is melted add flour. Stir into a smooth paste and add milk. Stir constantly and cook over low flame for 10 to 12 minutes. Sauce should have the consistency of very thick cream. Add salt and stir. Remove from heat and rapidly stir in cheese and egg yolk. Drain beans and rinse in cold water. Drain and place in skillet with rest of butter and sauté gently for 3 minutes, stirring occasionally. Put beans through a sieve. Mix with white sauce. Fold in egg whites. Place mixture in a buttered baking dish (filling baking dish only ¾ full). Even top with spoon and bake in 350° oven for 30 to 35 minutes. Serve immediately or mixture will fall. Serves 4.

Peas Roman Style

PISELLI ALLA ROMANA

2 boxes frozen sweet peas or 2 pounds of fresh peas	3 slices of prosciutto, diced (bacon can be substituted)
2 chopped onions	½ cup water
6 tablespoons olive oil	1 teaspoon salt
	½ teaspoon pepper

Place oil, onions and prosciutto in pan and simmer for 5 minutes. Add peas, water, salt and pepper. Cook uncovered over low flame for 30 minutes. Serves 8.

Celery Milanese

SEDANO ALLA MILANESE

1 large bunch of celery, cut in 2-inch pieces	1 recipe Heavy White Sauce (page 35)
	¼ cup grated Parmesan cheese

Cook celery in salted water until tender but still firm, about 25 to 30 minutes. Drain. Place in buttered baking dish, cover with sauce and sprinkle with cheese. Bake at 350° for 30 minutes. Serves 4.

Spinach in Butter

SPINACI AL BURRO

1½ pounds fresh spinach or 2 boxes frozen spinach	6 tablespoons butter salt and pepper to taste

Place spinach in a small quantity of boiling salted water, cover and cook about 10 to 20 minutes. Follow directions on package for frozen spinach. Drain well. Melt butter in skillet, then add spinach, sprinkle with pepper and sauté gently, stirring occasionally until excessive moisture has evaporated, about 5 minutes. Serves 4.

Spinach with Lemon Dressing

SPINACI ALL'OLIO E LIMONE

1½ pounds fresh spinach or 2 boxes frozen spinach	juice of one lemon salt and pepper to taste
⅓ cup olive oil	

Place spinach in small quantity of boiling salted water and cook for about 10 to 20 minutes, if using fresh spinach. Follow directions on package for frozen spinach. Drain well, season with oil and lemon juice and serve hot or cold. Serves 4.

Broccoli Roman Style

BROCCOLI ALLA ROMANA

1½ pounds fresh broccoli or 2 boxes frozen broccoli stalks	2 cloves garlic
½ cup olive oil	1½ cups dry white wine
	salt and pepper to taste

Sauté garlic in oil until golden but not brown. Remove garlic if desired, then add broccoli and simmer uncovered for 4 to 5 minutes, stirring occasionally. Add salt, pepper and wine; cover and cook for about 10 to 15 minutes if using frozen broccoli, or about 25 minutes if using fresh broccoli. Serves 4.

Cauliflower may be prepared the same way, using a medium-size head of fresh cauliflower or 2 boxes of frozen cauliflower.

Broccoli Sauté

BROCCOLI IN PADELLA

1½ pounds fresh broccoli, rinsed in cold water or 2 boxes frozen broccoli	2 large cloves of garlic
	⅓ cup olive oil
	salt and pepper to taste

Cook broccoli in boiling salted water until tender but still firm, about 15 to 25 minutes for fresh, and 7 to 8 minutes for frozen. Drain well. Sauté garlic in oil until golden. Discard garlic and add broccoli. Simmer for 5 minutes, stirring often. Serves 4.

Brussels Sprouts Parmigiana

CAVOLETTI ALLA PARMIGIANA

| 1½ pounds fresh Brussels sprouts or 2 boxes frozen Brussels sprouts | ¼ pound butter, melted |
| | ¼ cup grated Parmesan cheese |

Cook sprouts in salted water, 5 minutes if frozen, 12 to 15 minutes if fresh. Drain. Place in buttered baking dish, pour butter over them, sprinkle with cheese and bake at 350° for 20 minutes. Serves 4-6.

Stuffed Tomatoes alla Romana

POMODORI RIPIENI ALLA ROMANA

- 4 large firm tomatoes
- ¼ cup rice
- 6 tablespoons butter, melted
- 3 tablespoons grated Parmesan cheese
- ½ tablespoon parsley, chopped
- ⅓ cup finely diced mozzarella cheese
- ¼ teaspoon salt
- ⅛ teaspoon pepper

Cook rice in salted water for 10 minutes. Drain. Mix with 4 tablespoons butter, Parmesan and mozzarella cheeses, parsley, salt and pepper. Cut a slice about ⅓ inch thick from the stem end of each tomato. Remove the center, being careful not to break the wall. Sprinkle the inside of each tomato lightly with salt and pepper and stuff with rice mixture. Place tomatoes in large buttered baking dish, sprinkle top of each with remaining butter and bake in oven at 350° for 25 minutes. Serves 4.

Stuffed Onion Hector

CIPOLLE RIPIENE ALLA ETTORE

- 4 large Bermuda onions
- 3 tablespoons butter
- 2 slices bread, soaked in milk and squeezed dry
- ⅓ cup grated Parmesan cheese
- 2 eggs
- 3 almond macaroons, minced (optional)
- 2 tablespoons parsley, minced
- 1 teaspoon sugar
- salt and pepper to taste

Peel onions, and remove a slice about ¾ of an inch thick from top of each. Parboil in salted water for 15 minutes. Remove from stove and let stand in cooking water until cool enough to handle. Then drain and remove center of each onion with the help of a soup spoon, leaving a shell about ½ inch thick. Mince the scooped-out part of the onions and place in skillet with butter. Cook over medium-low flame, stirring for 15 minutes. Do not allow onion to brown. Remove from stove and cool. Blend with cheese, egg, parsley, soaked bread and macaroons. Season to taste, and fill onion shells. Place in greased baking dish. Beat remaining egg with sugar and spoon it over onions. Bake in 325° oven for 1½ hours, or until tender. Serves 4.

Stuffed Acorn Squash

ZUCCHE RIPIENE

- 3 large acorn squash
- 4 slices white bread, soaked in milk and squeezed dry
- 1 large egg, beaten
- 1/3 cup parsley, minced
- 1/3 cup celery, minced
- 1 large clove garlic, minced
- 1 7-ounce can tuna fish
- 1 7-ounce can salmon
- 6 slices of bacon
- 1/2 cup water
- salt and pepper to taste

Cut squash in half crosswise, remove seeds and sprinkle inside of each with salt and pepper. Blend into a smooth paste the bread, garlic, egg, parsley, celery, tuna and salmon, seasoning to taste. Fill squash with this mixture, place in greased baking dish, topping each with one strip of bacon. Pour water in baking dish and bake in 350° oven for one hour. Serves 6.

Creamed Mushrooms

FUNGHI ALLA PANNA

- 1½ pounds mushrooms, sliced
- 3 tablespoons butter
- 1½ tablespoons olive oil
- 2 tablespoons chopped onion
- ¼ cup heavy cream
- ½ teaspoon lemon juice
- salt and pepper to taste
- dash of paprika

Place oil, butter and onion in saucepan and simmer for 3 to 4 minutes or until onion is soft. Do not brown. Add mushrooms and cook over medium flame for 5 minutes. Season to taste, add cream and lemon juice. Simmer about 5 minutes more, or until mushrooms are free of excessive moisture. Serves 4.

Mushrooms Trifolati

FUNGHI TRIFOLATI

- 1½ pounds mushrooms, sliced
- 1 clove garlic
- ¼ cup olive oil
- 3 anchovy fillets, chopped
- 3 tablespoons butter
- 1 lemon, cut in wedges
- salt and pepper to taste

Sauté garlic in oil until golden. Discard garlic. Add mushrooms and sauté, stirring occasionally, for 5 minutes. Mix butter and anchovies together and add to mushrooms. Mix well, season to taste and sauté one minute more. Remove mushrooms to hot serving plate. Serve with lemon wedges. Serves 4.

Stuffed Mushrooms Piedmont Style

FUNGHI RIPIENI ALLA PIEMONTESE

- 16 large firm mushrooms
- 2 anchovies, finely chopped
- 1 medium-size onion, finely chopped
- 2 teaspoons parsley, chopped
- 2 tablespoons olive oil
- 4 tablespoons bread crumbs
- 1 egg, slightly beaten
- 2/3 cup olive oil
- 1/2 tablespoon salt
- 1/2 teaspoon pepper

Clean and wash mushrooms. Drain caps and dry carefully. Put stems through food chopper.

Cook parsley, anchovies and onions in 2 tablespoons olive oil until onions are golden. Add chopped mushroom stems, salt and pepper and simmer very slowly for 5 minutes. Remove from stove and cool. Add egg and bread crumbs and mix thoroughly. Stuff caps with this mixture. Arrange stuffed caps in large baking dish, allowing space between each cap. Sprinkle with remaining olive oil and very lightly with salt and pepper. Bake for 20 minutes in moderate oven, basting occasionally. Serves 6.

Baked Zucchini with Prosciutto

ZUCCHINI GRATINATE AL PROSCIUTTO

- 2 pounds unpeeled zucchini, each about 5 inches long and 2 to 3 inches wide
- 3 slices prosciutto, diced fine
- 3 slices bacon, minced
- 3 tablespoons parsley, chopped
- 1/2 onion, minced
- 1/4 cup melted butter
- salt and pepper

Rinse zucchini in cold water. Cook in boiling salted water for 3 minutes. Drain. Slice in half lengthwise and place in single layer in large buttered baking dish. Mix prosciutto, bacon, parsley and onion. Season zucchini lightly with salt and pepper and place bacon mixture on top of zucchini. Pour butter over all and place in 350° oven for 30 to 45 minutes. Serves 4.

Golden Zucchini

ZUCCHINI DORATI

8 small zucchini, unpeeled
2 cups olive oil
1 cup flour
salt and pepper

Wash zucchini. Cut in narrow strips lengthwise. Sprinkle with salt and let stand for one hour in colander. Roll in flour and fry in hot oil until golden and crisp. Sprinkle with pepper and salt and serve immediately. Serves 4-6.

Zucchini Madeleine

ZUCCHINI ALLA MADDALENA

3 zucchini, peeled and diced
5 tablespoons olive oil
2 onions, diced
4 potatoes, peeled and diced
1 large tomato, peeled and diced
salt and pepper to taste

Place oil in small pan. Add all ingredients and simmer covered for 30 to 45 minutes. Add some hot water if vegetables become too dry. Serves 4.

Fried Cauliflower

CAVOLFIORE DORATO

1 large cauliflower
½ recipe Batter No. 1 (page 159)
olive oil for deep frying

Cut off any bruised spots from cauliflower. Place in cold salted water, top downward, for 30 to 45 minutes. Drain and break into flowerets. Cook in boiling salted water for 15 minutes. Drain carefully and cool. Dip flowerets in batter and fry a few at a time in hot oil, until golden. Serve hot or cold. Serves 6.

Cauliflower Soufflé

SOUFFLÉ DI CAVOLFIORE

- 2 packages frozen cauliflower, or 1 fresh cauliflower, about 2 pounds
- 1 teaspoon butter
- 1 teaspoon flour
- ¼ cup light cream
- 4 egg yolks, beaten
- 2 tablespoons grated Parmesan cheese
- 4 egg whites, beaten stiff
- ⅛ teaspoon pepper
- ½ teaspoon salt

If using fresh cauliflower, remove leaves and cut off any bruised spots and wash. Cook cauliflower in salted water for 30 minutes. If using frozen vegetable, cooking time should be about 20 minutes. Drain. Mash with vegetable masher to a smooth paste. Make a white sauce by placing butter in very small saucepan, over low flame. When butter is melted, add flour and stir for a few seconds. Add cream and continue stirring until sauce thickens. Remove from heat and add to cauliflower together with salt, pepper, cheese and egg yolks. Mix into a smooth paste. Fold in egg whites. Taste for seasoning. Bake in buttered pan for 20 minutes in 350° oven. Must be served immediately. Serves 8.

Eggplant Parmigiana

MELANZANE ALLA PARMIGIANA

- 2 eggplants (about 1 pound each), peeled
- 2¼ cups olive oil
- 1 clove garlic
- 3 pounds very ripe Italian egg tomatoes, peeled and diced or 1⅓ cups tomato paste diluted in 2 cups warm water
- 2 leaves fresh sweet basil or ¼ teaspoon dried basil
- ½ recipe for Batter No. 1 (page 159)
- 1 cup grated Parmesan cheese
- ½ cup mozzarella cheese, diced (optional)
- 3 tablespoons butter
- salt and pepper to taste

Sauté garlic in ¼ cup oil until golden. Discard garlic. Add tomatoes or tomato paste, basil, salt and pepper and simmer, stirring occasionally, for 30 minutes. Slice eggplants crosswise in ⅓-inch thick slices. Dip in batter and fry in hot oil until golden on both sides. Line one large casserole or smaller individual ones with tomato sauce. Make a layer of eggplant, cover with sauce, sprinkle with Parmesan and a few pieces of mozzarella cheese. Repeat layers until all ingredients are used. Dot with butter and bake in 350° oven for 30 minutes.

(For individual casseroles 15 minutes will be enough.) Serve hot. Serves 6.

Baked Eggplant

MELANZANE GRATINATE

4 very small eggplants, unpeeled (about 1¼-1½ pounds in all)
2 cloves of garlic, chopped
3 basil leaves, chopped or ¼ teaspoon dried basil
⅔ cup olive oil
salt and pepper to taste

Remove stems from eggplant, rinse in cold water. Slice in half lengthwise. Make small crisscross cuts on meat side of eggplant halves. Mix garlic, basil, salt and pepper. Spread the garlic mixture on cut side of eggplant halves. Place in single layer in baking dish, sprinkle with oil and bake for 25 to 30 minutes in 375° oven. Serves 4.

Asparagus Milanese

ASPARAGI ALLA MILANESE

2 pounds fresh asparagus
⅓ cup grated Parmesan cheese
½ cup hot butter

Clean asparagus and cut off tough part of stalk. Tie in 4 bunches and boil in 3 quarts salted water for about 15 to 20 minutes, or until tender. Drain. Remove string. Place in hot oval serving platter so that asparagus bunches are tip to tip in the center of the platter. Sprinkle tips with cheese. Pour hot butter over asparagus. Serves 6-8.

Asparagus Polonese

ASPARAGI ALLA POLONESE

1 pound fresh asparagus
1 hard-boiled egg
5 tablespoons butter
1½ tablespoons bread crumbs

Clean asparagus and cut off tough part of stalk. Tie in two bunches and cook in 2½ quarts salted water for 15 to 20 minutes, or until tender. Drain. Remove string. Place asparagus in hot serving dish and keep warm. Mash the yolk of the hard-boiled egg. Place butter in small frying pan and, when hot, add yolk and bread crumbs. Cook over medium-high flame for 2 minutes, stirring. Add to asparagus and serve immediately. Serves 4.

Asparagus Madeleine

ASPARAGI ALLA MADDALENA

- 1 pound fresh or frozen asparagus
- 3 slices bacon
- 3 tablespoons olive oil
- ½ cup water
- ½ teaspoon salt
- ⅛ teaspoon pepper
- a dash of crushed red pepper

Place bacon in small saucepan and simmer till it becomes almost crisp. Add oil, water, salt and pepper. Let boil for 2 minutes. Add asparagus, cover and simmer for about 20 minutes. Remove bacon before serving. Serves 4.

Artichokes Roman Style

CARCIOFI ALLA ROMANA

- 8 medium artichokes
- juice of a large lemon
- ⅓ cup bread crumbs
- 8 anchovy fillets, chopped
- 4 tablespoons minced parsley
- 5 leaves minced mint or ½ teaspoon dried mint
- 1 teaspoon salt
- ½ teaspoon pepper
- ½ cup olive oil
- 2 cups water

Cut off stalks and tips of artichokes and remove tougher outer leaves. Press artichokes down, holding them by the stems to spread leaves. With small sharp knife remove spiny chokes, if necessary. Place artichokes in bowl of water to which lemon juice has been added. Mix together bread crumbs, anchovies, parsley, mint and pepper. Moisten with enough water or oil to make a paste. Drain artichokes and fill their centers with anchovy mixture. Place in saucepan, add water, salt and oil, cover tightly and cook slowly for 30 to 45 minutes, depending on tenderness of artichokes. These are delicious hot or cold. Serves 4.

Artichokes Elpidiana

CARCIOFI ELPIDIANA

8 small artichokes
juice of 2 large lemons
2 sweet Italian sausages
2 tablespoons black truffle, diced fine
2 pounds mushrooms, sliced
⅓ cup olive oil
⅓ cup chicken or beef broth
salt and pepper

Cut off stalks and tips of artichokes and remove tough outer leaves. Press open center of artichokes and remove and discard chokes if necessary. Place in bowl of water to which lemon juice has been added. Remove sausages from casing. Mix sausage meat and truffle. Drain artichokes and stuff center with truffle mixture. Place artichokes, standing up close together, in small saucepan. Sprinkle with salt and pepper, a few drops of lemon juice and add mushrooms. Add oil and broth. Cover tightly and cook over low flame for 30 to 40 minutes. Serve plain or sprinkled with chopped parsley. Serves 4-8.

Golden Artichokes

CARCIOFI DORATI

12 small artichokes
juice of 2 lemons
½ recipe for Batter No. 1 (page 159)
olive oil for deep frying

Cut off stalks and tips of artichokes and remove tough outer leaves, leaving only tender ones. Cut in half lengthwise, discarding chokes from center. Slice each half in 3 slices. Place artichokes in large bowl with water and lemon juice to cover. Drain. Dip in batter and fry a few at a time in hot olive oil until golden. Serve hot. Serves 4-6.

Artichokes Jewish Style

CARCIOFI ALLA GIUDIA

Here is the most famous and most generally liked way of preparing artichokes. Its secret lies in their tenderness and in the right cooking time. Each leaf should look golden and be as crisp as a potato chip.

12 artichokes
4 cups olive oil
juice of 2 lemons
1 teaspoon salt
½ teaspoon pepper

Peel stalks and cut off tips of artichokes. Remove all tough outer leaves and spread remaining ones open by pressing artichoke down and holding by stem. Remove spiny choke from center with a small sharp knife. Wash artichokes in water to which lemon juice has been added. Drain. Sprinkle inside leaves with salt and pepper. Place oil in deep skillet or saucepan. Fry artichokes a few at a time over medium flame, for 8 to 10 minutes, turning occasionally. Remove artichokes to absorbent paper. Let artichokes stand for at least ½ hour (even as long as 3 hours) before continuing preparation. Then reheat oil in skillet and, when hot, hold each artichoke by the stalk and dip it in. The artichoke will open, its leaves will curl and become a dark golden color. Remove to absorbent paper, sprinkle lightly with salt and serve hot. Serves 4-6.

Artichokes and Peas

CARCIOFI CON PISELLI

6 small artichokes
juice of one large lemon
1 box frozen peas, or 10 ounces fresh shelled peas
3 tablespoons butter
2 tablespoons olive oil
¼ cup prosciutto, diced (lean bacon can be substituted)
½ small onion, minced
about ½ cup beef or chicken broth (if needed)
salt and pepper to taste

Cut off stalks and tips of artichokes and remove tough outer leaves. Cut in half lengthwise, discarding chokes from center. Slice lengthwise in thin slices. Place artichokes in a bowl of water to which lemon juice has been added. Drain. Place butter, oil and prosciutto or bacon in saucepan. Sauté gently for about 3 minutes, add onion and sauté a few more minutes. Do not allow onion to brown. Add artichokes and peas, salt and pepper, cover and simmer for 30 to 40 minutes, adding the broth if necessary. Serve hot. Serves 6.

Peppers Ticinese

PEPERONI ALLA TICINESE

- 4 large green sweet peppers
- ¼ pound Swiss cheese, diced
- 1½ pounds potatoes, peeled and sliced paper-thin
- 1 large onion, diced
- 1 pound ripe Italian egg tomatoes, peeled and diced
- ¼ cup olive oil
- salt and pepper

With a sharp knife cut peppers inside the depression containing the stem. Remove this portion and set aside. Carefully remove the seeds and rinse peppers in cold water. Stuff peppers with cheese and replace stems to close openings. Place onion in large casserole. Make a layer of the potatoes, and sprinkle with salt and pepper. Add tomatoes, salt and pepper. Place stuffed peppers on top of tomatoes and sprinkle with salt, pepper and oil. Cover and bake in moderate oven (350°) for 45 minutes. Remove cover and cook 15 minutes more. Serves 4.

Peppers and Potatoes

PEPERONATA CON LE PATATE

- 1 pound sweet green peppers
- 5 large potatoes, peeled and coarsely diced
- 5 tablespoons olive oil
- 1 clove garlic
- 3 tablespoons tomato paste diluted in 1 cup lukewarm water
- 1 large onion, sliced
- salt and pepper to taste

Remove stems and seeds from peppers. Slice each pepper lengthwise in 6 or 8 slices and rinse in cold water. Sauté garlic in oil. Discard garlic when golden. Add rest of ingredients, cover and cook slowly for 45 minutes. Add a little water if necessary. Correct seasoning. Serves 4.

Fried Apples

MELE FRITTE

- 2 pounds large cooking apples
- 1 recipe of Batter No. 1 (page 159)
- 2 cups olive oil

Rinse apples in cold water and dry. Cut in thin wedges, removing the cores. Place 5 or 6 wedges in the batter. Remove with fork and place in hot oil. Fry on both sides till lightly brown. Repeat operation until all apples have been fried. Serve hot. Fried apples can be served with roast meats. Serves 8.

Fried Potatoes Home Style

PATATE FRITTE ALLA CASALINGA

2 pounds potatoes, peeled
⅔ cup olive oil
¼ teaspoon rosemary
salt

Cut potatoes into cubes about ¾ inch square. Fry in hot oil, over medium flame, stirring often, for 5 minutes. Add rosemary and continue frying until potatoes are done, about 10 minutes more. Sprinkle with salt before serving. Serves 4.

Potatoes with Cream

PATATE ALLA PANNA

3 pounds potatoes, peeled and sliced thin
2 large onions, peeled and sliced fine
4 slices of bacon, diced
5 tablespoons butter
2 cups chicken or beef broth, or water
¾ cup heavy cream at room temperature
1 teaspoon salt
¼ teaspoon pepper

Place onions, bacon and butter in saucepan. Sauté gently for 5 to 8 minutes, or until onions are soft but not brown. Add potatoes and broth or water, salt and pepper. Cover and cook over medium-high flame for 20 to 30 minutes. Carefully stir in cream, remove from stove and serve. Serves 6-8.

Delfino Potatoes

PATATE DEL DELFINO

2 pounds potatoes, peeled
1 large egg, beaten
1⅓ cups cold milk or cream
1⅓ teaspoons salt
⅓ teaspoon black pepper
¾ teaspoon nutmeg

Slice potatoes very thin. Place in well-buttered casserole. Mix egg with milk, salt, pepper and nutmeg. Pour over potatoes. Bake uncovered in oven at 400° for 45 to 55 minutes. Serve hot. Serves 6.

Potato Ring

CIAMBELLA DI PATATE

2 pounds potatoes, peeled	1 tablespoon parsley, chopped
5 tablespoons butter	bread crumbs
3 eggs, beaten	salt and pepper
¼ pound diced cooked ham	

Boil potatoes in salted water until tender. Drain well and mash. Blend in eggs, butter, parsley, ham, salt and pepper. Butter a 1½ quart ring mold, sprinkle sides and bottom with bread crumbs, add potato mixture, level off top with spoon and sprinkle with bread crumbs. Dot with butter. Bake in oven at 350° for 30 minutes. Unmold on serving dish. Serves 8.

Potatoes Maria Luisa

SFORMATO DI PATATE MARIA LUISA

4 pounds potatoes	3 tablespoons butter
3 eggs, beaten	6 slices prosciutto (cooked ham or salami may be substituted)
½ cup grated Parmesan cheese or ⅓ cup grated Romano cheese	¼ pound provolone or mozzarella cheese, diced
½ teaspoon pepper	¼ cup bread crumbs
½ teaspoon salt	

Wash potatoes and boil unpeeled in salted water until tender. Peel and mash while hot, taking care that they do not become cold. Put in mixing bowl with eggs, grated cheese, salt, pepper, diced provolone or mozzarella and 2 tablespoons butter. Mix well. Sprinkle greased 8" x 3" or 9" x 2" baking dish with one half of bread crumbs. Pour in half of potato mixture. Level off top with spoon and cover with layer of prosciutto or substitute. Cover with remaining potato mixture. Even top with spoon, sprinkle with remaining bread crumbs, dot with butter and bake in 300° oven for 35 minutes. Cool for 15 minutes. Turn out on serving dish. Cut in wedges and serve. Serves 6 to 8. If desired, it can be served hot immediately, using a spoon for serving. It is also delicious served cold.

Potatoes and Sausage

PATATE RIPIENE DI SALSICCIA

4 large Idaho potatoes, unpeeled	1 tablespoon butter
2 sweet Italian sausages, with casing removed	2 tablespoons parsley, chopped
	1 egg yolk
2 slices of bread soaked in milk and squeezed dry	salt and pepper to taste

Make a forcemeat of the sausages, bread, butter, parsley, egg yolk, salt and pepper. Rinse potatoes in cold water. Pat dry. With a sharp knife scoop out a deep hole for the stuffing. (Potatoes should look like boats.) Stuff potatoes with forcemeat and place in baking pan. Bake in 475° oven for 45 to 50 minutes. Serves 4.

Potato Croquettes

CROCCHETTE DI PATATE

2½ pounds unpeeled potatoes	1½ tablespoons parsley, chopped
2 eggs, beaten	⅔ cup bread crumbs
½ cup grated Parmesan cheese or ⅓ cup grated Romano cheese	2 cups olive oil
	1 teaspoon salt
	⅛ teaspoon pepper

Boil potatoes in slightly salted water until done. Peel and mash while hot. Add eggs, cheese, salt, pepper and parsley. Mix well. Make sausage-shaped patties about 2½ inches long and 1 inch thick. Roll in bread crumbs and fry, a few at a time, in hot oil, until golden brown. Serves 6-8.

Cabbage Home Style

CAVOLO ALLA CASALINGA

1 cabbage of about 2 pounds, shredded	2½ cups water
	1 tablespoon wine vinegar
½ cup bacon, diced fine	salt and pepper to taste

Sauté bacon gently for a few minutes until soft but not crisp. Add rest of ingredients, cover and cook over medium flame for 25 minutes or until tender. Stir occasionally and add more water if necessary. When cabbage is cooked, there should not be more than a couple of tablespoons of liquid in the pan. Serves 4.

SALADS

INSALATE

Maria Luisa's Salad

INSALATA MARIA LUISA

- 1 head escarole, or enough mixed salad greens for four
- 2 hard-boiled eggs
- 8 anchovy fillets, diced
- ½ teaspoon prepared mustard
- ½ cup olive oil
- 2½ tablespoons wine vinegar
- salt and pepper to taste

Rub the yolks of the hard-boiled eggs through a sieve, and add to anchovy fillets, mustard, oil, vinegar, salt and pepper. Dice egg whites and add to dressing. Mix well. Pour over escarole and toss. Serves 4.

Escarole Salad

INSALATA DI SCAROLA

- 1 small head escarole, shredded
- 1 egg yolk
- ½ teaspoon dry English mustard
- ⅓ cup olive oil
- 2 tablespoons wine vinegar or lemon juice
- salt and pepper to taste

Place yolk and mustard in salad bowl. Beat with a spoon or wire whisk and slowly add oil and vinegar, continuing to beat until dressing is creamy. Season to taste, add greens and toss well. Serves 2-4.

Romaine Salad all'Italiana

INSALATA VERDE ALL'ITALIANA

1 large head romaine, cleaned, and broken into 2-inch lengths
1 clove garlic
⅓ cup olive oil
1½ tablespoons wine vinegar
salt
freshly ground black pepper

Rub salad bowl with garlic, add greens, sprinkle with oil and vinegar, salt and pepper, and toss briskly. Serves 4.

Combination Salad Italian Style

INSALATA MISTA ALL'ITALIANA

1 small cucumber, peeled and sliced
1 medium tomato, diced
½ small carrot, diced
1 medium head escarole
1 clove garlic
4 tablespoons mayonnaise
4 tablespoons olive oil
1 tablespoon wine vinegar
salt and pepper to taste

Rub bowl with garlic. Mix mayonnaise, oil and vinegar. Pour over the greens, adding salt and pepper to taste. Toss and serve. Serves 4.

Three-Color Salad

INSALATA TRICOLORE

1 pound potatoes
2 large firm tomatoes, diced
½ pound fresh string beans, cut in two-inch pieces, or
one box regular cut frozen string beans
3 tablespoons wine vinegar
7 tablespoons olive oil
salt and pepper to taste

Cook potatoes in jackets in salted water until tender but still firm, about 20 to 25 minutes. At the same time cook string beans in salted water until tender but still firm, about 20 to 30 minutes for fresh beans. Follow directions on the box if using frozen vegetable. Drain potatoes, and string beans, and rinse in cold water, separately. Peel and slice potatoes. Place vegetables in salad bowl. Add oil, vinegar, salt and pepper and toss. Place in refrigerator for at least 2 hours. Serves 4.

Molded Salad

INSALATA RUSSA

- 2 boxes frozen mixed vegetables
- 2 large potatoes
- 4 tablespoons olive oil
- 1 tablespoon wine vinegar
- ⅔ cup mayonnaise
- 1 envelope unflavored gelatine
- ¼ cup cold water
- 1 cup boiling water
- salt and pepper to taste

Cook vegetables in salted water according to directions on the box. Drain well and cool. In the meantime, cook potatoes unpeeled in salted water for about 20 minutes, or until tender but still firm. Drain, peel and cool. Dice when cold. Mix vegetables, potatoes, oil, vinegar, mayonnaise, salt and pepper. Soften gelatine in ¼ cup cold water. Add boiling water and stir until gelatine is dissolved. Place in refrigerator for a few minutes until gelatine is thoroughly chilled and is slightly thickened, then pour a thin layer on bottom of chilled one quart mold, and place in refrigerator until set. Now coat the sides of the mold with a thin layer of gelatine. This is done by pouring enough gelatine on one side of the mold, about ¼ inch thick, and placing it in the refrigerator until set. When mold is completely coated with gelatine, place vegetables in mold, pressing down gently with a spoon to avoid spaces, even top with a spoon, pour in rest of the gelatine and place in refrigerator to set for at least 3 hours. When ready to serve, wring out a cloth dipped in very hot water, wrap it around the mold for a moment and turn out salad carefully on serving dish. Serves 6-8.

If desired when mold is completely coated with gelatine, decorate bottom and sides with pickled slices of carrots, cauliflower, and slices of hard-boiled egg, black truffles, etc.

The following recipe comes from one of the most famous restaurants in Florence, the Buca Lapi, which is located in what used to be the stables of the sixteenth century palace of Marchesi Antinori. At one time, the stables had also been used as a charcoal store; and it is said that the owner of the store hanged himself on a bell that is still in the restaurant.

Orazio Lapi opened a small *osteria* (wine store) there in 1880. After a while, he began to serve soup with the wine. His clientele at the time was made up only of coachmen, but as time went by, the clientele grew, the place was enlarged and different kinds of food were served. At first, Orazio Lapi and his three sons were able to take care of the customers, but as business prospered, additional personnel had to be hired.

The décor in the restaurant is very striking. Its walls and ceilings are covered with travel posters, but you will never guess why. In winter the ceiling used to drip from humidity, and Mr. Lapi covered it with travel posters, as this was an easy way to cover up the stains and, at the same time, to give the restaurant an unusual appearance at practically no expense. And as some gay customers under the influence of Bacchus delighted in covering the walls near their tables with sketches not meant for the eyes of ladies, he ended by covering the walls with posters too.

Bruno Lapi, one of the sons of Orazio, is today the owner of the restaurant. The place has an international clientele, very good food and service, and naturally the cellar is stocked with the best of wines.

Buca Lapi Salad

INSALATA BUCA LAPI

- 1 medium romaine or escarole, shredded
- 1 clove garlic
- ⅓ cup olive oil
- 1½ tablespoons wine vinegar
- 1 teaspoon prepared mustard
- 3 ounces Gorgonzola or Roquefort cheese, crumbled
- salt and pepper to taste

Rub salad bowl with garlic. Discard garlic. Mix oil, vinegar, mustard, salt and pepper and cheese, add greens and toss. Serves 4.

Fennel Salad

INSALATA DI FINOCCHI

- 4 medium stalks fennel, thoroughly chilled
- ⅓ cup olive oil
- salt and pepper to taste

Trim fennel, wash and drain well, and slice very thin. Place in salad bowl, add oil, salt and pepper, toss and serve. Serves 4-6.

Fennel and Celery Salad

INSALATA DI FINOCCHI E SEDANI

4 medium-size stalks fennel, washed and sliced fine
1 celery heart, cut julienne
⅓ cup walnut meats, coarsely diced
lettuce leaves
about ½ cup heavy cream, thoroughly chilled
salt and pepper

Cover salad bowl with lettuce leaves, then add fennel and celery. Sprinkle with salt, pepper and walnut meats, then pour heavy cream over all. Serves 4-6.

Tomato Salad

INSALATA DI POMODORI

4 large firm tomatoes, chilled and sliced
⅓ cup olive oil
2 tablespoons wine vinegar
4 fresh large basil leaves, minced or 1 clove garlic, minced
salt and pepper

Arrange tomatoes on platter, then sprinkle with rest of ingredients. Serves 4-6.

Bella Elena Salad

INSALATA ALLA BELLA ELENA

2 cups chilled celery hearts, diced
1 cup chilled cooked beets, sliced
2 hard-boiled egg yolks
1 raw egg yolk
1 dozen walnuts, shelled
¼ cup and 1 tablespoon olive oil
1½ tablespoons wine vinegar or lemon juice
salt and pepper to taste

Put hard-boiled yolks through a sieve, add to it the raw yolk, oil and vinegar or lemon juice. Beat slowly with a spoon or wire whisk until dressing is well blended and creamy. Season to taste, add celery and toss well. Then place celery and half the walnuts, coarsely chopped, in the center of a round platter, place the sliced beets all around, and arrange the walnut halves on the beets. Serves 4.

Salad Country Style

INSALATA PAESANA

1 small head romaine	1 clove garlic
⅓ head escarole	2 leaves fresh basil or ¼ teaspoon dried basil
2 hard-boiled eggs	3 small onions, sliced
6 small potatoes boiled in jackets	½ cup olive oil
5 radishes	2 tablespoons wine vinegar
2 firm red tomatoes	salt and pepper
½ small cucumber	

Peel potatoes while still hot and let them cool. Slice tomatoes, radishes, cucumbers and potatoes. Wash and dry romaine and escarole and cut into 2-inch lengths. Place salt, pepper, garlic and basil in bowl. Mash with wooden spoon and add vinegar, then oil. Beat with fork. Add salad ingredients and toss. Serves 8.

Cauliflower Salad Neapolitan Style

INSALATA DI RINFORZO ALLA NAPOLETANA

This is the traditional salad served in Naples at Christmas dinner.

1 cauliflower of about 3 pounds	1 tablespoon capers
8 anchovy fillets, chopped fine	8 tablespoons olive oil
1½ dozen black Italian olives, pitted and chopped	4 tablespoons wine vinegar
	salt and pepper to taste
	Eels Carpionata (page 11), optional

Remove green leaves from cauliflower and cut off any bruised spots. Break into flowerets, cook in salted water for about 5 minutes. Drain and place in bowl of cold salted water for half an hour or more. Drain. Mix anchovies, olives, capers, oil and vinegar together, add cauliflower and season to taste. Decorate with slices of eel. Serves 6.

Garden Salad

INSALATA AL BOSCO

1 pound fresh string beans
1 pound potatoes
½ cup celery, diced
2 medium tomatoes
4 hard-boiled eggs, peeled
8 slices cooked ham
⅓ cup olive oil
2½ tablespoons wine vinegar
1 clove garlic (optional)
salt and pepper to taste
mayonnaise

Cook string beans in salted water until tender but still firm, about 20 to 30 minutes. Cook potatoes in jackets in salted water until tender but still firm, about 20 to 25 minutes. Drain vegetables, rinse in cold water separately and let cool. Peel and dice potatoes, add garlic, well-drained string beans and celery, season with oil, vinegar, salt and pepper to taste, and toss. Place in refrigerator. When ready to serve, remove garlic and place vegetables on round platter. Cut hard-boiled eggs in half, roll each half in a slice of ham and place like spokes on top of vegetables. Cut tomatoes in halves, place them cut side down in the center on top of the vegetables and dot with mayonnaise. Serves 4. Very appropriate for a summer lunch or as an antipasto.

String Bean Salad

FAGIOLINI ALL'AGRO

2 pounds fresh string beans, cut into 2-inch lengths
½ cup olive oil
1 tablespoon wine vinegar
1 large clove of garlic
salt and pepper
dash of crushed red pepper

Cook string beans in slightly salted water until tender but still firm, about 30 minutes. Drain. While beans are cooling, rub salad bowl with garlic. Place garlic in bowl with oil, vinegar, red pepper, salt and pepper, and let stand till beans have reached room temperature. Add beans to ingredients in bowl and mix well. Place in refrigerator for 1½ hours. Remove garlic before serving. Serves 6.

Pepper Salad

INSALATA DI PEPERONI ARROSTITI

2 pounds large firm peppers, preferably yellow and pink
2 cloves garlic, chopped fine
⅓ cup olive oil
salt and pepper to taste

Place peppers, one or two at a time, directly over gas burner, on medium flame. Turn often. Remove pepper when skin has turned black and has a burned look. Repeat till all peppers are done. Under cold running water remove burned skin. Remove stems and seeds. Cut lengthwise into about 1-inch strips. Rinse well and let drain. Place in bowl with oil and garlic, salt and pepper. Toss and place in refrigerator for at least one hour before serving. Serves 6 to 8. May also be served as part of antipasto.

Turnip Green Salad

INSALATA DI BROCCOLETTI DI RAPA

2 pounds turnip greens
3 slices bacon
6 tablespoons olive oil
2 tablespoons wine vinegar
salt and pepper to taste

Wash greens thoroughly. Cook in 4 quarts of water for 2 hours, over low flame, with the bacon and 1 tablespoon of salt. Drain. Add oil, vinegar, pepper and salt. Mix well and serve. Serves 4-6.

PIZZA, BREAD, ROLLS AND BATTERS

PIZZE, PANE, PASTELLE

Pizza Dough

PANE PER PIZZA

- 2 cups sifted flour
- ½ teaspoon salt
- 1 egg yolk
- 1 teaspoon powdered yeast or half cake of yeast dissolved in ½ cup and 1 tablespoon lukewarm water

Place flour and salt in large mixing bowl. Make a hole in the middle of flour. In it place the egg yolk and yeast. Beat lightly with fork, gradually adding flour. When ¾ of the flour is used, mix with hands. Place dough on floured board and knead till smooth. Place dough in large mixing bowl which has been sprinkled with flour, cover with damp kitchen towel and let rise in warm place for 2 hours. Dough should double in bulk. Damp towel will prevent dough from forming a hard crust. Use as directed.

Pizza Neapolitan Style

PIZZA NAPOLETANA

- 1 recipe Pizza Dough (page 154)
- 5 tablespoons olive oil
- 2 ripe peeled tomatoes, diced fine
- 2 cloves garlic, chopped to a pulp
- ½ cup grated Parmesan cheese
- salt and pepper

Cut dough in half and spread with hands in two greased 9-inch pie tins. Perforate each pizza dough with a fork in 8 places. Using a small brush grease pizzas with oil. Sprinkle each pizza with salt and pepper, half of the tomatoes, garlic, cheeze and remaining oil. Place in 400° oven for about 20 minutes. Serves 2 as main dish.

Pizza with Anchovies and Mozzarella Cheese

PIZZA CON ACCIUGHE E MOZZARELLA

- 1 recipe Pizza Dough (page 154)
- 5 tablespoons olive oil
- 2 ripe peeled tomatoes, diced fine
- 1 cup mozzarella cheese, diced
- 8 fillets of anchovies, diced
- ¼ teaspoon oregano
- salt and pepper

Cut dough in half and spread with hands in two greased 9-inch pie tins. With a fork perforate each pizza dough in 8 places. Grease pizza with oil, using a small brush. Sprinkle each pizza with half of the tomatoes, mozzarella cheese, anchovies, oregano, remaining oil, salt and pepper. Bake in 400° oven for 20 to 25 minutes. Serves 2 as main dish.

Pizza with Onions and Olives

PIZZA CON CIPOLLE ED OLIVE

- 1 recipe Pizza Dough (page 154)
- 5 tablespoons olive oil or melted butter
- 2 large peeled and parboiled onions, sliced fine
- 1½ dozen Italian black olives, pitted
- salt and pepper

Cut dough in half and spread with hands in two greased 9-inch pie tins. Perforate each pizza dough with a fork in 8 places. Using a small brush, grease pizzas with oil. Pour remaining oil in small skillet, add onions and cook over low flame, stirring occasionally, for 10 minutes. Season onions to taste. Cover pizzas with onions and olives. Sprinkle with pepper and bake in 400° oven for about 20 minutes. Serves 2-4.

Bread

PANE

- 3 cups sifted flour
- 1½ teaspoons dry powdered yeast
- 1 cup lukewarm water
- 1½ teaspoons salt

Dissolve yeast in ⅓ cup water. Place one cup flour and salt in mixing bowl and add yeast. Mix and place on floured board. Knead until smooth. Place dough in floured mixing bowl, cover with damp towel and let stand in warm place for 2 hours. Mix rest of flour and water into a smooth dough, place on floured board and add to original dough. Knead until smooth and satiny. Place dough again in large floured bowl. Cover with a damp towel and let stand in warm place for 4 hours. Place dough on floured board, knead for 3 to 4 minutes, shape into a loaf and place on greased cookie sheet. Brush top with olive oil or melted butter, cover with towel and let rise. Bake in 425° oven for 35 minutes. Makes 1 pound loaf.

Homemade Milk Rolls

PANINI AL LATTE

4 cups sifted flour
2 teaspoons salt
3 tablespoons butter
1½ teaspoons powdered yeast dissolved in ¼ cup lukewarm water
1¼ cups lukewarm milk
1 beaten egg yolk

Sift flour and salt together. Place in large mixing bowl and cut in butter with pastry blender. Make a hole in center of flour about the size of an orange and pour water and milk in it. Beat with fork, slowly blending flour. When about two-thirds of flour is used, mix with hands. Place dough on floured board. (If dough is too soft add a little flour.) Knead for 5 minutes. Place dough in large deep pan which has been lightly greased with butter, cover pan with damp clean kitchen towel and let it stand in warm place for about 2 hours. Dough should double in volume. Place dough on floured board. Knead for a minute or so. Cut it into pieces about the size of a small egg. Shape dough into rolls by rolling and patting it with palms of hands. Place on greased cookie sheets about 2 inches apart. Brush top with egg yolk. Let stand for 3 to 4 hours. Bake in hot oven at 425° for 15 to 20 minutes. Makes about two dozen rolls.

Sandwich Rolls

PANETTI PER TARTINE

2 cups sifted flour
3 tablespoons melted butter
1 teaspoon sugar
1 teaspoon salt

1 teaspoon dry yeast, diluted in 1/3 cup lukewarm water
1/4 cup lukewarm milk

Place one cup flour in mixing bowl, blend in yeast mixture, then place on lightly floured board and knead until smooth. Place dough in floured bowl, cover with damp towel and let stand in warm place for 2 to 3 hours or until doubled in bulk. Mix rest of ingredients together into a soft smooth dough, and place on floured board. Add to it the risen dough and knead until smooth and satiny. Place dough in large floured bowl, cover with damp towel and let stand until doubled in bulk. Then return dough to floured board and knead for a few minutes until it is elastic and does not stick to unfloured board. Divide dough in 24 pieces and shape each piece into croquette-like rolls about 2 or 2½ inches long. Place on greased baking sheets about 2 inches apart and let double in bulk. Brush with melted butter or milk and bake in 450° oven for 10 to 12 minutes. Makes 2 dozen.

To freeze rolls: Bake for 6 minutes, remove from oven and cool. Wrap in freezer paper and freeze. When ready to use remove from freezer and let stand at room temperature for one hour, then place in 350° oven for 5 to 6 minutes or until golden.

Bread Sticks

GRISSINI

Originally a specialty of Torino, in the past few years bread sticks have become well-known all over Italy and even in the United States. Use the recipe for the Sandwich Rolls (page 157). Here is how it is done:

Divide dough into 24 pieces. Shape each piece by rolling dough between hands into a thin rope about 6 to 7 inches long. Place on buttered baking sheets one inch apart, brush with milk and bake at 425° for 6 to 8 minutes, or until golden and crisp. Makes 2 dozen.

Breakfast Buns Roman Style

MARITOZZI ROMANI

- 1 envelope yeast diluted in ½ cup lukewarm water
- 4 cups pastry flour, sifted
- ½ teaspoon salt
- 2 large eggs
- 4 tablespoons olive oil
- ½ cup lukewarm water
- ½ cup sugar
- ½ cup seedless raisins
- 2½ tablespoons of sugar blended with 2½ tablespoons water, or: 1 large egg beaten with 1 tablespoon water and ¼ teaspoon flour

Blend yeast with water. Place 1 cup flour in mixing bowl, add yeast mixture and mix thoroughly. Place on floured board and knead for 5 minutes. Shape dough into a ball, place in floured bowl, cover with a damp towel and let stand in warm place for about 1 hour or until doubled in bulk. Place remaining 3 cups of flour on pastry board, form a well in center and in it place salt, eggs, oil and ½ cup lukewarm water. Beat egg mixture with fork, slowly mixing about half of the flour with it. Mix in rest of the flour by hand. Knead for 2 minutes, add yeast dough and knead until smooth. Add sugar and work it in well. Shape dough into a ball, place in floured bowl, cover with a damp towel and let stand in warm place for 3 hours. Then place dough on floured board, add raisins, and knead for a few minutes. Shape dough into balls the shape and size of small eggs. Place on buttered cookie sheets about 4" apart, brush with egg or sugar mixture and let stand in warm place for 4 hours or until doubled in bulk. Bake in 375° oven for 15 minutes. Makes about 2 dozen buns.

Batter for Frying Meats

PASTELLA PER FRITTI DI CARNE

- 4 tablespoons flour
- 2 tablespoons olive oil
- 2 whole eggs, slightly beaten
- ¼ teaspoon salt

Beat all ingredients together until they make a smooth paste.

Batter for Frying No. 1

PASTELLA PER FRIGGERE NO. 1

1 cup flour
2 egg yolks
¼ cup dry white wine
⅓ cup water
1 tablespoon olive oil

2 egg whites, beaten stiff with ½ teaspoon salt
¼ teaspoon grated lemon peel (optional), or ¼ teaspoon nutmeg

Beat together salt, flour, egg yolks, oil, wine and ¼ cup cold water till you have a smooth paste. Let stand for 2 hours. Fold in beaten egg whites and lemon peel or nutmeg. Use as directed. Generally used for vegetables, fish, etc.

Batter for Frying No. 2

PASTELLA PER FRIGGERE NO. 2

1 cup flour
2 tablespoons melted butter
2 egg yolks
1 tablespoon sugar
grated peel of half a lemon

½ cup water
2 tablespoons brandy
½ teaspoon salt
2 egg whites beaten stiff

Beat together salt, flour, butter, yolks, sugar, lemon peel, brandy and water till they make a smooth paste. Let stand for 2 hours. Fold in egg whites and use as directed. Generally used for fruits.

DESSERTS AND CANDY

FRUTTA, BUDINI, GELATI, CONFETTERIA

Apples Priscilla

MELE ALLA PRISCILLA

- 4 firm Roman Beauty or Golden Delicious apples
- 2 cups sugar
- 3 cups water
- ½ teaspoon vanilla extract
- 1 recipe Pasticcera Cream (page 168)
- ½ cup chopped almonds

Peel and core apples. Slice in half lengthwise. Place water, sugar and vanilla in saucepan. Bring to a boil. Add apples and cook uncovered for 10 minutes or until just tender, but still firm. Drain apples carefully and place in single layer in buttered baking dish. Pour Cream Pasticcera over them. Sprinkle with chopped almonds and bake in oven at 350° for 20 minutes. Serve hot. Serves 8.

Stuffed Baked Apples

MELE RIPIENE

- 6 firm Golden Delicious apples
- 1 cup sugar
- ½ teaspoon vanilla extract
- ½ cup Pasticcera Cream (page 168), boiled for 3 minutes
- ½ recipe Italian Meringue (page 204)
- ¼ cup Almond Pralinée (page 180), chopped (optional)

Core apples carefully. Place 1½ quarts water, sugar and vanilla in saucepan. Bring to a boil and boil for 5 minutes. Add apples and simmer for 2 to 3 minutes. Remove apples with flat skimmer to buttered baking dish. Fill apples with Pasticcera Cream, coat with Italian Meringue and sprinkle with chopped Pralinée. When ready to serve, place in 300° oven for about 5 to 7 minutes, until Meringue is pale gold. Remove to individual hot dishes and serve immediately. Serves 6.

Fried Apples with Rum

MELE FRITTE AL RUM

2 pounds large cooking apples	2 cups olive oil
1 recipe Batter No. 2 (page 159)	⅓ cup confectioner's sugar
	½ cup dark rum

Rinse apples in cold water and dry. Cut in thin wedges, removing the cores. Place a few wedges in the batter. Remove with fork and place in hot oil. Fry on both sides till light brown. Repeat operation until all apple wedges are fried. Place on hot serving dish, sprinkle with rum and sugar and serve immediately. Serves 8.

Fried Bananas with Rum

BANANE FRITTE AL RUM

2½ pounds ripe bananas	2 cups olive oil
1 recipe Batter No. 2 (page 159)	⅓ cup confectioner's sugar
	½ cup dark rum or kirsch

Peel bananas. Slice in ⅔-inch rounds. Place 5 or 6 slices in the batter. Remove with fork and place in hot oil. Fry on both sides till light brown. Repeat operation until all bananas are cooked. Place in hot serving dish, sprinkle with sugar and rum or kirsch and serve. Makes a delicious dessert. Serves 8.

Banana Whip

SPUMA DI BANANE

½ cup sugar	1½ ounces dark Jamaica rum
4 egg yolks	½ pint heavy cream
1 teaspoon cornstarch	1 tablespoon sugar
1 cup lukewarm milk	⅓ teaspoon vanilla extract
1 tablespoon gelatine	⅓ cup chopped pistachio nuts
3 bananas	

Place yolks, sugar and cornstarch in mixing bowl. Beat with egg beater until eggs are creamy and smooth. Add milk slowly. Pour egg mixture in saucepan and cook over low flame stirring constantly, until mixture has the consistency of heavy cream (about 3 to 4 minutes). Do not allow to boil. Remove from stove and stir in gelatine which has been softened in 1 tablespoon cold water and dissolved in 2 tablespoons hot water. Pour egg mixture into a bowl and cool. Peel and mash bananas and put them through a sieve. Whip cream with 1 tablespoon sugar. As soon as egg mixture starts to thicken, blend in the bananas, cream and rum. Pour into a serving bowl, sprinkle with pistachio nuts and place in refrigerator for not less than 2 hours. Serves 6-8.

Here is a recipe given me by Mrs. Alfredo Zoppi who, together with her husband, owns one of the best restaurants in Venice, La Taverna Fenice. The restaurant has been in the family for over 40 years and was named by the poet Gabriele D'Annunzio for the Theater La Fenice. Mrs. Zoppi, who not only supervises all the cooking but who herself also prepares some of her own famous dishes, comes from Aqui, in Piedmont, so that La Taverna's cuisine has a touch of the Piedmontese.

Peaches Fenice

PESCHE FENICE

8 large peaches, ripe but firm
1 cup shelled almonds
¾ cup sugar
6 tablespoons water
1½ cups macaroons, crumbled
3 tablespoons peach or apricot preserves
5 drops vanilla
⅛ teaspoon almond extract
2 tablespoons confectioner's sugar
3 ounces dark Jamaica rum

Place almonds in boiling water and let stand for 5 minutes. Drain and remove skins. Place in 375° oven on cookie sheet for 10 minutes. Remove from oven and chop. Boil sugar and water together in small saucepan for 10 minutes. Add almonds and macaroons. Cook for 2 minutes, add preserves and cook, stirring, for 2 minutes more. Remove from stove and cool. Blend in vanilla and almond extract. Cut peaches in half and remove pits. Place in large, well-buttered baking dish which has been lightly sprinkled with sugar. Bake at 375° for 20 minutes. Remove from oven, and fill peaches with almond mixture. Replace in oven and bake for 7 minutes. Remove peaches to hot unbreakable serving dish. Sprinkle with confectioner's sugar and rum. Serve immediately. Light rum at the table. Serves 8-16.

Peaches Maria Luisa

PESCHE MARIA LUISA

6 large ripe firm peaches	1½ cups heavy cream
3 cups sugar	2 ounces Cognac or brandy
4½ cups water	3 tablespoons confectioner's sugar
¼ teaspoon vanilla	

Place peaches in large bowl or pan and cover with boiling water. Let stand for 5 minutes. Remove peaches from hot water and peel. Carefully cut peaches in half, removing pits. Place sugar, water and vanilla in saucepan. Bring to a boil and boil for 5 minutes. Remove from stove and add peaches. Cool. Place in refrigerator for not less than 2 hours. Remove peaches from syrup and place in a glass or silver bowl. Place bowl in a larger one filled with ice. Mix Cognac with cream. Pour a few tablespoons over peaches and sprinkle with confectioner's sugar. Serve remaining cream separately. Peaches can also be served in individual bowls. Serves 6.

Peach halves canned in syrup can be used if fresh ones are not available. Just chill, remove from syrup and serve according to above directions.

Apricots Bishop Style

ALBICOCCHE ALLA CARDINALE

12 large firm ripe apricots	1 teaspoon lemon juice
2½ cups sugar	chopped Almond Pralinée (page 180) or
3½ cups water	
¼ teaspoon vanilla	½ cup blanched and toasted almonds, coarsely chopped
1 box frozen raspberries	

Place apricots in large bowl and cover with boiling water. Let stand for 5 minutes. Drain. Cool and peel. Cut apricots in half, removing pits. Place 2 cups sugar, water and vanilla in saucepan. Bring to a boil and boil for 5 minutes. Remove from stove and add apricots. Cool. Remove to a bowl and place in refrigerator for 2 hours. Thaw raspberries and put through a sieve. Stir in ½ cup sugar and lemon juice. Place in refrigerator for about 2 hours. Place drained apricots in chilled serving dish. Pour raspberry mixture over fruit and sprinkle with almonds. Serves 6.

Peaches can be served the same way.

Apricot halves canned in syrup can be substituted if fresh ones are not available. Just chill, remove from syrup and serve according to above directions.

Melon Oriental Style

MELLONE ALL'ORIENTALE

4 very small cantaloupes	10 large strawberries, cut in half
4 medium bananas, diced	
8 slices of fresh pineapple ¼ inch thick, diced	8 tablespoons sugar
	1 cup kirsch

Cut a ½ inch slice from top of each cantaloupe. With silver spoon remove seeds and discard. Remove all pulp from cantaloupes, being careful not to break melon shell. Mix pulp with bananas, pineapple and strawberries, and refill melons. Top each cantaloupe with 2 tablespoons sugar. Pour ¼ cup kirsch into each melon and close each melon with the slices previously cut from them. Put melons in coldest part of refrigerator for 5 hours. Remove sliced tops before serving. Serves 4.

Strawberries in Wine

FRAGOLE AL VINO

3 cups strawberries
2 tablespoons sugar
½ cup dry red or white wine, or champagne, chilled

Pick strawberries carefully, wash, hull and drain. Sprinkle with sugar and let stand in refrigerator for 2 hours before serving. Cover with wine and serve. Serves 4.

Cherries Flambées

CILIEGE FIAMMEGGIATE

2 pounds Bing cherries, rinsed in cold water and pitted
2 cups dry red wine
7 tablespoons sugar
¼ teaspoon cinnamon
1 teaspoon cornstarch
1½ tablespoons blackberry jelly
3 ounces kirsch or dark rum

Place cherries in saucepan with wine, sugar and cinnamon. Let come to a boil and cook for 3 minutes. Drain. Cook wine-sugar mixture until it is reduced to ¾ of a cup. Blend in cornstarch and jelly. Remove from stove and add to cherries which have been placed in a hot ovenproof dish. Sprinkle with kirsch or rum. Bring to the table and light with a match. Canned Bing cherries may be substituted if desired. Serves 6-8.

Rum Pears

PERE ALLA FIAMMA

6 Bartlett pears, rinsed in cold water and dried
3 cups sugar
4 cups water
½ teaspoon vanilla extract
3 tablespoons apricot preserves
1 teaspoon cornstarch
½ cup Jamaica rum

Place water, sugar and vanilla in deep saucepan, over medium-high flame. Let come to a boil and boil for 5 minutes. Add pears and boil for 5 to 20 minutes, according to ripeness of fruit, until pears are tender but still firm. Remove pears from syrup and place in hot serving dish. Keep warm. Boil 1½ cups syrup until candy thermometer reads 215°, or until syrup coats the spoon. Remove thermometer and add apricot preserves and cornstarch, mixing well. Cook for about 5 minutes or until syrup thickens, stirring occasionally. Pour over pears, sprinkle with rum and bring to the table. Light the rum with a match and let flame burn out. Serves 6.

Pineapple Veneziana

ANANAS ALLA VENEZIANA

- 1 recipe Kirsch Gelatine (page 168)
- 1 No. 2½ can sliced pineapple
- juice of half a lemon
- 1 tablespoon unflavored gelatine
- ¼ cup cold water
- 1 cup heavy cream, beaten stiff

Drain pineapple, reserving the syrup. With a sharp knife cut each slice in two horizontally so that you will have twice as many slices. Place them on a cake rack to drain well. Then coat 1-quart mold with ¾ of the Kirsch Gelatine and place in refrigerator to set. Remove mold from refrigerator and line bottom and sides of mold with pineapple slices overlapping each other. Soften unflavored gelatine in cold water, and blend with ¾ of a cup of pineapple syrup that has been scalded. Let cool, then blend with lemon juice and whipped cream. Fill mold with this mixture and top with remaining Kirsch Gelatine. Place in refrigerator to set for at least 5 hours. When ready to serve wrap a towel dipped in hot water around the mold and unmold on a round platter. Serves 6-8.

Sweet Potatoes and Apples

DOLCE DI PATATE E MELE

- 2 pounds sweet potatoes
- 3 apples, peeled, cored and sliced
- ½ cup sugar
- juice of 1½ oranges
- ¼ teaspoon salt
- 1 teaspoon nutmeg
- 2 tablespoons melted butter
- 1 ounce Jamaica rum, kirsch or any desired liqueur (optional)

Cook sweet potatoes in salted water for twenty minutes or until tender. Drain, cool and peel. Cut into ½-inch slices, and arrange in buttered baking dish with alternate layers of apples, sprinkling each layer with sugar and nutmeg. Then pour butter and orange juice over all and bake in 325° oven for 30 minutes. Sprinkle with rum or desired liqueur before serving. Serves 6.

Roman Cheese Pudding

BUDINO DI RICOTTA ALLA ROMANA

½ pound ricotta cheese
½ cup sugar
2 egg yolks
3 whole eggs

¼ teaspoon cinnamon
grated peel of a small lemon
¼ teaspoon salt

Put ricotta cheese through a sieve. Add sugar and mix well. Blend in yolks, and add whole eggs, one at a time, beating constantly. Blend in rest of ingredients. Place mixture in a 1-quart buttered mold, lightly sprinkled with bread crumbs. Place mold in a pan of water and bake in 325° oven for one hour or until a toothpick or straw inserted in the pudding comes out dry. If desired, pudding can be cooked in individual molds. Serves 6.

Baked Custard Maria Luisa

CREMA ROVESCIATA MARIA LUISA

2 eggs
4 egg yolks
⅔ cup sugar
2½ cups hot milk
½ teaspoon vanilla
peel of lemon, about 2 inches long and 1 inch wide

1½ cups heavy cream, beaten stiff, with 1 teaspoon sugar and a few drops vanilla
⅓ cup finely chopped Almond Pralinée (page 180)

Beat whole eggs, yolks and sugar together for 2 minutes with electric beater at egg-beating speed or 10 minutes with hand beater. Fold in milk, vanilla and lemon peel. Let stand for 5 minutes. Remove lemon peel and foam from top. Put through a fine sieve and place in 1½-quart ring mold. Place ring in larger pan, about 2 or 3 inches high, containing about one inch of water. Place in 275° oven and bake for about 1½ to 1¾ hours. Custard will be done when a knife blade comes out clean. Remove from oven and cool. Turn on serving dish and place in refrigerator till ready to use. A few minutes before serving, pile whipped cream in center of custard, sprinkle with Almond Pralinée and serve. Serves 8-10.

Bavarian Cream

CREMA BAVARESE

- 3 egg yolks
- ⅓ cup sugar
- 1 cup cold milk
- ⅛ teaspoon vanilla
- 1 tablespoon unflavored gelatine
- 1 cup heavy cream
- 1 tablespoon sugar

Beat yolks and sugar together with hand or electric beater until light and foamy. Blend in milk and vanilla. Place in saucepan over very low flame and simmer (do not boil) for 5 minutes, stirring constantly with a wooden spoon. Remove from heat. Soften gelatine in 2 tablespoons cold water and dissolve in 4 tablespoons boiling water. Stir into hot mixture and put through a fine sieve. Cool, stirring occasionally. Whip cream with 1 tablespoon sugar and fold in. Use as directed or chill and serve with berries, cut fruit or any desired sweet sauce.

Pasticcera Cream

CREMA PASTICCERA

- 1 cup lukewarm light cream
- 4 egg yolks
- ½ cup sugar
- ¼ teaspoon vanilla or a piece of lemon peel about 3"x1"
- 1½ teaspoons potato flour

Beat yolks and sugar together until mixture is lemon-colored. Mix in potato flour, then add cream, vanilla or lemon peel and mix thoroughly. Place mixture in saucepan over low flame and cook, stirring constantly, until cream reaches the boiling point. Remove from stove, put through a sieve and use as directed. If cream is to be used for filling pies, cakes, pastry or fruit, double the amount of flour, and boil for 3 minutes so that it will acquire the correct thicker consistency. Makes about 1½ cups.

Kirsch Gelatine

GELATINA AL KIRSCH

- 1 tablespoon unflavored gelatine
- ¼ cup cold water
- ½ cup water
- ½ cup sugar
- ¼ teaspoon vanilla
- 1 ounce kirsch liqueur

Soften gelatine in ¼ cup cold water. In the meantime place sugar and ½ cup water in small saucepan, bring to a boil and boil for 5 minutes. Remove from stove and add rest of ingredients, blending well. Cool until consistency of unbeaten egg white. Use for coating molds for fruit desserts. Enough for 1-quart mold. The Gelatine may be flavored with any preferred liqueur.

Torino Pudding

BUDINO TORINESE

- 1 pound chestnuts
- 6 tablespoons butter
- ½ cup sugar
- ¼ teaspoon vanilla
- 3 ounces sweet chocolate, grated

Peel chestnuts and cook in salted water for ten minutes. Drain and remove second skin rapidly so that they do not become cold. Place peeled chestnuts in boiling salted water and cook for 30 minutes more or until they are very soft. Drain and put through a sieve. Cream butter and sugar together with electric mixer or egg beater until completely blended. Add chestnut paste, grated chocolate, and vanilla and blend well. Line a mold with foil or waxed paper, and fill with chestnut mixture. Even top with a spoon, cover mold with lid or foil, and place in refrigerator for at least 4 hours. Remove cover from mold, turn on serving dish and carefully peel off foil or waxed paper. It is quite a delicacy! Serves 8. Can be kept covered in refrigerator for a week; flavor improves with time.

Iced Zabaglione

ZABAGLIONE GELATO

- 8 egg yolks
- ½ cup and 1 tablespoon granulated sugar
- sliced peel of ½ lemon
- 1 cup dry Marsala wine (preferably imported)
- 1 teaspoon unflavored gelatine
- 3 tablespoons Cognac
- 1 pint heavy cream whipped stiff with ½ teaspoon vanilla and 1 tablespoon sugar

Beat egg yolks, lemon peel and sugar for 3 minutes with electric beater at beating-eggs speed, or 9 minutes with hand beater. Remove lemon peel. Fold in Marsala wine. Place egg mixture in top of double boiler. (The water in the double boiler should be boiling slowly.) Cook for about 6 minutes continuing to beat with beater. Zabaglione is cooked when it stands in soft peaks. Remove from fire. Soften gelatine in 1 tablespoon cold water and dissolve in 2 tablespoons boiling water and add to zabaglione, stirring slowly. When zabaglione is at room temperature, blend in Cognac and heavy cream. Place in individual glasses or in a crystal or silver bowl and place in refrigerator for 4 to 5 hours. Serve with cookies or French pastry. Serves 8.

ICE CREAM

To freeze ice cream in refrigerator:
Pour mixture into trays. Place in freezing unit of refrigerator until mixture starts freezing around edges. Transfer to chilled bowl; whip until smooth and replace in trays. Freeze until firm. Stir occasionally to insure smooth texture.

To freeze ice cream in a crank freezer:
Have enough crushed ice ready and mix it with rock salt. (One part salt to 8 parts crushed ice.) Fill ice-cream container not more than three-fourths full. Place in the freezer pail, cover and adjust the top. Be sure that the cover fits tight. Fill freezer with crushed ice mixture well above the line of the mixture in ice-cream container. Turn the crank slowly until the mixture begins to freeze; then turn it more rapidly. Ice cream takes from 12 to 20 minutes to freeze in a crank freezer.

Vanilla Ice Cream

GELATO ALLA VANIGLIA

1 pint light cream
1 cup sugar
4 eggs
2 teaspoons vanilla extract

Beat eggs and sugar together with hand or electric beater until creamy and lemon-colored. Place light cream and vanilla in saucepan and scald. Slowly add to beaten eggs, blending well. Place in saucepan and bring to a boil over low flame, stirring constantly. Put mixture through a sieve and stir until it has reached room temperature. Freeze as usual. Makes 1 quart of ice cream.

Coffee Ice Cream

GELATO AL CAFFE

1 recipe Vanilla Ice Cream (page 170)
½ cup Coffee Espresso (page 206)
½ recipe Italian Meringue (page 204)

Follow directions for Vanilla Ice Cream, and add coffee with vanilla when scalding cream. Slowly add to egg mixture, blending well. Place in saucepan and bring to a boil over low fire, stirring constantly. Put mixture through a sieve and stir until it has reached room temperature. Fold in Italian Meringue and freeze.

Chocolate Ice Cream

GELATO DI CIOCCOLATA

1 recipe Vanilla Ice Cream (page 170)
1½ squares unsweetened chocolate

Follow instructions for Vanilla Ice Cream and, instead of vanilla, add the chocolate to the cream when scalding. Makes about 1 quart.

Vanilla Spumoni

SPUMONI ALLA VANIGLIA

4 egg whites beaten stiff but not dry
¾ cup sugar
⅛ cup water
1 cup heavy cream, whipped
1½ teaspoons vanilla extract
¼ cup toasted almonds or pistachio nuts, chopped or Almond Pralinée (page 180)

Place sugar and water in saucepan and cook until a few drops in cold water form a soft ball. Remove from heat and pour gradually over stiffly beaten egg whites, beating constantly. Continue beating gently until cool. Then fold in vanilla and whipped cream. Fill chilled quart mold with mixture, close mold and pack in salt and ice for 2 hours, or freeze for 2 hours in freezing compartment of refrigerator. Dip mold briefly in hot water to unmold. Sprinkle with chopped nuts and serve. If desired, spumoni can be sprinkled with any chilled liqueur before serving. For Chocolate Spumoni, use 1½ squares melted unsweetened chocolate instead of vanilla. For Coffee Spumoni, use ½ cup very strong coffee instead of vanilla.

Strawberry Ice Cream Neapolitan Style

GELATO DI FRAGOLE ALLA NAPOLETANA

- 2 pints strawberries
- 2 cups water
- 1½ cups sugar
- 1 teaspoon lemon juice
- ⅛ teaspoon vanilla extract
- 2 cups heavy cream

Place water and sugar in saucepan, bring to a boil and cook for 10 minutes. Remove from stove and cool. Wash, drain and hull the strawberries, then put them through a sieve and add to syrup together with vanilla and lemon juice. Blend in cream and freeze as usual. Any other fruit may be used in place of strawberries. Makes 2 quarts.

White Lady Ice Cream

GELATO DAMA BIANCA

- 1 cup shelled almonds, blanched
- 2½ cups milk
- 1 cup granulated sugar
- ¼ teaspoon vanilla extract
- ½ pint heavy cream

Dip almonds in cold water, drain and put through a food grinder or nut chopper twice, so that they will be as fine as possible. Scald milk with sugar and vanilla, stirring occasionally, then add the almonds and let cool completely. Put mixture through a sieve, mashing down almonds with a spoon or other instrument, add cream, and freeze as usual. Makes about 1½ quarts.

Peach Melba

COPPA MELBA

- vanilla ice cream
- 4 large canned peach halves
- ½ cup heavy cream, whipped stiff
- 1 ounce brandy
- 4 maraschino cherries
- 2 tablespoons pistachio nuts, minced

Place peaches in 4 dessert or champagne glasses, and arrange one scoop of ice cream on top of each, then sprinkle with brandy and pile whipped cream on top. Place a cherry on each mound and sprinkle with pistachio nuts. Serves 4.

Strawberry Cup

COPPA ALLE FRAGOLE

1 pint small ripe strawberries	pistachio ice cream
1 ounce Jamaica rum	1 cup heavy cream, whipped stiff

Place strawberries in small bowl together with rum and let stand for one hour. Drain. Place ice cream in dessert or champagne glasses, add whipped cream and arrange strawberries on top. Serves 6.

Wine Sherbet Roman Style

PUNCH ALLA ROMANA

1 cup sugar	juice of 3 lemons
1 cup water	4 cups dry white wine
1 teaspoon grated orange peel	½ recipe Italian Meringue (page 204)
1 teaspoon grated lemon peel	
juice of 2 oranges	Jamaica rum (optional)

Place sugar and water in saucepan, bring to a boil for 5 minutes. Remove from stove and cool. Place in ice-cream-freezer container, together with wine, grated lemon peel, grated orange peel, and orange and lemon juice. Cover tightly and pack with crushed ice and rock salt, turning the freezer slowly until mixture begins to freeze, then turn it more rapidly. Mixture will take 20 to 30 minutes to freeze. Then blend in Italian Meringue and keep packed in ice for 2 hours before serving, or store in freezing compartment of refrigerator. Makes about 2 quarts. Sprinkle with a little rum before serving.

Witch's Bombe

BOMBA STREGA

- 1½ pints Chocolate Ice Cream (page 171)
- ¾ cup heavy cream
- ¼ teaspoon vanilla
- 1 tablespoon confectioner's sugar
- ¼ cup minced dates
- 1 tablespoon Jamaica rum (optional)
- ½ recipe Italian Sponge Cake (page 182) baked in 10"x 15" tin at 325° for 25 minutes, or until dry in center
- 1 cup Chocolate Fondant (page 203) or about 8 ounces dipping chocolate

Marinate dates in rum for at least one hour. Line one-quart mold with sheet of cake, trimming edges. Now make a layer of ¾ of the Chocolate Ice Cream. Drain dates and add to cream which has been whipped with vanilla and confectioner's sugar, folding gently. Fill *bombe* center with whipped cream and top with a layer of the remaining ice cream. Cover this with a piece of waxed paper, then with mold cover and seal with butter. Pack in ice and salt or place in freezing compartment of refrigerator for 3 hours. Melt Fondant or dipping chocolate over hot water, unmold *bombe* and very quickly cover it with Fondant or dipping chocolate. Remove to serving dish and serve immediately. If a freezer is available, *bombe* may be prepared in advance and stored in freezer until ready to use. Makes 1 quart.

Snowball Bombe

BOMBA PALLA DI NEVE

- 1 quart White Lady Ice Cream (page 172), or Vanilla Ice Cream (page 170)
- ½ cup mixed candied fruit peel
- ¼ cup kirsch
- 1 cup heavy cream
- 1 tablespoon confectioner's sugar
- ½ teaspoon vanilla
- 8 candied violets

Add kirsch to mixed candied fruit peel and let stand covered for 2 hours. Drain and blend with ice cream. Pack ice cream in one-quart mold, cover it with a piece of waxed paper, then with mold cover, and seal with butter. Pack in ice and salt or place in freezing compartment of refrigerator for 3 hours. Unmold *bombe* on serving dish, and very quickly decorate it with cream whipped with confectioner's sugar and vanilla, by covering it with small "kisses" with the help of a pastry bag or cookie press. Arrange violets all over and serve.

CANDY

Walnut Bonbons

NOCI AL CIOCCOLATO

1 cup shelled walnuts	4 ounces dipping chocolate
½ cup sugar	2 ounces grated sweet chocolate, or 3 ounces chocolate sprinkles
2 tablespoons water or kirsch or any desired liqueur	

Grind nuts in nut grinder or use a mortar. Blend with sugar, water or liqueur and shape into balls the size of cherries. Melt dipping chocolate in top of double boiler, dip bonbons in it one by one with a candy fork or a regular fork, roll in grated chocolate or chocolate sprinkles, and place on platter or tray covered with foil. Store in a cool place or refrigerator for 5 hours. Makes about 2½ dozen.

Rum Filbert Bonbons

NOCCIOLINE AL RUM

1 cup shelled filberts, lightly toasted	2 tablespoons Jamaica rum
½ cup sugar	about 1 tablespoon water
	4 ounces dipping chocolate

Grind nuts thoroughly and blend with rum, sugar and just enough water to make a firm paste. Shape into firm balls the size of cherries, and let stand for ten minutes. Place chocolate in double-boiler top and melt. Remove from heat, but keep over hot water. Have ready a large tray or platter lined with foil. Gently dip bonbons in chocolate one by one with a candy fork or a regular fork, and place on lined platter or tray, leaving some space between each. Place in refrigerator or any cool place for a few hours, until completely dry. Makes about 2½ dozen.

Chocolate Covered Filberts

NOCCIOLINE MASCHERATE

1 cup shelled filberts, lightly toasted   4 ounces dipping chocolate

Place chocolate in top of double boiler over hot water and melt. Remove from heat, but keep over hot water. Have ready a large tray or platter lined with foil. Dip two filberts at a time in chocolate and remove to platter, making sure that enough chocolate coats the nuts. Place in refrigerator or any cool place for a few hours so that chocolate will be completely dry. Makes about 3½ dozen.

Cherry Bonbons

CILIEGE AL COGNAC

1 cup maraschino cherries   3 ounces dipping chocolate
⅓ cup cognac or brandy

Sprinkle cherries with brandy and let stand for 2 hours. Drain and place on brown paper to dry for at least one hour. Melt chocolate over hot water, remove from heat, and dip cherries in chocolate one by one and remove to tray lined with foil.

Almond Chocolate Bonbons

MARCHESINE

1 cup shelled almonds   4 ounces sweet chocolate
½ cup sugar   1 tablespoon water
2 egg yolks

Grind almonds in nut grinder or use a mortar. Grate chocolate and add half of it to almonds together with yolks, water and sugar, blending into a firm workable paste. Shape into balls the size of cherries and roll in remaining grated chocolate. Place on a platter in a cool place or in refrigerator for five hours. Makes about 4 dozen.

Strawberries in Fondant

FRAGOLE AL FONDENTE

1 pint strawberries
1/3 cup Jamaica rum
about 2 cups Fondant (page 202)
1/2 teaspoon vanilla
a few drops pink food coloring
1-ounce bonbon cups

To prepare this recipe about 2½ dozen one-ounce containers are required; that is, a container for each strawberry. They can be bonbon cups if you can find them, or Dixie cups that can be lined and covered with silver foil and decorated to taste, or even paper baking cups, or so-called muffin cups. (Just remember that *these* are 2-ounce containers.) One-ounce liqueur glasses may also be used if necessary.

Wash and hull strawberries. Place in a bowl, sprinkle with rum, and let stand for one hour. Drain strawberries well. Melt Fondant over hot water, blending in vanilla and enough pink food coloring to make the Fondant a very light pink. Place a strawberry in each bonbon cup, or whatever container you have decided to use, and pour just enough Fondant over it to cover the strawberry completely.

Place in refrigerator overnight, and serve with a teaspoon within the next twelve hours. Keep in refrigerator until ready to serve. You will find that each container will be filled with a liquid made of the melted strawberry and Fondant under a thin top of Fondant.

Almond Crunch

CROCCANTE DI MANDORLE

3½ cups sugar
juice of half a lemon
2 cups almonds
½ cup white corn syrup
1 pint heavy cream

Place one cup sugar and lemon juice in saucepan and cook over medium flame, stirring constantly until sugar reaches the caramel stage (338°). Add the almonds, mixing thoroughly. Remove from stove and drop mixture on marble slab or dish that has been sprinkled with water. Cool. Place mixture, a little at a time, in a mortar and grind it fine. Now place rest of sugar, corn syrup and cream in heavy saucepan over low flame, bring to a boil, stirring constantly. Continue cooking, still stirring, until a drop of the mixture in cold water forms a hard ball (250-255°), being careful that mixture does not boil over. Keep sides of saucepan clean by brushing them with a pastry brush dipped in water. Remove mixture from stove, blend in ground almonds and pour it in two 8"x8" baking tins which have been lined with foil. Cool completely. Then remove from tins, peel off foil, and cut into 2-inch squares. Wrap in tin foil or waxed paper and store in a jar. If desired, it can be cut into smaller squares or into fingers 2 inches long and then dipped in dipping chocolate. Makes about 2½ pounds.

Vanilla Nougat Candy

TORRONE ALLA VANIGLIA

- ⅓ cup honey
- ½ cup sugar
- 2 tablespoons water
- 2 tablespoons shelled pistachio nuts
- ½ cup shelled hazelnuts
- 2 cups blanched almonds
- white of a large egg, beaten stiff with ¼ teaspoon salt
- 1 teaspoon vanilla extract
- wafers (ostie) *

Ostie are made of a mixture of wheat and water. They can be obtained at many confectioner's supply stores. *Ostie* have the appearance of thin sheets of white paper.

Place honey in top of double boiler over boiling water and cook, stirring constantly, until a drop of honey in cold water forms a hard ball. Add egg white, a little at a time, blending well. Continue stirring for about 15 minutes or until honey mixture reaches the "hard ball" stage. Then place sugar, vanilla and water in small saucepan and let cook until candy thermometer reads "crack" or until a few drops in cold water crack when pressed between the fingers. Blend sugar with honey mixture and continue cooking and stirring for a few minutes, until a few drops in cold water crack when pressed between fingers (280° on candy thermometer). Remove from heat, quickly add nuts and mix well. Have ready a loaf pan, or an ice tray with cube partitions removed, lined with wafers. Pour mixture in pan or tray, even top with a spoon and cover with more wafers. Press with hands or put a weight on top and let stand until almost cold. Remove from pan or tray and cut in half, lengthwise. Cut each piece crosswise in 4 pieces and wrap individually in tin foil. Store in covered jar in a cool place.

Preserved Marrons

MARRONI CANDITI

4 pounds large marrons (Spanish or Italian chestnuts)	7½ cups sugar
	½ teaspoon vanilla
	½ cup sugar
2 quarts water	1 cup corn syrup

Here is a dish that requires time and patience; but the results are quite rewarding. Get somebody to help with the peeling and the job can be done in half the time.

Rinse marrons in lukewarm water. Place in large saucepan of hot water and let boil for 10 minutes. Remove from stove. Do not drain. With a tablespoon remove each marron from hot water and as carefully as possible, so as not to bruise or break meats, remove first skin. Do not worry about second skin as it will be removed much more quickly and with less danger of breaking meats when they are completely cooked. It is important not to allow marrons to get cold; therefore as soon as each meat is peeled, place it in large pan of hot water. If necessary, change water to keep it hot. Some of the meats will break while being peeled no matter how careful one is, but with care and patience the number of broken ones will be very small. The broken nut meats can be put to many uses. When all are peeled, boil for 20 to 25 minutes. (Exact cooking time depends on how fresh marrons are.) Test one for tenderness. They should be very soft, but still firm. While marrons are cooking, place water and 7½ cups sugar in large flat saucepan (about 14"x4"). Bring to a boil and boil for 4 minutes. Cool. With a tablespoon remove each marron from hot water, carefully remove second skin and place meats on large platter or table top. When all meats are peeled place them carefully in the syrup. Put over medium flame and bring to a boil. Remove from stove, cover and let stand in cool place (NOT IN THE REFRIGERATOR) until next morning. Drain syrup from pan and place it in small saucepan. Add vanilla and ¼ cup sugar. Place over medium-high flame and boil for 5 minutes. Pour over marrons. Cover and let stand until evening. Again drain syrup and place it in small deep saucepan. Add rest of sugar and corn syrup. Insert candy thermometer. Boil until thermometer reads "jelly" (215°). Add to meats. Immediately fill sterilized glass jars with whole nut meats, reserving one jar for broken meats, and cover with syrup to overflowing. Seal. Turn jars upside down until cold. Make sure jars do not leak. Store in cool place. Makes 6 pints.

Almond Pralinée

MANDORLE TOSTATE

(First introduced by the Venetians centuries ago.)

1⅔ cups sugar
12 ounces shelled almonds
¼ cup water

Place sugar and water in saucepan. Attach candy thermometer, if you have one, inside the pan. Cook over medium-high flame stirring constantly with a wooden spoon. When thermometer reads "soft ball" (when a drop of the syrup forms a soft ball in cold water) add the almonds. Remove thermometer now as it will be much easier to stir without it. Continue stirring. After a few minutes the sugar will dry up completely and become sandy. Continue stirring. Slowly, the sugar will become liquid again. When you have a clear golden brown syrup, a minute or so after all sugar has become liquid, remove from heat. Place almonds on top of a marble slab or a metal cookie sheet previously greased with butter. Quickly, with a soup spoon, separate almonds from each other before sugar hardens. Each almond should have a separate coat of syrup. When almonds are cold place them in airtight jars. Stored in a cold place they will keep for months. They are delicious as candy, or chopped fine and sprinkled on cakes, ice cream and other desserts.

Hazlenuts Pralinée

NOCCIOLINE PRALINATE

2 cups shelled hazlenuts
1 cup sugar
¼ cup water
4 to 5 drops pink or green vegetable food coloring

Place sugar and water in saucepan and cook over medium-high flame until candy thermometer reads "soft ball," or until a few drops in cold water form a soft ball. Add nuts and food coloring and continue cooking, stirring constantly, until sugar becomes sandy. Continue stirring for a moment or so longer. Nuts are done when a sandy coat of sugar covers each individual nut and sugar at bottom of pan starts to melt again. Place nuts on flat surface separating them if necessary. When cold, place in airtight sterilized jars and store in cool place. They keep fresh for months. Makes about 2 pints.

CAKES, PASTRIES, PIES, AND ICINGS

TORTE, PASTICCINI, CROSTATE, GHIACCE

Genoese Cake

PASTA GENOVESE

- ¾ cup sugar
- 6 eggs at room temperature
- 1½ cups self-rising cake flour, sifted 4 times
- 6 tablespoons melted butter
- 1 teaspoon almond extract or 1½ tablespoons dark rum

Place sugar and eggs in top of double boiler. Water in bottom of double boiler should be hot but not boiling. Beat eggs with hand or electric beater until mixture is lukewarm. Remove eggs to a mixing bowl and continue beating until mixture is light and foamy. Gradually sift in flour, stirring well after each addition. Add butter, mixing lightly until ingredients are well blended. Stir in almond extract or rum. Pour batter in 3 nine-inch cake pans, previously buttered and lightly floured. It is advisable to line bottom of pans with waxed paper. Bake in 375° oven for 20 minutes. Remove cake from oven when a toothpick inserted in cake comes out clean. Invert on cake racks and cool. This is a basic recipe for different kinds of layer cakes and pastry.

Maddalena Cake

PASTA MADDALENA

- 1 cup sugar
- 3 eggs
- 1 egg yolk
- ¾ cup sifted self-rising cake flour
- ¼ cup sifted potato flour
- 2 egg whites, beaten stiff

Sift together cake and potato flours. Place eggs, egg yolk

and sugar in top of double boiler. Water in bottom of double boiler should be hot but not boiling. Beat egg mixture with rotary beater until lukewarm. Remove eggs to mixing bowl and beat with rotary or electric beater until mixture is light and foamy. Gradually sift in flour, then fold in beaten egg whites. Pour batter in 3 nine-inch buttered cake tins and bake in 375° oven for 15 to 20 minutes. Turn tins on cake racks and cool. Use as directed, or use your favorite cake filling and icing.

Italian Sponge Cake

PAN DI SPAGNA

- 5 egg whites beaten with ¼ teaspoon salt until stiff but not dry
- 5 egg yolks
- 1 cup sugar
- 1 cup cake flour sifted with ½ teaspoon cream of tartar
- grated peel of one large lemon
- ⅛ teaspoon vanilla

Beat egg yolks and sugar together 15 minutes with hand beater or 5 minutes with electric beater (at egg-beating speed). Add vanilla, lemon peel and fold in egg whites. Beating constantly with either electric or hand beater, sift flour slowly over the egg mixture. After all flour is used, beat 2 minutes by electric beater or 4 minutes by hand. Bake in buttered and lightly floured 9"x4" cake pan, for about 35 to 40 minutes in 375° oven. Test cake with toothpick or straw. Cake should be dry in center. Do not overcook cake. Just a few minutes more in the oven will make the difference between a good cake and a poor one. When cake is done, invert pan on cake rack and let stand until cool. Serves 8-10.

Genoa Almond Cake

PAN DI GENOVA

- ½ cup sugar
- ¼ pound butter
- 1 cup Almond Paste (page 191)
- 2½ tablespoons flour
- 3 eggs
- ¼ teaspoon salt
- 2½ tablespoons kirsch
- confectioner's sugar

Cream butter and sugar for 3 or 4 minutes with hand beater or about 1 minute with electric beater (at cream-butter speed). Add almond paste and beat with electric beater at same speed for 2 minutes, or 5 minutes with hand beater. Add eggs one at a time, continuing to beat at same speed 4 minutes, or 15 minutes with hand beater. Add flour, salt and kirsch. Beat for 3 minutes at blending speed or 5 minutes by hand. Place in a buttered 8-inch pie pan, the bottom of which has been lined with waxed paper. Bake at 300° for about 45 minutes. Turn out on cake rack and cool. Place on serving dish and sprinkle generously with confectioner's sugar. Place in refrigerator for a couple of hours. Serves 8.

Coconut Cake

TORTA AL COCCO

- 1 recipe Genoese Cake (page 181)
- ½ recipe Vanilla Butter Cream (page 204)
- shredded sweetened coconut
- 1 ounce maraschino liqueur

Spread tops of 2 layers of cake with Butter Cream and sprinkle with coconut. Then place layers one on top of the other, the third plain layer on top. With a small pastry brush, brush top and sides of cake with liqueur. Cover cake with Butter Cream, and sprinkle top and sides with coconut. Serves 8-10.

Butter Cream Cake

TORTA CON CREMA AL BURRO

- 10 egg yolks
- 10 egg whites beaten stiff with ½ teaspoon salt
- 2 cups sugar
- 2 cups sifted cake flour
- grated peel of 2 lemons
- 1 teaspoon vanilla extract
- 1 recipe Chocolate Butter Cream (see p. 205)
- ¾ cup toasted almonds, coarsely chopped

Beat egg yolks and sugar together for 15 minutes with rotary beater or 5 minutes with electric beater at high speed. Add vanilla, lemon peel and fold in beaten egg whites. Beating constantly, sift flour slowly over the egg mixture. After all flour is used, beat 2 minutes by electric beater or 4 minutes by hand. Bake in 3 buttered and lightly floured 9"x12" cake tins for 25 to 30 minutes at 375°. Test with toothpick or straw. Cake should be dry in center. Remove from oven, invert on cake rack and let stand until cake is cool. When cake has reached room temperature, spread the tops of 2 layers with a thin layer of Chocolate Butter Cream. Then place layers one on top of the other, plain layer at top. Spread cake well all over with Butter Cream, reserving a few tablespoons. With the help of a knife cover sides of cake with chopped almonds. Use cake decorator to decorate top of cake with rest of Butter Cream. Keep in refrigerator until ready to serve. Serves 18-20.

Birthday Cake

TORTA PER COMPLEANNO

- 10 egg yolks
- 10 egg whites beaten with ½ teaspoon salt until stiff but not dry
- 2 cups sugar
- 2 cups sifted cake flour
- grated peel of 2 large lemons
- 1 teaspoon vanilla extract
- 1 recipe cold Pasticcera Cream (page 168)
- 1 pint heavy cream
- 1 tablespoon sugar
- 1½ teaspoons unflavored gelatine
- vegetable coloring

Soak gelatine in 3 tablespoons cold water for 5 minutes. Scald 5 tablespoons heavy cream and add to the gelatine, stirring until dissolved. Stir in the rest of heavy cream and mix well. Place in refrigerator for about 2 hours.

Beat egg yolks and 2 cups of sugar together for 15 minutes, with hand beater, or 5 minutes with electric beater. Add ½ teaspoon vanilla, lemon peel, and fold in beaten egg whites. Beating constantly, sift flour slowly over the egg mixture. When all flour is used, beat 2 minutes by electric beater or 4 minutes by hand. Bake in 3 buttered and lightly floured 9"x12" cake tins for 25 to 30 minutes at 375°. Test with toothpick or straw. Cake should be dry in center. Remove from oven, invert tins on cake rack and let stand until cake is cool. When cake has reached room temperature, spread the tops of two of the layers with Cream Pasticcera. Then place layers one on top of the other, plain layer at top. Place in refrigerator for half hour.

Whip cream, 1 tablespoon sugar and rest of vanilla together until stiff enough to stand in peaks. Spread cake with ⅔ of whipped cream. Add red vegetable coloring to rest of whipped cream, until delicate pink. Use cake decorator to decorate top of cake with tinted cream. Place in refrigerator for at least two hours before serving. Serves 20.

Zuppa Inglese

BUDINO ALL'ITALIANA

- 1 recipe Italian Sponge Cake (page 182), baked in four 9" layer pans
- 1 4-ounce package of lady fingers, split
- 1½ recipe Bavarian Cream (page 168)
- ½ cup dark rum
- 1 cup small strawberries or drained fruit cocktail } optional
- 1 tablespoon kirsch or maraschino liqueur
- 1 cup heavy cream, whipped stiff

Place Bavarian Cream in refrigerator and let stand until thick, but not firm. If fruit and liqueur are to be used, mix the two and place in refrigerator until needed. When Cream has reached right consistency, brush one side of each cake layer and bottom of lady fingers with rum, using a pastry brush. Place one cake layer, rum side up, on a large round plate. Make a collar of several strips of strong paper, about 3 inches high, around the circumference of the cake, and secure with paper clips. Line inside of paper with lady fingers, placed vertically, and with rum-brushed side facing the center of the plate. Mix fruit and Bavarian Cream and place one fourth of this mixture inside ladyfinger shell. If fruit and liqueur are not used, simply use Cream. Cut remaining cake layers to fit inside lady fingers, cutting off about ½ inch around. Alternate layers of cake with Cream mixture, ending with a layer of Cream. Place in refrigerator for not less than 4 hours. When ready to serve, remove paper very carefully, and pile whipped cream on top of Cream mixture. Can be prepared the day before, especially if fruit mixture is not used. Serves 10-12.

Mont Blanc Maria Luisa

MONTE BIANCO MARIA LUISA

- 1½ pounds chestnuts
- 1 quart milk
- vanilla extract
- 1 cup sugar
- ¼ cup water
- 2 tablespoons sweet butter
- 2½ tablespoons Cognac
- 1½ cups heavy cream beaten stiff with 1 teaspoon sugar and 2 or 3 drops of vanilla

Peel chestnuts. Place in pan of cold water, bring to a boil and cook for 10 minutes. Drain and remove second skin rapidly so that chestnuts do not become cold. Place nuts in very hot milk to which 3 or 4 drops of vanilla have been added. Simmer until chestnuts are very soft (about ½ hour) and drain. Place sugar, water and 4 drops of vanilla in small pan and cook over low flame for about 10 minutes, stirring often. Put chestnuts through a fine sieve. Combine chestnuts, sugar syrup, butter and Cognac and mix into a smooth paste. On a round crystal or silver dish about 9 or 10 inches wide make a bird's nest of the chestnut paste with a cake decorator, leaving in center a space the size of a grapefruit. Place in refrigerator for 2 to 4 hours. When ready to serve place whipped cream in the middle. Serves 8-10.

Fruit Chest Palermitana

CASSATA ALLA PALERMITANA

- 1 recipe Italian Sponge Cake (page 182), baked in loaf pan
- 1¼ pounds ricotta cheese
- ¾ cup sugar
- ⅓ cup water
- rum or any favorite liqueur
- ⅓ cup pistachio nuts, peeled and chopped
- 1 tablespoon candied citron peel, diced
- 1 tablespoon candied orange peel, diced
- ¼ cup chocolate bits
- ⅛ teaspoon cinnamon
- apricot or peach preserves

Cook sugar and water until the syrup forms a soft ball (about 10 minutes). Put ricotta cheese through a sieve and slowly stir into it the syrup and ½ ounce liqueur, blending into a smooth paste. Add, blending well, the pistachio nuts, candied citron and orange peel, chocolate and cinnamon. Place in refrigerator until ready to use. Cut one slice about ½ inch thick from top of cake. Cut out center leaving wall about ½ inch thick. Sprinkle inside of chest with liqueur, place back in loaf pan and fill with ricotta mixture. Close with top slice, sealing edges with preserves. Place in refrigerator for about 4 hours. Remove cake from pan and ice with your favorite icing. Serve cold, sliced. Serves 6.

Note: Cut-out center can be used for Genoese Meringues, Pastry, etc.

White Fruit Cake

PANETTONE DI MILANO

- 6½ cups sifted flour
- 1 envelope yeast
- ½ cup lukewarm water
- 7 tablespoons butter, melted
- ¾ cup sugar
- 3 tablespoons corn syrup
- 1 teaspoon salt
- 4 egg yolks, at room temperature
- 1 whole egg
- ½ cup candied citron peel, cut in small pieces
- ½ cup seedless raisins

The preparation of this cake is very simple but quite long. Blend yeast with water. Place one cup flour in small mixing bowl. Add yeast and water and mix thoroughly. Place on floured board and knead for 5 minutes. Form dough into a ball. Make a cross mark with knife on top of dough and place it in a floured bowl. Cover with kitchen towel and let stand in warm place for one hour. Place one cup of flour in clean mixing bowl, add ⅓ cup lukewarm water and ball of dough. Mix well. Place on floured board and knead for 5 minutes. Make a ball of this dough and make a cross mark with knife on top of dough. Place again in a floured bowl. Cover with towel and let stand for 2 hours. Mix 1½ cups flour and ½ cup lukewarm water in a bowl. Add to dough and knead on floured board for 5 minutes. Place dough in a large floured bowl, cover and let stand 2 more hours. Place butter and salt in large mixing bowl of electric beater, add egg yolks and dough and beat at lowest speed lifting beaters up and down, until you have a smooth paste. Mix sugar, corn syrup and 3 tablespoons lukewarm water and add to dough. Beat at lowest speed, lifting beaters up and down, until dough is smooth. If an electric mixer is not available, place butter, salt and dough in large bowl, add egg yolks and mix with a spoon or with hand until a smooth paste is obtained. Mix sugar, corn syrup and 3 tablespoons lukewarm water and add to dough. Mix well with spoon.

Add ¾ of the remaining flour, mixing with a spoon. Place dough on floured board, make a hole in the middle of dough and add whole egg. Knead for a minute or so and gradually add rest of flour. Knead 10 minutes, if electric beater was used, or 20 minutes otherwise. Add raisins and citron peel and knead 5 minutes more. Cut dough in half, and shape into balls. Place on buttered baking sheets. Wrap sides of each panettone with a collar of strong paper about 5 inches wide, secured on the sides with either paper clips or pins. If desired, one large panettone can be made instead of 2 small ones. Also panettone can be baked in a buttered baking pan 9"x5", the bottom of which has been lined with waxed paper, or in two baking pans about 6"x5". Cover with damp towel and let stand in warm place for 4 to 6 hours. (Exact time depends on dampness and warmth of the place.) Make a cross with a knife on top of each and place in 350° oven. Place a small pan of water in the oven: this will help the cake to rise and will make the crust glossy. (Bakeries in Italy have special ovens equipped with steam valves for this purpose.) After 10 minutes, gently enlarge the center of the crossmarks with finger tips, and place in ½ teaspoon butter. Bake 20 to 25 minutes more. (Allow a few minutes more if baking pans are used.) For one large panettone reduce heat after 15 minutes to 325° and bake about 40 minutes longer. Panettone is done when a straw inserted in the middle of it comes out clean. Let cool on cake rack. This cake keeps for days and is delicious with coffee.

The town of Genoa claims that Panettone was first made there and given the name of Pandolce, and that the famous Panettone of Milan, the Panettone of Venice and the Panettone of Turin are just imitations. Panettone of Milan has been for years the most popular. Before the last war it was used only during Christmas holidays, but since then its use has spread throughout the year and to many parts of the world, including the United States.

Savarin al Rum

- 2½ cups sifted cake flour
- 1 cup melted butter
- ⅓ cup sugar
- 1 teaspoon powdered yeast dissolved in ¼ cup lukewarm water
- 3 eggs at room temperature, beaten
- ¾ cup lukewarm milk

SAUCE:

- 1½ cups sugar
- ¾ cup water
- ½ teaspoon vanilla
- ½ cup Jamaica rum
- ¼ cup candied orange peel, diced
- ¼ cup candied citron peel, diced
- 8 candied or maraschino cherries

Place ½ cup flour in mixing bowl. Add yeast and water and mix into a smooth paste. Place in floured bowl, cover with kitchen towel and let stand for one hour. Place rest of flour in large mixing bowl together with the sugar, eggs and milk. With a tablespoon mix into a smooth paste. Add flour and yeast mixture, then add melted butter. Mix with hand beater or electric beater until dough is smooth. Cover with damp towel and let stand for 3 hours. Mix dough with a spoon, just long enough to deflate it, cover it and let stand. Repeat this operation after 2 hours, and let it rise for 2 hours more. Butter a 3-quart ring mold and line bottom with waxed paper. Place dough in ring. Let it rise till it reaches top of pan (about 2 hours). Bake in oven at 300° for 18 to 20 minutes. Test cake with toothpick after 15 minutes. Turn on cake rack for a few minutes, until cake has cooled a bit. Place sugar, water and vanilla in small deep saucepan. Insert candy thermometer and let cook till thermometer reads 200°. Remove from heat and add ¼ cup rum. Carefully remove cake from ring and place on warm serving dish. Pour sauce on top of cake. Sprinkle with rest of rum and decorate with orange and citron peel and cherries. Serve warm. Serves 10-12.

Fruit Cake Siena Style

PANFORTE DI SIENA

This specialty of Siena is very similar to Torrone but at the same time it resembles a fruit cake. It is usually eaten during the Christmas holidays. It is sent all over Italy, and in the past few years it has been exported to many foreign countries. Here is the original recipe:

- ⅓ cup granulated sugar
- ½ cup honey
- ⅔ cup sifted flour
- 1½ cups shelled almonds, coarsely chopped and lightly toasted
- ⅔ cup hazelnuts, coarsely chopped and lightly toasted
- 3 ounces candied orange peel
- 3 ounces candied citron peel
- 4 ounces candied pumpkin or melon peel
- ¼ cup powdered unsweetened cocoa
- ⅙ teaspoon black pepper
- 2½ teaspoons cinnamon
- ⅛ teaspoon vanilla extract
- 2 tablespoons confectioner's sugar

Mix together flour, almonds, hazelnuts, candied orange, citron, pumpkin or melon peel, cocoa, pepper, 1½ teaspoons cinnamon and vanilla. Place granulated sugar and honey in large saucepan over low flame, insert candy thermometer and cook, stirring constantly with a wooden spoon, until thermometer reads "soft ball," or until a drop of sugar mixture dropped in cold water forms a soft ball. Remove from stove and add nut mixture. Mix well. Line bottom and sides of a 9" cake pan with greased waxed paper. Add cake mixture, even top with a spoon and bake in 300° oven for 35 minutes. Remove from oven and cool in cake pan. When cake has reached room temperature, remove from pan and carefully remove waxed paper. Sprinkle with rest of cinnamon and confectioner's sugar. Wrap in waxed paper and store in cool place. This cake keeps fresh for a couple of months. Serves 8-12.

Short Pastry

PASTA FROLLA

1½ cups flour	yolks of 2 eggs
¼ pound and 2 tablespoons cold butter or shortening	1 egg, beaten
⅓ cup sugar	¼ teaspoon salt

Sift flour, sugar and salt together and place in mixing bowl. Cut in butter or shortening, then add whole egg and yolks, blending quickly. Wrap dough in waxed paper and place in refrigerator for not less than 2 hours but preferably overnight. This will improve the texture of the pastry. Use as directed and for tarts, pastry, pies, etc.

Neapolitan Pastry

PASTICCINI NAPOLETANI

1 recipe Short Pastry (see above)	jam or jelly confectioner's sugar

You will need 2 sizes of cookie cutters, one about 2½" in diameter and the other the size of a nickel.

Roll dough ¼ inch thick on floured board and cut into rounds with larger cutter. Now remove center of half of the rounds with smaller cutter. Knead quickly all leftover dough, roll out and cut into more large rounds, removing center of half of the rounds with smaller cutter. Bake on cookie sheets lined with waxed paper at 375° for 10 minutes or until light golden. Remove from oven and let cool. Spread whole rounds with a thin layer of jam or jelly, and top with the doughnut-like rounds. Fill depression of each pastry with additional jam or jelly. Sprinkle with confectioner's sugar. Makes about 2 dozen.

Cream Puff Paste

PASTA REALE

1 cup sifted cake flour
1 cup hot water
4 whole eggs

½ cup butter
pinch of salt

Place water, butter and salt in saucepan and heat to the boiling point. Lower heat and pour in flour all at once, stirring until mixture leaves sides of pan. Remove from stove and cool. Add eggs, one at a time, when mixture is lukewarm, beating well after each addition. Use as directed.

Black Truffles Surprise

TARTUFI NERI IN SORPRESA

1 recipe Cream Puff Paste (see above)
2 teaspoons powdered sweet cocoa

1 recipe Chocolate Butter Cream (page 205)
¼ cup superfine sugar
¼ cup unsweetened cocoa

Blend 2 teaspoons sweet cocoa with Cream Puff Paste. Drop batter on lightly greased cookie sheets by the teaspoonful, leaving 2 inches between each. Bake in 450° oven for 10 minutes, lower heat to 300° and bake for 15 minutes more. Remove from oven and cool. Make a very small slit in each puff and with the help of a cake decorator, using the tip with the smallest opening, fill each puff with Butter Cream. Mix together sugar and cocoa and roll puffs in it. Keep in refrigerator until ready to serve. Makes about 4 dozen.

Almond Paste

PASTA DI MANDORLE

2 cups blanched almonds (about 8 ounces)

1 cup sugar
2 egg whites, lightly beaten

Drop almonds in egg white. Remove almonds and put them through a food grinder twice. Blend left-over egg white with chopped almonds and the sugar. Use as directed and as a base for pastry.

Filbert Cookies

PASTINE CON LE NOCCIOLE

1 recipe Almond Paste (page 191)
2 tablespoons dark rum
⅓ cup shelled filberts, slightly toasted and chopped fine

Blend rum with Almond Paste. Shape paste into patties of equal size, about 1½ inches wide. Roll on one side in toasted filberts. Place on buttered and floured baking sheets, filbert side up, about one inch apart. Let stand for 2 hours. Bake in 400° oven for 5 to 8 minutes or until light brown in color. Makes about 3½ dozen.

Macaroons

AMARETTI

1 recipe Almond Paste (page 191)
½ teaspoon almond extract
granulated sugar

Blend paste and almond extract together and shape into patties about 1½ inches wide and ¼ inch thick. Place on buttered and floured baking sheets about one inch apart. Sprinkle lightly with sugar and let stand for 2 hours. Bake in 400° oven for 12 to 15 minutes or until light brown. Remove with metal spatula while still warm. Makes about 3 dozen.

Pine Nut Cookies

PASTINE CON I PIGNOLI

Pignoli or pine nuts are imported from Italy and can be bought in all Italian food stores and also in many delicatessen stores.

1 recipe Almond Paste (page 191)
2 tablespoons kirsch or any favorite liqueur
1 egg white lightly beaten
¼ cup pine nuts

Blend liqueur with Almond Paste. Shape paste into patties of equal size, about 1½ inches wide. Place on buttered and floured baking sheets about one inch apart. Brush top of each with egg white and place 5 to 6 pine nuts on top of each cookie. Let stand for 2 hours. Bake in oven at 400° for about 5 to 8 minutes or until light brown in color. Makes about 3½ dozen.

Fancy Cookies Milanese

PASTINE FANTASIA ALLA MILANESE

4 ounces shelled almonds, blanched	1 small egg, beaten
⅓ cup granulated sugar	¼ teaspoon vanilla
¼ cup confectioner's sugar	or 1½ teaspoons dark rum
1 egg white, beaten	or 1½ teaspoons Crème de Cacao

Drop almonds in egg white, drain and put through a food grinder twice. Blend chopped almonds with rest of egg white, the beaten egg, sugar and seasoning. Pack almond mixture in cookie press or pastry tube and shape on buttered and lightly floured baking sheet. Make cookies small and dainty, in different forms. Decorate with walnut halves, or blanched almonds, or candied fruit peel, or jam. Bake in 375° oven for 15 minutes. Makes about 2 dozen cookies.

Basic Cookie Dough

PASTA ZUCCHERATA

1 cup flour, sifted	¼ teaspoon salt
¼ cup cold butter, diced	1 small egg
¼ cup sugar	

Sift flour, salt and sugar together in mixing bowl. Cut in butter and blend in egg. Place on floured board and knead briefly into a smooth dough, adding a little more flour if dough is too soft. Wrap in waxed paper and place in refrigerator for at least 3 hours. Use as directed.

Venetian Cookies

VENETI

2 recipes Basic Cookie Dough (see above)	½ recipe Royal Icing (page 203)
	apricot jelly

Roll out pastry about ¼ inch thick on floured board. Cut in 2-inch squares, place on greased cookie sheets and bake in 375° oven for 10 to 12 minutes. Remove from oven and cool. Spread top of each with a thin layer of Royal Icing. Place apricot jelly in cake decorator and with it form a large X on top of the icing. Makes 2 dozen cookies.

Variation: Instead of forming an X with the jelly, drop about ⅓ of a teaspoon of it in the center of each cookie and place half a pecan on it.

Honey Cookies

PASTINE AL MIELE

1 recipe Basic Cookie Dough (page 193)	honey
3 tablespoons mixed candied fruit peels, diced fine	confectioner's sugar (optional)

Add candied peels to dough and knead briefly to insure even distribution. Then roll out on floured board and cut in 24 rounds about 2 to 2½ inches in diameter. Place on greased cookie sheets and bake in 375° oven for 10 to 12 minutes. Do not allow to brown. Remove from oven and cool. Spread a thin layer of honey on one side of half of the rounds, top with rest of rounds and sprinkle with confectioner's sugar. Makes a dozen cookies.

Orange Cookies

BISCOTTI ALL'ARANCIO

1 cup sugar	6 drops red food coloring
4 large eggs at room temperature	3 drops yellow food coloring — optional
2 cups sifted flour	
1 tablespoon grated orange peel	

Place half of the sugar and 2 eggs in mixing bowl. Beat with hand or electric beater, slowly adding rest of sugar. Beat for a few more minutes and add one egg. Beat for 3 minutes and add fourth egg. Beat till eggs are light and foamy (about 5 minutes by electric beater or 15 minutes by hand). Fold in flour, orange peel and food coloring. Press through a pastry bag on to baking sheets covered with greased aluminum wrap or waxed paper, one inch apart. Give cookie a round shape about 1 inch wide or a long shape about 1½ inches long. Sprinkle with sugar and let stand for 3 hours. (This way the cookies will keep their shape much better and their tops will also become shiny.) Bake in oven at about 350° for about 10 minutes.

Lemon Cookies

BISCOTTI AL LIMONE

Follow recipe for Orange Cookies (see above). Substitute lemon peel and 3 drops of yellow food coloring.

Lady Fingers

SAVOIARDI

3 egg yolks	¼ teaspoon vanilla extract
3 egg whites beaten stiff with ¼ teaspoon salt	2 tablespoons granulated sugar
⅔ cup sugar	2 tablespoons confectioner's sugar
⅔ cup cake flour	

Beat yolks and ⅔ cup sugar with hand or electric beater until yellow and foamy. Sift in flour and continue beating until thoroughly blended. Fold in beaten egg whites and vanilla. Butter cookie sheets and sprinkle very lightly with flour. Brush off excess flour with pastry brush. Press dough through pastry bag on to cookie sheets in 3-inch-long fingers, placing them about 1½ inches apart. Mix confectioner's and granulated sugars and sprinkle half of it over lady fingers. Let stand for 15 minutes. Sprinkle with remaining sugar and let stand for 10 minutes more. Bake in 375° oven for 8 minutes, or until golden. Remove from baking sheets with a metal spatula and let cool on cake rack. Makes about 2 dozen.

Coconut Cookies

PASTINE AL COCCO

¼ cup sugar	1 egg white beaten stiff with ⅛ teaspoon salt
2 egg yolks	4 ounces shredded coconut

Beat yolks and sugar together until creamy. Then fold in

coconut and beaten egg white. Drop by teaspoonful on greased cookie sheet. Bake in 300° oven for 15 minutes, lower heat to 250° and bake for 30 minutes more or until thoroughly dry. Makes about 1½ dozen.

Bolognese Ring

CIAMBELLA BOLOGNESE

3¼ cups self-rising cake flour, sifted	¼ cup lukewarm milk
1¼ cups sugar	1 teaspoon cream of tartar
¼ teaspoon salt	2 eggs, beaten
2 tablespoons melted butter	2 teaspoons grated lemon peel

Sift flour, sugar and salt in mixing bowl. Add rest of ingredients, blending well. Knead dough on floured board, adding more flour if dough is sticky, until a soft, smooth dough is obtained. Shape into a large ring or two small ones, and place on buttered and lightly floured baking sheet. Sprinkle with one tablespoon granulated sugar and bake in 375° oven for 25 minutes. This ring is usually sliced thin and is very appropriate for children's snacks.

Anise Cookies

BISCOTTI ALL'ANICE

4 egg yolks	2½ cups sifted cake flour
2 small eggs	2 teaspoons anise extract
1 cup sugar	

Beat whole eggs, yolks and sugar until foamy and lemon-colored. Blend in flour and anise extract. Drop by the teaspoonful on greased cookie sheets about one inch apart, and bake in 375° oven for 15 minutes or until light brown. Makes about 3 dozen.

Genoese Meringues

MARENGHE GENOVESI

1 recipe Genoese Cake (page 181)	apricot jam or jelly
about 1½ ounces dark rum or Crème de Cacao, or any desired liqueur	1 recipe Italian Meringue (page 204)

Cut cake layers in 2-inch rounds, using a cookie cutter. Lightly sprinkle top of each with rum or desired liqueur and place about 1 teaspoon of jam in the middle of each. Place Italian Meringue in a cookie press or pastry bag and form a cone of meringue about 2½ inches high on top of each round. Carefully place pastry on cookie sheets and bake in 300° oven for about 5 minutes or until meringue is lightly golden. Remove from oven and let cool. Makes about 2 dozen.

Petits Fours

PASTICCERIA CON PAN DI SPAGNA

1 recipe Italian Sponge Cake (page 182) baked in tin 10"x14" (cooking time 20-25 minutes at 375°)	1 ounce kirsch
	1 ounce Crème de Cacao
	apricot jam, as needed
	Fondant for icing (page 202)
1 ounce rum	

Cut cake in 6 pieces crosswise. Cut each piece in 3 pieces crosswise. Divide in three groups. Slice each piece in half. Sprinkle inside of each piece of one group with rum, the second group with Crème de Cacao, and the last with kirsch. Spread half the pieces (on the same side that has been sprinkled with liqueur) with a thin layer of jam, and top each piece with its other half. Ice with Fondant, using a different color for each group.

Anise Bread

PANE ALL'ANICE

1 cup sugar	2½ cups sifted cake flour
3 eggs	1½ teaspoons anise extract
1 yolk	¼ teaspoon minced aniseed
¼ cup butter	2 teaspoons baking powder

Cream whole eggs, yolk, sugar and butter. Sift in flour, blending well. Mix in anise extract, aniseed and baking powder. Bake in buttured baking tin 8"x12", at 350° for 20 minutes, or until cake is dry in center. Turn on cake rack and cool. Remove from pan, cut in half lengthwise and slice crosswise in ¾ inch slices. Arrange slices on cookie sheets, and place in 450° oven for 2 to 3 minutes, or until lightly toasted. Makes about 2½ dozen.

Saint Joseph Cream Puff

SFINGI DI SAN GIUSEPPE

- 1 recipe Cream Puff Paste (page 191)
- 1 pound ricotta cheese
- ⅓ cup milk-chocolate bits
- 1 tablespoon candied orange peel
- 2 tablespoons pistachio nuts, minced
- ½ cup sugar

Drop Cream Puff Paste on lightly greased cookie sheets by the teaspoonful, leaving 2 inches between each. Bake in 450° oven for 10 minutes, lower heat to 300° and bake 15 to 20 minutes more. Remove from oven and cool. Blend together rest of ingredients. Make a slit on one side of each puff and fill with mixture. Keep in refrigerator until ready to use. Makes about 4 dozen. Serve sprinkled with confectioner's sugar.

Sweet Chestnuts Lazio

CASTAGNOLE LAZIALI

A specialty of the province of Rome, they are so named because, when cooked, the dough shapes itself into small chestnut-like balls.

- 2 eggs
- 2 heaping tablespoons sugar
- ⅓ teaspoon salt
- grated peel of a lemon
- 2 tablespoons brandy
- about ¾ cup flour
- 1 tablespoon olive oil
- oil or shortening for deep frying
- confectioner's sugar or honey

Cream eggs and sugar. Blend in oil and brandy, salt, grated lemon peel and flour. The exact amount of flour is hard to give as some flour absorbs more moisture than others; therefore add flour slowly, until you have a paste of "dropping consistency." The amount of flour given above will only be a tablespoon more or less than the exact amount. Drop mixture in hot fat (but not so hot that fritters will brown too quickly on the outside and fail to cook in the center), ½ teaspoon at a time. Fry a few at a time over medium-high flame until golden and puffy. With perforated spoon remove to absorbent paper. Serve hot, sprinkled with confectioner's sugar or warm honey. Serves 4-6.

Shrove Tuesday Sweet Knots

CENCI PER IL BERLINGACCIO

A popular sweet that is traditional in Tuscany at dinner on Shrove Tuesday, or Feast of the Berlingaccio as it is called locally. The Sweet Knots are sprinkled with confectioner's sugar and served with plain whipped cream.

2 cups flour, sifted	1 teaspoon baking powder
2 tablespoons butter, diced	2 tablespoons brandy
1/3 cup sugar	oil or shortening for deep frying
2 eggs	
1/4 teaspoon salt	1 pint heavy cream, whipped

Sift flour, sugar, baking powder and salt together on to pastry board. Make a depression in center and add eggs, butter and brandy. Beat with a fork, mixing in most of the flour. Then mix with hands and knead into a smooth paste. Wrap dough in waxed paper and keep in warmest part of refrigerator for one hour. Then roll out paper-thin on floured board. Cut into strips about 1½ inches wide and 5 inches long. Tie a knot in each and fry over medium flame in hot fat, a few at a time, until puffed and light golden. Serves 6-8.

Homemade Pie Crust

PASTA PER CROSTATE

2¼ cups sifted flour	grated peel of a small lemon
2/3 cup cold butter or shortening	1 large egg, lightly beaten
1/4 cup sugar	1 to 2 tablespoons cold water, as necessary

Sift flour and sugar together. Place in mixing bowl and cut in butter. Add egg and lemon peel and mix quickly until mixture holds together. Add water as needed if mixture is too dry. Divide dough in 2 parts; if butter has been used, place in refrigerator for at least 30 minutes. Roll out quickly on lightly floured board. Use as needed. Makes 2 nine-inch shells, or 1 two-crust pie.

Quick Pie Crust

1 package pie crust mix	grated peel of a lemon
2 tablespoons sugar	

Add sugar and grated lemon peel to pie crust mix and follow directions on package.

Coconut Bavarian Cream Pie

CROSTATA BAVARESE AL COCCO

1 nine-inch baked Pie Crust (page 199)	1 teaspoon almond extract shredded coconut
1 recipe Bavarian Cream (page 168)	

Add almond extract to Bavarian Cream when adding the gelatine. Fill pie crust with Bavarian Cream and chill for one hour. Sprinkle top of pie with coconut and replace in refrigerator until ready to serve.

Strawberry Pie

CROSTATA DI FRAGOLE

½ recipe Pie Crust (page 199)	2 cups apple sauce
⅓ cup apricot jelly or jam blended with	1 pint fresh strawberries

Line a nine-inch pie pan with dough, then ruffle edges. Prick crust thoroughly with fork. Fill ⅔ of pie shell with apple sauce and jelly mixture. Bake at 375° for 25 to 30 minutes, or until crust is golden and crisp. Remove pie from oven and let cool. Fill rest of pie with strawberries and sprinkle with confectioner's sugar. If desired strawberries can be previously marinated in dry red or white wine to which 2 tablespoons of sugar have been added.

Apple Pie No. 1

CROSTATA DI MELE NO. 1

1 recipe Pie Crust (page 199)	grated peel of small lemon
1 No. 2½ can apple sauce	or ⅓ teaspoon vanilla extract
5 tablespoons sugar	

Line pie pan with ½ of dough. Blend apple sauce, sugar and lemon peel or vanilla. Add apple mixture and cover with strips of crust in lattice design. Bake at 375° for about 30 minutes or until crust is crisp and golden in color. Serves 6.

Apple Pie No. 2

CROSTATA DI MELE NO. 2

1 recipe Pie Crust (page 199)
½ cup apricot jam or jelly
3 large apples, peeled, cored and sliced thin
3 tablespoons sugar
1 ounce dark rum or kirsch

Mix rum or kirsch with jam. Line pie pan with ½ of pie dough, fill with sliced apples, sprinkle with sugar and pour jam mixture over all. Cover with strips of crust in lattice design. Bake at 375° for 30 to 40 minutes or until crust is crisp and golden in color. Makes a 9-inch pie. Serves 6.

Pear Pie Milanese

CROSTATA DI PERE ALLA MILANESE

1 recipe Pie Crust (page 199)
12 canned pear halves, well drained
6 tablespoons apricot jam or jelly
2 ounces dark rum or Crème de Cacao

Line a 9-inch pie pan with one half of dough. Mix jam and rum or Crème de Cacao together, pour over pears and mix. Place pears in pie pan, cover with top crust and press edges together. Prick crust thoroughly with a fork to allow steam to escape while baking. Bake in 375° oven for about 30 minutes, or until crust is crisp and golden in color.

Sicilian Pie

CROSTATA ALLA SICILIANA

½ recipe Pie Crust, baked (page 199)
2 recipes Pasticcera Cream at room temperature (page 168)
½ cup chopped pistachio nuts
⅓ cup candied orange peel, diced
1 cup heavy cream, beaten stiff

Mix Pasticcera Cream with pistachio nuts and diced orange

peel. Place in pie crust. Keep in refrigerator for about 4 hours before serving. Top with whipped cream.

Neapolitan Pie

CROSTATA ALLA NAPOLETANA

½ recipe Pie Crust (page 199)
1 recipe Pasticcera Cream (page 168)
1 square unsweetened chocolate, melted
¼ cup candied citron peel, diced fine
about 16 fresh or canned apricot halves

Add chocolate to Pasticcera Cream together with citron peel, mixing well. Line a 9-inch pie pan with unbaked crust and pour into it the cream mixture. Cover with a layer of apricot halves and sprinkle with confectioner's sugar. Bake in 350° oven for 30 to 35 minutes. Serve hot or cold. If desired, pie may be decorated with whipped cream if served cold.

Fondant for Icing Cakes and Pastry

IL FONDENTE PER GHIACCIARE

2 cups sugar
¾ cup water
¾ cup white corn syrup
6 drops fresh lemon juice

Fondant is one of the best and most practical of pastry decorations. It is a superior icing for cakes and pastry; it is also an important ingredient in the preparation of many sweets of the highest quality. Fondant used for icing requires at least ¾ cup white corn syrup or glucose for each pound of sugar. It can be made in great quantity, as it keeps for a long time when stored in airtight jars. If Fondant should become too thick, dilute it with a small amount of milk while it is being warmed. To warm Fondant, place necessary quantity in double boiler over hot water. Stir constantly until completely melted and keep it over hot water while in use, to avoid hardening. Never overheat Fondant, as excessive heat will cause it to lose much of its shine and to become grainy.

Place sugar in deep saucepan. Add water and stir. Insert candy thermometer and place over medium-high flame. Add lemon juice and corn syrup when sugar comes to a boil. Keep sides of pan damp with a pastry brush dipped in hot water. Cook until thermometer reads "soft ball" or until a drop of the sugar mixture in cold water makes a soft ball. Remove from heat and pour on any smooth nonpainted surface which has been dampened with cold water. Let stand until lukewarm. Stir with a metal spatula by picking up the mixture and working toward the center. Continue the operation for about 15 minutes, or until mixture has become very white and smooth. Place in jar, cover tightly and let stand in cool place for at least 24 hours before using. Makes 1 pint.

Chocolate Fondant

FONDANT AL CIOCCOLATO

Add 1 ounce unsweetened chocolate and 1 tablespoon butter for each cup of Fondant (page 202) when melting.

Fondant may be made in any desired flavor, adding one tablespoon of any preferred liqueur or flavoring for each cup of Fondant. Flavoring and coloring should be added when melting Fondant.

Royal Icing

GHIACCIA REALE

1 cup confectioner's sugar
white of a small egg
¼ teaspoon fresh lemon juice

Place ingredients in a bowl and beat with rotary beater or electric mixer until white, creamy and thick. Enough to cover a 9-inch cake.

Roman Cream

CREMA ROMANA

½ pint heavy cream
4 ounces milk chocolate, cut in small pieces

Place ingredients in saucepan. Bring to a boil, mixing constantly, and simmer for one minute. Remove to mixing bowl and cool, stirring occasionally. Place bowl in saucepan half filled with cracked ice and beat with rotary or electric beater, until mixture is completely whipped. Cream will have the consistency of whipped butter. Use as filling, icing and decoration of cakes. Enough for filling and icing two 9-inch cake layers.

Italian Meringue

MARENGA ALL'ITALIANA

2 egg whites beaten stiff but not dry
1⅓ cups sugar
¼ cup water
½ teaspoon vanilla extract

Place sugar, water and vanilla in saucepan and cook until candy thermometer reads "soft ball" or until a soft ball forms when a small amount of syrup is dropped into cold water. Pour sugar syrup gradually over egg whites, beating constantly. Cool and use as directed. Can be used for decoration of cakes and pastry and can be added to many desserts to make them lighter.

Butter Cream

CREMA AL BURRO

8 ounces whipped sweet butter
2 tablespoons superfine sugar
8 tablespoons cold Pasticcera Cream (page 168)

Place butter in bowl and let stand at room temperature until soft. Beat butter with hand or electric beater, gradually adding sugar and Pasticcera Cream, until mixture is smooth and almost doubled in bulk (about 20 to 25 minutes by hand beater, and 10 minutes by electric, at medium-high speed). Enough for icing and filling two 9-inch cakes.

Vanilla Butter Cream

CREMA AL BURRO VANIGLIA

1 recipe Butter Cream (see above)
½ teaspoon vanilla extract

Blend vanilla extract with Butter Cream.

Chocolate Butter Cream

CREMA AL BURRO CIOCCOLATO

| 1 recipe Butter Cream (page 204) | ½ square bitter chocolate |

Melt bitter chocolate and add to Butter Cream, blending well.

Butter Cream Torinese

CREMA AL BURRO ALLA TORINESE

| 1 recipe Chocolate Butter Cream (see above) | ¼ cup Almond Pralinée, chopped fine (page 180) |

Blend chopped Almond Pralinée with Chocolate Butter Cream.

Hazelnut Butter Cream

CREMA AL BURRO NOCCIOLE

| ½ recipe Butter Cream (page 204) | 24 hazelnuts, shelled and lightly roasted |

Pound hazelnuts in a mortar until pulverized and add to Butter Cream, blending well. Enough for a 9" layer cake.

COFFEE

CAFFÈ

In the past few years as Americans have become more and more familiar with Italian food, they have acquired a taste for Italian coffee. There is, however, one misconception about Italian coffee, and that is the widespread belief that it is all *espresso*. Even in Italy, until a few years ago, because it is brewed in a special machine, *espresso* could generally be had only in coffee shops and restaurants. No one knows exactly how the name *espresso* originated, but I have heard that it was so named to mean not only expressly made but also because it requires a very short time.

Espresso is more delicate, aromatic and flavorful than the everyday coffee of the Italian home. It is made in a large electric urn in which steam (or *very* hot water) under pressure are forced through the powdered coffee. But in the past few years, *espresso* machines for home use, electric or plain (that is, they can be used on any stove burner), have been manufactured and imported to this country. They come in different shapes, sizes and makes, with instructions attached, and at a moderate price. Italian coffee as such—the drink served here in restaurants—is almost always drip coffee made in the Neapolitan coffee-maker.

To make Italian coffee, one needs not only a Neapolitan drip-coffee maker, or an *espresso* machine, but also Italian roasted coffee, either in cans or freshly roasted and ground. The amount of coffee to use is determined by the size of your coffee-maker. No matter what kind you happen to have or its size, the coffee-maker has a special container that has to be filled with coffee.

On page 207 are shown the three most common types of machines for making Italian coffee.

Whether or not it is *espresso* or drip, Italian coffee, black as it is, can be drunk with sugar and/or a small piece of lemon peel, or a tablespoon of Anisette, brandy or Grappa.

The only time our coffee is drunk with milk or cream is

ESPRESSO　　　　ESPRESSO　　　NEAPOLITAN
　　　　　　　　　　　　　　　　　　DRIP

when it is served as a *cappuccino*. This is *espresso*, to which, after it has been poured in a cup, a teaspoon or so of hot milk is added. *Cappuccino* is never served after a meal but is very appropriate for breakfast or between meals, and it should be served in cups that are larger than a demi-tasse and smaller than the regular American coffee cups. Half coffee and half hot milk—*caffè latte*—also is a drink commonly served at breakfast, especially for children. *Caffè latte* is generally made with drip coffee, but it can also be made with *espresso*.

WINES

VINI

⁄⁄⁄

Italy is among the world's largest and greatest producers of wines. The products of its vineyards are famous the world over. France produces more wine annually than Italy, but Italy has more land dedicated to the cultivation of its vineyards. This is the largest industry in Italy, employing about twelve million people, roughly a quater of the entire Italian population.

It has been said that no country can supply a greater variety of exquisite wines. This richness and variety go back at least two thousand years. In the first century A.D. Pliny declared that Italy produced the best wines in the world, surpassing even Greece, which up to almost that date had been predominant in the production of rare wines. "Of the 80 types of fine wines known in the entire world, Italy produces more than two thirds: *longe propterea ante cunctas terras.*"

What is the number of rare wines produced in Italy today —one hundred? two hundred? Nobody seems to know exactly, which is a great shame, but efforts are being made and have been made in the past few years to ascertain the number, not only for the Italian trade, but also for the benefit of connoisseurs abroad.

It is not known exactly where and when the first wine was made. References to vineyards are to be found in the Bible and also in the works of Virgil and Homer. It is common belief that grapevines were first introduced in Europe by the Phocaeans about 600 B.C.

In the first century, the cultivation of grapevines had become so widespread in the Mediterranean regions that the Emperor Domitian, fearing grain scarcity, restricted their cultivation in Italy. Later the Romans introduced the vines in England, where their cultivation never had great success. Italy, France, Spain, the Rhineland, Portugal, Greece, North Africa, the Canary Islands and the Azores were most successful in tending vines. In the seventeenth century the *Vitis vini-*

fera was also introduced in the New World, but the vine-growers had very little success. Experts from Tuscany and the Rhineland working in Virginia and Pennsylvania for Thomas Jefferson also failed. In the nineteenth century, it was discovered that the cause for the failure of grapevines in the United States was due to a louse called the phylloxera. Viticulture finally became successful in the United States when the Catawba and Concord grapes were introduced in the last century.

Of the innumerable wines made in Italy, comparatively few are exported to this country. But even so, there is still a wide choice, especially if one knows what and where to buy. Good Italian wine is comparatively low in price, ranging from about $1.50 to $2.50 a bottle. It is as important to have a good wine merchant as, let us say, a good butcher; somebody who knows our taste and who can also tip us off on good buys. For example, a good vintage-year wine might be on the market now for just a little over a dollar a bottle, while in a few years that same wine, nicely aged, will cost quite a bit more. As everybody knows, aged wines are very expensive. But by shrewd buying practically everybody can build up a "cellar," small or large, according to one's pocketbook and the space available. Small wine cellars can be made in a cool closet (the ideal temperature for storing wines is 55° F. and should be kept constant) either by transferring wine to whiskey cases and standing the cases on end, or by building compartmented shelves as near the floor as possible.

White wines and sparkling wines go on the bottom shelves, then the red wines. Fortified wines (sherry, Madeira, Marsala, etc.) can stand upright with the spirits. If one has a house cellar the wine can be properly stored in compartmented shelves in a cool dark corner. Many department stores carry wine shelves of various sizes that can be bought quite inexpensively. They are especially appropriate for natural wines, which should be stored horizontally. In this way the cork, kept damp by the wine, will not dry and shrink and, most important of all, the wine will not spoil. Wines to be served in a month or so may be kept upright.

Serving Wines

Care should be taken in the serving of wines. Red wines, especially fine aged ones, cast a deposit. This is a natural sediment, completely harmless, indicating only that the wine is old. When serving wines that have cast a sediment, let the bottle stand upright without agitation for a few hours, or set the bottle in a wine cradle, which holds it so that the deposit settles in the angle of the bottle. If too much sediment is present, the wine should be decanted; it should be poured very gently, after letting the sediment settle, into a different container, taking care that the deposit does not get in the new container.

The foil wrapping around the mouth of the bottle should be removed and the top of the bottle should be wiped with a damp cloth. The cork should be removed with care so that bits of it do not fall into the wine. But at times, despite all the care in the world, this will happen, especially with old wines, where the cork is not well preserved. Etiquette therefore requires the host to pour a little wine from the newly opened bottle into his glass, not only to smell it and taste it to see if the wine is good, but also in case there should be bits of cork. Also, the cork should be removed an hour or so before the wine is to be served, to allow the wine to come into contact with air. Only then can its fine bouquet be really tested. For the same reason, wine should be served in large glasses only half filled.

According to experts, the best wine glasses are tulip-shaped and made of clear rather than colored crystal.

The time of ten-course meals has practically disappeared even in Italy. But for the Italians any meal, from the everyday repast to a dinner party, still requires wine, with the difference that in an everyday family meal one kind of wine is served as a rule, while at a formal dinner or luncheon, even the smallest, at least three kinds are required: a medium-dry white wine for the antipasto and soup, followed by a red wine with the meat course (replaced by a good, aged dry white wine if fish is served, or a *generoso* red wine for roast meats and fowl), and a light, sweet wine to be served with desserts. It should be stressed here that in Europe sparkling wines are not served throughout the entire meal, but it is not unusual to see a dry champagne served before dinner.

TYPE OF WHITE WINE TO BE SERVED WITH ANTIPASTO:

Capri
Soave
Frascati (medium dry)
Chianti
Marino
Est-Est-Est (semi-dry)

TYPE OF RED WINE FOR MEATS:

Bardolino
Valpolicella
Light Chianti
Freisa
Grignolino
Lambrusco
Merlot

TYPE OF WHITE WINE TO BE SERVED WITH FISH:

Capri
Lacrima Christi
Orvieto
Etna
Terlano
Est-Est-Est (dry)

TYPE OF RED WINE TO BE SERVED WITH ROAST MEATS AND FOWL:

Barbera
Barberesco
Barolo
Chianti Classico Superiore
Nebbiolo
Santa Maddalena
Lago di Cordaro

PRESERVED AND PICKLED VEGETABLES

CONSERVE

Preserved Tomatoes No. 1

POMIDORI CONSERVATI NO. 1

10 pounds very ripe Italian egg tomatoes	12 fresh basil leaves sterilized jars

Rinse tomatoes thoroughly and cut each into 4 pieces. Fill jars with tomatoes, adding 2 basil leaves for each jar, and leaving ½ inch head space. Divide juice among jars and seal. Place jars in high pan of cold water. Bring to a boil, cover and simmer for one hour. Remove jars from pan when they have reached room temperature. Dry and store in cool, dry place. Use for sauce as fresh tomatoes after straining them.

Preserved Tomatoes No. 2

POMIDORI PELATI CONSERVATI NO. 2

10 pounds very ripe Italian egg tomatoes	sterilized jars

Place tomatoes in large pan of hot water and let stand for 5 minutes. Drain, peel and dice. Pack carefully in jars, leaving ½ inch head space. Divide juice among jars and seal. Place jars in high pan of cold water. Bring to a boil, cover and simmer for one hour. Remove jars from pan when they have reached room temperature. Dry and store in cool, dry place. Use for sauces as fresh tomatoes.

Preserved Tomato Sauce

SALSA DI POMIDORO

- 10 pounds very ripe Italian egg tomatoes, diced
- 4 medium-size onions, peeled and sliced
- 2 large carrots, peeled and diced
- ½ cup diced celery
- 8 leaves of fresh basil (or ⅓ teaspoon dried basil)
- ¾ cup olive oil
- 1 cup canned vegetable juice
- about 2 tablespoons of salt
- about ½ teaspoon pepper
- sterilized jars

Gently sauté onions, carrots and celery in oil, stirring occasionally, for 10 minutes. Add tomatoes, basil and vegetable juice. Bring to a boil and simmer uncovered for 2 hours. Season to taste. Remove from stove, cover and cool. Strain mixture through a sieve. Fill jars, leaving ½ inch head space. Add 1 tablespoon olive oil for each jar, seal and place in pan of cold water. Bring slowly to a boil, cover and simmer for one hour. Remove jars from pan when they have reached room temperature. Dry and store in cool, dry place. The sauce is ready to use any time. Just heat, add some butter and use.

Pickled Mushrooms

FUNGHI SOTTO ACETO

- 2 pounds button mushrooms
- 1 lemon
- 3 cups white wine vinegar
- 1 teaspoon salt
- 1 onion
- 8 peppercorns
- 2 cloves of garlic
- 3 bay leaves
- 2 cloves
- ⅓ cup olive oil

Choose very fresh mushrooms. Cut off ends of stems. Rinse quickly in pan of salted water to which juice of one lemon has been added. Place 3 cups vinegar and same amount of water in saucepan, together with salt, onion, garlic and bay leaves. Add mushrooms when vinegar comes to a boil. Boil for 5 minutes. Drain. Remove onion, garlic and bay leaves. Place mushrooms in 2 one-pint sterilized jars with peppercorns and cloves, leaving ½ inch head space. Fill jars with fresh wine vinegar, leaving ¼ inch head space. Pour olive oil to overflowing. Seal and store in cool, dry place. Ready in 6 weeks.

Mushrooms in Olive Oil

FUNGHI SOTTO OLIO

2 pounds button mushrooms	6 peppercorns
1 lemon	2 bay leaves
1 teaspoon salt	4 cloves
2 quarts white vinegar	olive oil

Choose young button mushrooms. Rinse them quickly in pan of salted water to which juice of one lemon has been added. Drain. Place in saucepan with vinegar, cloves and salt. Bring to a boil and cook for 5 minutes. Drain and cool. Place in 2 one-pint sterilized jars with bay leaves and peppercorns. Fill jars to overflowing with olive oil. Seal and store in cool, dry place. Ready in 4 weeks.

Pickled String Beans

FAGIOLINI SOTTO ACETO

1 pound fresh string beans, cleaned and cut into 2-inch pieces	2 whole cloves
	4 scallions
	8 peppercorns
4 basil leaves or ½ teaspoon dried basil	about 3 cups hot wine vinegar, which has been allowed to boil for a few minutes
2 cloves garlic	

Place string beans in boiling salted water and boil from 10 to 20 minutes according to thickness of beans. Beans should be only half-cooked. Drain well. Place in 2 one-pint sterilized jars with basil, scallions (cut in pieces), garlic, cloves and peppercorns. Fill jars with vinegar. Seal and store in cool place. Ready in 4 weeks.

Pickled Cucumbers

CETRIOLINI IN ACETO

24 cucumbers about 2 to 3 inches long, or 12 long ones cut into two-inch pieces	8 small onions, peeled
	2 bay leaves
	4 basil leaves or ½ teaspoon dried basil
6 cups wine vinegar	wine vinegar
3 tablespoons salt	
8 peppercorns	

Clean cucumbers with damp towel and place in a bowl. Place 6 cups vinegar and the salt in saucepan and boil for 2 minutes. Remove from fire and cool. Add to cucumbers. Cover and let stand for 4 days, stirring occasionally with a wooden spoon. Remove cucumbers from vinegar, place on paper towel and let stand until dry (about 1 hour). Place in sterilized jars with peppercorns, onions, bay leaves and basil. Fill jar with vinegar to overflowing. Seal and store in cool place. Ready in 2 months.

Pickled Peppers

PEPERONI SOTTO ACETO

24 sweet peppers	3 cloves garlic
about 3 quarts wine vinegar	6 basil leaves

Place peppers on large tray. Let stand in the sun for 3 days, turning them occasionally. Rub peppers gently with damp towel to remove dust. Place in jars with garlic and basil leaves. Add vinegar to overflowing. Seal and store in cool place. Ready in 2 months. Change vinegar every 4 months. Makes about 4 quarts.

Artichoke Hearts in Olive Oil

CARCIOFINI SOTTO OLIO

100 young small artichokes (about the size of a large egg)	1 lemon, sliced
	6 bay leaves
	6 cloves
juice of 12 lemons	black peppercorns
1 cup white vinegar	about 1 quart and 1 cup olive oil
about 2 quarts dry white wine	
1 tablespoon salt	bay leaves

For best results follow directions strictly. Above all never use water during process.

Cut off stalks and tips of artichokes. Remove all outside leaves, leaving only the tender white ones of the heart. Dip in lemon juice as you prepare them. This will prevent discoloration. Pour wine in large saucepan and add artichokes. Be sure wine covers artichokes. Add salt, 1 cup vinegar, bay leaves, peppercorns, cloves and lemon. Bring to a boil, cover and simmer from 30 to 45 minutes, depending on tenderness of artichokes. Artichokes should be cooked but still very firm. Drain all wine from pan. Remove cloves, lemon, bay leaves and peppercorns. Place artichokes in colander, cover and cool. Place artichokes in sterilized jars together with a few peppercorns and 2 bay leaves for each jar, leaving 1 inch head space. Pour oil to overflowing. Cover with silver foil and let stand for a week. Artichokes will have absorbed some of the oil. Add more oil, leaving ¼ inch head space. Seal, wipe off jars and store in cool, dry place. Ready in 4 weeks. Makes 7 pints.

Pickled Mixed Vegetables

GIARDINIERA DI LEGUMI IN ACETO

- 1 dozen small carrots
- 1 small cauliflower
- 2 dozen small white onions
- ½ pound fresh string beans cut in one-inch pieces
- 1 box frozen cut corn
- 8 small cucumbers, about 2 or 3 inches long
- 3 white turnips, peeled and diced
- 12 peppercorns
- wine vinegar
- salt

Scrape and slice carrots in ⅓ inch slices, rinse in cold water and cook for 10 minutes in slightly salted water. Drain. Remove leaves from cauliflower and cut off bruised spots. Place top down in a deep bowl of cold salted water and let stand 30 minutes. Drain and break into flowerets. Place in lightly salted boiling water and cook for 13 minutes. Drain. Place onions in a bowl, cover with boiling water and let stand for 5 minutes. Drain. Cover with cold water and peel. Place peeled onions in pan of boiling water and boil for 2 minutes. Drain. Cook beans in slightly salted water for 15 minutes. Drain. Boil corn in salted water for 2 to 3 minutes. Drain. Wash cucumbers in cold water. Boil turnips in salted water for 10 minutes. Drain. Gently mix vegetables and place in sterilized jars, adding peppercorns. Add vinegar to overflowing. Seal jars. Turn upside down to make sure there is no leakage. Store in cool place. Ready in a month. Makes about 6 pints.

JAMS AND JELLIES

Quince Jam

MARMELLATA DI COTOGNE

5 pounds quinces
sugar
3 tablespoons lemon juice

Rub quinces with wet towel to remove dust. Place in large saucepan, cover with water, bring to a boil, cover and cook for 45 minutes or until tender. Drain, peel, dice and put through a sieve or food chopper. Measure pulp and add ¾ cup of sugar for each cup of pulp. Place over medium flame, insert candy thermometer and simmer, stirring frequently, until the thermometer reads "jelly" (220°). Pour into sterilized jars, seal with wax, cover and store in cool place. Makes about 4 pints.

Quince Paste

COTOGNATA

5 pounds quinces
¾ cup sugar for each cup of quince pulp
½ cup water

Rub quince with damp towel to remove dust. Place in large saucepan, cover with water, bring to a boil and cook for 45 minutes or until tender. Drain and cool. Peel and dice and put through a sieve or food chopper. Measure pulp and place it in top of double boiler over boiling water and cook, stirring frequently with long wooden spoon for about 1¾ hours or until mixture has lost most of its moisture and practically stands up in soft peaks. Place sugar and water in saucepan, insert candy thermometer and cook until thermometer reads "crack" or until mixture cracks when tested in cold water. Blend immediately with quince. Line a baking pan 10"x12" with waxed paper. Place quince mixture in it, smooth top with a spoon and let stand in a dry place for 24 hours. Then place in 200° oven for one hour or until dry on top. Turn quince paste on paper-lined cookie sheet and return to oven for another hour or until dry on other side. Remove from oven and cool. Cut quince paste into squares 2"x2" and, if desired, roll in granulated sugar.

Cantaloupe Jelly

CONFETTURA DI MELLONE

2½ pounds cantaloupe, peeled and diced
2½ cups sugar
½ teaspoon vanilla or peel of a tangerine or an orange

Place cantaloupe, covered with sugar, in a covered bowl and put in refrigerator for 24 hours. Drain cantaloupe, pouring off the sugar and liquid into large saucepan. Bring to a boil over medium flame and boil for 5 minutes. Add diced cantaloupe and vanilla or tangerine peel. Insert candy thermometer and simmer, stirring occasionally, until thermometer reads "jelly." Pour into sterilized jars, seal with wax, cover and store in cool place. Makes about 2 pints.

Chestnut Preserves

MARMELLATA DI MARRONI

2 pounds large chestnuts
1 cup milk
2½ cups sugar
½ cup water
½ teaspoon vanilla extract

Peel chestnuts and place in boiling water. Cook for 25 to 30 minutes or until tender. Drain and remove inner skin. Mash with potato masher, or put through food grinder. Place in saucepan with milk over very low flame and cook, stirring constantly, for a few minutes, until milk has been absorbed and chestnut mixture is quite dry and thick. Remove from stove and put through a sieve. Place sugar and water in saucepan and cook until candy thermometer reads "caramel" (338°). Pour immediately but slowly into chestnut mixture, mixing constantly. Add vanilla and blend thoroughly. Fill ½-pint sterilized jelly glasses, seal with wax, cover and store in cool place. Makes 3 pints.

Peach Jelly

MARMELLATA DI PESCHE

4 pounds peaches
grated rind of one lemon

5 cups sugar
⅓ teaspoon cinnamon

Place peaches in large pan or bowl. Cover fruit with boiling water and let stand for 5 minutes. Drain, peel and dice, discarding pits. Put fruit through a sieve and put in saucepan together with lemon rind, cinnamon and sugar. Insert candy thermometer and place over medium-high flame. Stir frequently with wooden or silver spoon. Remove foam that will form on top of fruit. Remove pan from fire when thermometer reads "jelly." Pour into hot jars. Seal at once with paraffin. Makes 3 pints.

CHEESE

Asiago Has a pungent aroma and sharp flavor and, like other grating cheeses, may be used as a table cheese when not aged more than 10 months. Imported and domestic.

Bel Paese Meaning "beautiful country," this is a soft, mild table cheese. Imported and domestic.

Caciocavallo A spindle-shaped cheese, with a pointed bottom and a neck and head at the top. One theory of the origin of the name is that the cheeses, which are tied in pairs and hung over poles to cure, look as if they were hung over a saddle; hence, cheese on horseback, or *cacio a cavallo*. It has a pleasant sharp flavor and is used as a table cheese and for grating. Imported.

Caciocavallo Siciliano Made in Italy and in small quantity in this country. A sharp cheese used for table and grating.

Cacio Reale A rich, creamy table cheese.

Dolce Verde A creamy, blue-vein mild table cheese.

Gorgonzola A blue-green veined cheese of Italy, which is said to have been made in the Po Valley since A.D. 870. Imported and domestic.

Incanestrato (Basketed) Cheese is so named because the curd often is pressed in wicker molds, and the imprint of the wicker remains on the cheese. A grating cheese. Imported and domestic.

Mozzarella A soft, white, mild, plastic-curd cheese used mostly in cooking. It originates from Latium and Campania in southern Italy but is made also in great quantity in the United States, especially in New York. Domestic.

Mozzarella Salata The same cheese with the addition of salt. Used in cooking and as a table cheese.

Parmesan Is the name used outside of Italy and sometimes in Italy, for a group of very hard, grating, mild cheeses: Parmigiano, Reggiano, Lodigiano, Lombardy, Emiliano, Veneto and Bagozzo or Bresciano, some of which are imported in great quantity to this country. Parmesan is also made domestically.

Pastorella A soft rich table cheese.

Pecorino A cheese made from ewe's milk. There are numerous kinds, the most common of which is Pecorino Romano. A grating cheese with a marked but pleasant sharp taste.

Pepato A Romano-type, spiced cheese made in Sicily and southern Italy. A cheese of this type is also made in northern Michigan.

Provolone A table cheese, first made in southern Italy and now also made in the United States. Light in color, mellow, smooth, with an agreeable flavor.

Provolette and Provoloncini Semi-hard table cheeses with a pleasant, piquant taste.

Ricotta A soft, creamy, white, mild cheese, resembling a cottage cheese, used in cooking and as a table cheese. Domestic.

Sardo or Sardo Romano Pecorino-type cheese made on the Island of Sardinia. It is now also made in the United States and in Argentina. Used for grating.

Scamozza or Scamorza A soft, mild cheese originally made in Abruzzi. It is also made in the United States and, like Mozzarella, is eaten while fresh. A table cheese, but also used in cooking.

Stracchino A generic name applied to several types of soft whole-milk table cheeses made in Italy.

Taleggio A soft, mild whole-milk table cheese. Imported.

MENUS

―――

///

BUFFET

In the past few years the Buffet has become a very popular way of entertaining charmingly and casually. In fact, for most of us, living in modern apartments, with no help or practically none, it seems to have become the only way of entertaining even a small group.

The buffet dinner can be very elaborate or quite simple according to the occasion, the space and the help available. Here are a few important facts to keep in mind for a successful party: Don't leave anything to chance. Have everything planned and prepared in advance. Avoid elaborate dishes unless you have good kitchen help. A tired and worried hostess makes it difficult for her guests to relax and enjoy themselves. Do not invite so many people that you cannot pay enough attention to them. A small, well-organized party is most successful for hostess and guests alike, and don't try out Aunt Hattie's delicious soufflé on your guests. It may turn out to be a bad surprise.

Here are a few menus to guide you.

Hot Weather Menus

1
Truffled Canapés
Melon and Prosciutto Rolls
Fish Chowder Fano

Escarole Salad
Snowball Bombe
A SEMI-DRY WHITE WINE

2
Fillet Woronoff
Mushrooms Trifolati
Brussels Sprouts Parmigiana

Vanilla Spumoni
A LIGHT RED WINE OR A ROSÉ

3
Antipasto platter
Egg Noodle Pie Bologna Style
Romaine Salad all'Italiana

Pineapple Veneziana
A SEMI-DRY WHITE OR RED WINE

4
Molded Salmon
Stuffed Tomatoes alla Romana
Combination Salad Italian Style
Assorted cheeses

Apple Pie No. 1
A SEMI-DRY WHITE WINE OR A ROSÉ

5
Flounder ai Ferri
Stuffed Mushrooms Piedmont Style

Buca Lapi Salad
Iced Zabaglione
A DRY, AGED WHITE WINE

6
Snails Marchigiana
Turkey Casserole alla Scarlatta
Molded Salad

Strawberries in Wine
A LIGHT RED WINE

Cool Weather Menus

1
Rice with Lamb or Veal Kidney
Peas Roman Style

Escarole Salad
Peaches Maria Luisa
A LIGHT RED WINE

2
Saltimbocca alla Romana
Asparagus Polonese
Baked Eggplant

Potato Croquettes
Assorted cheeses
A SEMI-DRY WHITE OR RED WINE

3
Veal Shoulder Carabiniera
Artichokes Elpidiana
Celery Milanese

Torino Pudding
A SEMI-DRY RED OR WHITE WINE

4
Chicken Tetrazzini
Broccoli Sauté
Artichokes Roman Style

Coconut Bavarian Cream Pie
A ROSÉ OR LIGHT RED WINE

5
Pork Chops Neapolitan Style
Maria Luisa Salad

Neapolitan Pie
A FULL-BODIED RED WINE

6
Stuffed Turkey Lombardy Style
Artichokes Jewish Style
Bella Elena Salad

Apricots Bishop Style
A FULL-BODIED RED WINE

Easter Menu

Egg Drop Soup	WHITE MARINO
Whole Roast Kid or Baby Lamb	VALPOLICELLA
Potatoes Maria Luisa	
Artichokes Jewish Style	
Romaine Salad	
Fruit in season	
Zuppa Inglese	LACRIMA CHRISTI SPUMANTE
Espresso	

Christmas Dinner Menu

Canapés with Chicken Liver Spread	DRY WHITE ORVIETO
Caps Romagnola Style	
Truffled Capon or Stuffed Turkey Lombardy Style	SANTA MADDALENA
Green Rice	
Celery Milanese	
Pears, apples, dates, oranges	
White Fruit Cake (Panettone)	NEBBIOLO SPUMANTE
or	
White Lady Ice Cream	
or	
Mont Blanc Maria Luisa	
Espresso	

Menus for formal luncheons or dinners can be based on the following rules:

ANTIPASTO: A simple one such as oysters, or grapefruit, shrimps, etc., if a soup follows it. In Italy there are different opinions on the subject. Some believe in serving antipasto followed by a soup; while some omit the soup, especially when a mixed antipasto is served—such as the one in the first menu—as they feel that the spicy food in the antipasto will kill the taste of the soup.

SOUP: A consommé or a creamed soup. At dinners a risotto, or macaroni, ravioli, etc. is often served instead.

FISH: Fish fillets or a whole baked fish, often stuffed, beautifully decorated.

MEAT, POULTRY OR GAME: This can be a roast or fillet of beef, game or poultry with vegetables.

SALAD: It is usually served at dinners, and almost always whenever a roast is served.

CHEESE: It used to be served at the end of the meal, but in the past few years it is usually served before the dessert.

DESSERT: Individual pastry, frozen dessert, fruit dessert, custards, etc.

FRUIT: Any fresh fruit.

COFFEE: Espresso, served with sugar if desired.

WINES: Three or more wines should be served. A semi-dry white wine with antipasto, soup or macaroni, and fish. But more often a more aged white dry wine is served with the fish course. Then a fine aged red wine goes with the meat, game or fowl course, followed by a sweet dessert wine or champagne.

Here are a few typical luncheon and dinner menus:

Formal Luncheon Menus for Eight

1

FIRST COURSE:

2 recipes Eggs with Pâté, 1½ recipes Eels Carpionata, about 3 dozen Pickled Mushrooms, about 3 dozen Artichoke Hearts in Olive Oil	RIESLING, EST-EST-EST

SECOND COURSE:

2 recipes Fillets of Sole Oltremare	SAME AS FOR FIRST COURSE OR WHITE SOAVE

THIRD COURSE:

2 recipes Roast Duck, 2 recipes Stuffed Tomatoes alla Romana, 1½ recipes Golden Zucchini	RED CHIANTI CLASSICO

FOURTH COURSE:

Romaine Salad all'Italiana

FIFTH COURSE:

Cheese

SIXTH COURSE:

Peaches Fenice Espresso	A MALVASIA OR MOSCATO WINE OR ASTI SPUMANTE

2

FIRST COURSE:

Molded Tuna	WHITE FRASCATI, CHIANTI OR VELLETRI

SECOND COURSE:
Consommé with Cheese Puffs

THIRD COURSE:
**2 recipes Fillets of Turkey Bolognese,
Artichokes Elpidiana**   VALPOLICELLA OR BARDOLINO

FOURTH COURSE:
2 recipes Bella Elena Salad

FIFTH COURSE:
Cheese

SIXTH COURSE:
**Genoese Meringues
Espresso**   LACRIMA CHRISTI SPUMANTE

Formal Dinner Menus for Eight

1

FIRST COURSE:
2 recipes Oysters Veneziana   WHITE CAPRI OR SOAVE

SECOND COURSE:
1 recipe Egg Drop Soup   SAME AS FIRST COURSE

THIRD COURSE:
2 recipes Mackerel Fillets Venetian Style   DRY WHITE ORVIETO

FOURTH COURSE:
**2 recipes Beef Fillets Rossini,
Cauliflower Soufflé,
Potato Croquettes**   NEBBIOLO OR BAROLO

FIFTH COURSE:
2 recipes Maria Luisa Salad

SIXTH COURSE:
Fruit

SEVENTH COURSE:
**Zuppa Inglese
Espresso**   MOSCATO D'ASTI SPUMANTE

2

FIRST COURSE:
Salmon Stuffed Tomatoes

WHITE FRASCATI OR
LACRIMA CHRISTI (STILL)

SECOND COURSE:
Cannelloni alla Nerone

THIRD COURSE:
2 recipes Flounder ai Ferri

WHITE FRASCATI OR
LACRIMA CHRISTI (STILL)
OR TERLANO

FOURTH COURSE:
**Leg of Lamb with Marsala,
2 recipes Celery Milanese,
Potatoes with Cream**

VALPOLICELLA, GRIGNOLINO,
OR BARBERA SUPERIORE

FIFTH COURSE:
2 recipes Escarole Salad

SIXTH COURSE:
**Iced Zabaglione
Espresso**

GRAN SPUMANTE

CASSEROLES

//

Here is a list of casseroles and one-dish meals. Each one, served with a mixed green salad, bread sticks or Italian bread, fresh fruit and/or one or several kinds of cheese, will make a delightful meal. Wine can be served if desired.

Old-Fashioned Neapolitan Lasagne	Page 54-55
Cannelloni alla Nerone	52
Manicotti all'Etrusca	53
Pork Chops Neapolitan Style	111-112
Rice and Kidney Casserole	71
Rice Casserole Genoa Style	71-72
Turkey Casserole alla Scarlatta	123
Fillet of Turkey Bolognese	123
String Bean Casserole	128
Squab and Macaroni Casserole	66
Egg Noodle Casserole	64
Chicken Tetrazzini	65
Macaroni Pie	67
Egg Noodle Pie Bologna Style	63-64
Polenta Casserole	73
Polenta Ring with Chicken Livers	74
Artichokes Elpidiana	139
Potatoes and Sausages	144
Potatoes Maria Luisa	143-144
Peppers Ticinese	141
Eggplant Parmigiana	136-137
Stuffed Tomatoes alla Romana	132
Risotto Fagiano	70-71
Rice and Shrimps Adriatic Style	72
Rice Finanziera	70
Chicken Diesola	115
Pork in Tuna Sauce	7
Veal in Tuna Sauce	6-7
Chicken and Peppers Roman Style	115
Fried Chicken and Mushrooms Tuscany Style	119
Duck Niçoise	120-121

Molded Salmon	Page 87
Fish Chowder Rimini	29
Fish Chowder Fano	29
Fish Chowder Lazio	28
Jellied Veal	103

STANDARD MEASUREMENTS

All the measurements in this book are level unless otherwise stated.

4 cups flour	1 pound
2 cups granulated sugar	1 pound
2 cups butter or shortening	1 pound
2 cups rice	1 pound
1 cup corn meal	5⅓ ounces
1 cup shelled walnuts	4 ounces
1 cup shelled almonds	4 ounces
1 cup shelled pecans	5½ ounces
1 cup powdered sugar	6 ounces
1 cup brown sugar	6 ounces
1 cup bread crumbs	2½ ounces
2 tablespoons liquid	1 ounce
3 teaspoons liquid	1 tablespoon

INDEX

A

Almond chocolate bonbons, 176
   crunch, 177-178
   paste, 191
   pralinée, 180
Anise bread, 197
   cookies, 196
Antipasti, see Hors d'oeuvres
Antipasto platter, 15
Apple pie, No. 1, 200-201
   pie, No. 2, 201
Apples, baked, stuffed, 160-161
   fried, 141-142
   fried, with rum, 161
   Priscilla, 160
Apricots Bishop style, 163-164
Artichoke hearts, preserved, in olive oil, 215-216
Artichokes and peas, 140
   Elpidiana, 139
   golden, 139
   Jewish style, 139-140
   Roman style, 138
Asparagus Madeleine, 138
   Milanese, 137
   Polonese, 137-138

B

Bagna Cauda, 16
Baked apples, stuffed, 160-161
   custard Maria Luisa, 167
   eggplant, 137
   zucchini with prosciutto, 134
Banana whip, 161-162
Bananas, fried, with rum, 161
Bass, fillets of, Massaia style, 81
Batter for frying meats, 158
   for frying, No. 1, 159
   for frying, No. 2, 159
Bavarian cream, 168
Bean soup, 25
   soup Venetian style, 25
Beans, shell, soup, 24
Beans, string
   casserole, 128
   Italian style, 127
   pickled, 214
   salad, 152
   sautéed, 127
   soufflé, 129
   with tomato sauce, 128
Beef patties Maddalena, 90-91
   broth, 17
   Certosina, 96
   fillet Chateaubriand, 93
   fillet of, Arlesiana, 93
   fillet of, Carignano, 94
   fillet of, Rossini, 94
   fillet Woronoff, 92-93
   loaf, 91-92
   patties, 91
   pot roast Lombardy style, 96
   roast, Italian style, 96-97
   short ribs Italian style, 89
   steak Florentine, No. 1, 95
   steak Florentine, No. 2, 95
   steak with caper sauce, 95
   stew, 89-90
   stew Romana, 90
Belle Elena salad, 150
Beverages, see name of beverage
Birthday cake, 184
Black truffle surprise, 191
Bolognese ring, 196
   sauce, 33
Bread, 155-156
Bread sticks, 157
Breakfast buns Roman style, 158
Broccoli sauté, 131
   Roman style, 131
Broth with egg flakes, 18
   with toasted croutons, 18
Brown Chaufroid sauce, 39
Brown stock, 38-39
Brussels sprouts Parmigiana, 131
Buca Lapi salad, 149
Bucatini with kidney, 62
Buffet, menus for, 222-224
Buns, breakfast, Roman style, 158
Butter cream, 204
   cream cake, 183-184
   cream Torinese, 205
   sauce, maître d'hôtel, 40

231

C

Cabbage and rice Lombardy style, 26
  home style, **144-145**
Cake, 181
  birthday, 184
  black truffle surprise, 191
  butter cream, 183-184
  coconut, 183
  fruit, Siena style, 189-190
  fruit chest Palermitana, 186
  Genoa almond, 182-183
  Genoese, 181
  lady fingers, 195
  Maddalena, 181-182
  meringues, Genoese, 196-197
  Mont Blanc Maria Luisa, 185-186
  petit fours, 197
  Savarin al rum, 188-189
  sponge, Italian, 182
  white fruit, 187-188
  zuppa Inglese, 185
Cake fillings
  almond paste, 191
  butter cream, 204
  butter cream Torinese, 205
  chocolate butter cream, 205
  cream puff paste, 191
  hazelnut butter cream, 205
  Roman cream, 203-204
  vanilla butter cream, 204
Cake icings
  butter cream, 204
  butter cream Torinese, 205
  chocolate butter cream, 205
  chocolate fondant, 203
  fondant for cakes and pastry, 202-203
  hazelnut butter cream, 205
  meringue, Italian, 204
  Roman cream, 203-204
  royal, 203
  vanilla butter cream, 204
Calf liver
  Genoa style, 107
  Italian style, 108
  with sage sauce, 107
  with wine sauce, 106-107
Canapés, suggestions for, 14-15
  See also Hors d'oeuvres
Candy
  almond chocolate bonbons, 176
  almond crunch, 177-178
  almond pralinée, 180
  cherry bonbons, 176
  chocolate-covered filberts, 176
  hazelnuts pralinée, 180
  preserved marrons, 179
  rum filbert bonbons, 175
  strawberries in fondant, 177
  vanilla nougat, 178
  walnut bonbons, 175
Cannelloni alla Nerone, 52-53
  homemade, 51
  stuffing, 51
Cantaloupe jelly, 218
  rolled in prosciutto, 9
Caper sauce, 41
Capon, roast, truffled, 124
Cappuccino, *see* Italian coffee
Caps Romagnola style, 20-21
Casseroles, 228-229
Cauliflower, fried, 135
  salad Neapolitan style, 151
  soufflé, 136
  soup, No. 1, 23
  soup, No. 2, 23-24
Celery Milanese, 130
Cheese
  gorgonzola cream spread, 14
  Parmesan cream spread, 13
  pudding, Roman, 167
  puffs, 13
  types, descriptions, uses for, 220-221
Cherries flambées, 165
Cherry bonbons, 176
Chestnut preserves, 218
Chicken and beef broth, 17
  and peppers Roman style, 115
  Cacciatora, 115-116
  Cacciatora Maddalena, 116
  Diesola, 115
  fried, and mushrooms Tuscany style, 119
  Finanziera style, 118
  Ghiottona, 118
  liver spread, 14
  Marengo, 117
  Priscilla, 116
  rolls, 118
  Tetrazzini, 65
  with cream, 117
Chocolate butter cream, 205
  covered filberts, 216
  fondant, 203
  ice cream, 171
Coconut cake, 183
  Bavarian cream pie, 200
  cookies, 195-196

Cod Benedettina, 85
  Biscaglia, 85
  fillets of, Florentine, 86
  Mistral, 85-86
  Vicentina, 84
Coffee, 206-207
  ice cream, 171
Combination salad Italian style, 147
Cookies
  anise, 196
  anise bread, 197
  basic dough for, 193
  Bolognese ring, 196
  coconut, 195-196
  fancy Milanese, 193
  filbert, 192
  honey, 194
  lemon, 195
  macaroons, 192
  orange, 194-195
  pine nut, 192-193
  Saint Joseph cream puff, 198
  Venetian, 193-194
Corn meal
  polenta ring with chicken livers, 74
  polenta casserole, 73
  polenta with sausage, 74
  soft polenta, 73
  thick polenta, 73
Creamed mushrooms, 133
  veal kidneys, 106
Cream puff paste, 191
  puffs, St. Joseph, 198
Croquettes, potato, 144
  rice, Roman style, 3-4
Cucumbers, pickled, 214-215
Custard, baked, Maria Luisa, 167
Cutlets, veal, Milanese, 97
Cuttlefish in tomato sauce, 81-82
  Veneziana, 81

D

Delfino potatoes, 142-143
Desserts, see also Cake, Candy, Cookies, Custard, Fruits, Gelatine, Ice creams and ice cream desserts, Pastry, Pie, and Puddings
  apple Priscilla, 160
  apricots Bishop style, 163-164
  banana whip, 161-162
  cherries flambées, 165
  melon Oriental style, 164
  peaches Fenice, 162-163
  peaches Maria Luisa, 163
  pineapple Veneziana, 166
  rum pears, 165
  Shrove Tuesday sweet knots, 199
  strawberries in wine, 164
  sweet chestnuts Lazio, 198
  sweet potatoes and apples, 166
Deviled eggs, 5
Duck fillets alla Dino, 121
  Niçoise, 120-121
  roast, 120
Dumplings Italian style, 56

E

Eels Carpionata, 11
  Marinara (hors d'oeuvres), 10-11
  Marinara, 87
Egg bows in broth, 18
  drop soup, 18
Egg noodle
  casserole, 64
  pie Bologna style, 63-64
  timbale, 65
Egg noodles
  green, Bologna style, 50-51
  homemade, Bologna style, 50
  homemade medium, 49
  homemade wide, 49
  majestic, al Triplo Burro, 49-50
  Rugantino, 50
Eggplant
  baked, 137
  Parmigiana, 136-137
  (Sicilian) relish, 12
Eggs
  and peas, 77
  deviled, 5
  Florentine, 78
  omelet, frog legs, 75
  omelet, mushroom, 75
  omelet, potato, No. 1, 76
  omelet, potato, No. 2, 77
  omelet, onion, 76
  omelet, spinach, 76
  pickled, 6
  scrambled with sausage, 77
  stuffed with anchovies, 6
  with paté, 5
Escarole salad, 146

Espresso, see Italian coffee

F

Fancy cookies Milanese, 193
Fennel and celery salad, 150
    salad, 149
Filbert cookies, 192
Fillet of bass Massaia style, 81
Fillet of beef,
    Arlesiana, 93
    Carignano, 94
    Rossini, 94
Fillet of cod Florentine, 86
Fillet of flounder,
    baked, 97
    with mushrooms, 80
Fillet of sole,
    Messalina, 82-83
    Oltremare, 82
Fillet of turkey Bolognese, 123
Fillings for cake, see Cake fillings
Fish, 79-88. See also name of fish
    chowder,
        Fano, 29
        Lazio, 28
        Rimini, 29
    bass, fillets of, Massaia style, 81
    cod,
        Benedettina, 85
        Biscaglia, 85
        fillets of, Florentine, 86
        Mistral, 85-86
        Vicentina, 84
    cuttlefish,
        in tomato sauce, 81-82
        Veneziana, 81
    eels Marinara, 87
    flounder,
        baked fillets of, 79
        broiled, 79
        fillet of, with mushrooms, 80
    lobster fra Diavolo, 87
    mackerel fillets Venetian style, 80
    salmon, molded, 87
    sauce, 36
    shrimps,
        di Sciullo, 83
        grilled, 84
    sole,
        fillet of, Messalina, 82-83
        fillets of, Oltremare, 82
    tunafish patties Nizzarda, 86
    whiting, baked, in green sauce, 80-81

Flounder, baked fillets of, 79
    broiled, 79
    fillet of, with mushrooms, 80
Fondant, chocolate, 203
    for icing cakes and pastry, 202-203
Fondue, Piedmont style (a soup), 21-22
Fried apples, 141-142
    apples with rum, 161
    bananas with rum, 161
    cauliflower, 135
    chicken and mushrooms Tuscany style, 119
    potatoes home style, 142
Fritto Misto, 15-16
Frog legs omelet, 75
Fruit cake, Siena style, 189-190
Fruit chest Palermitana, 186

G

Garden salad, 152
Garlic mayonnaise, 38
Gelatine, kirsch, 168-169
Genoa almond cake, 182-183
Genoese cake, 181
    meringues, 196-197
Golden artichokes, 139
    zucchini, 135
Gorgonzola cream spread, 14
Green egg noodles Bologna style, 50-51
    rice, 68
    sauce Genovese, 34
Grilled shrimps, 84

H

Ham, prosciutto and melon, 8
Hazelnut butter cream, 205
Hazelnuts pralinée, 180
Homemade Cannelloni, 51
    egg noodles Bologna style, 50-51
    egg noodles, medium, 49
    egg noodles, wide, 49
    lasagna, 53-54
    manicotti, 51
    milk rolls, 156
    pie crust, 199
Hors d'oeuvres, 3-16

antipasto platter, 15
Bagna Cauda, 16
cantaloupe rolled in prosciutto, 9
cheese puffs, 13
chicken liver spread, 14
eggs, deviled, 5
eggs, pickled, 6
eggs, stuffed with anchovies, 6
eggs with paté, 5
eels Carpionata, 11
eels Marinara, 10-11
Fritto Misto, 15-16
gorgonzola cream spread, 14
molded tuna, 9-10
mozzarella in Carozza, 4
mussels in anchovy sauce, 10
oysters Veneziana, 9
Parmesan cream spread, 13
pepper relish, 11-12
pizza, miniature, di Sciullo, 4-5
pork in tuna sauce, 7
prosciutto and melon, 8
rice croquettes Roman style, 3-4
salmon-stuffed tomatoes, 12-13
Sicilian eggplant relish, 12
snails Marchigiana, 7
snails, St. John's, 8
truffled canapés, 3
veal in tuna sauce, 6-7
Honey cookies, 194
Horseradish sauce, 36
Hunters' sauce, 40-41
Housewife's sauce, 40

I

Ice cream, chocolate, 171
coffee, 171
vanilla, 170
Ice creams and ice cream desserts
peach Melba, 172-173
preparation of, 170
snowball bombe, 174-175
strawberry cup, 173
strawberry, Neapolitan style, 172
vanilla, 170
vanilla spumoni, 171-172
white lady, 172
wine sherbet Roman style, 173
witch's bombe, 174
Iced zabaglione, 169-170
Icings for cakes, see Cake icings
Italian coffee, 206-207

meringue, 204
sponge cake, 182

J

Jams
quince, 217
quince paste, 217-218
Jellied veal, 103
Jellies
cantaloupe, 218
chestnut preserves, 218
peach, 219

K

Kidneys, creamed veal, 106
veal, Madeira, 106
Kirsch gelatine, 168-169

L

Lady fingers, 195
Lamb Cacciatora, spring, 110
chops, breaded spring, 109
leg of, with marsala, 110
roast baby, 111
roast, spring, with new potatoes, 110-1 1
spring, in egg sauce, 109
Lasagne, homemade, 53-54
old-fashioned Neapolitan, 54-55
Lemon cookies, 195
Lentil soup, 24
Linguine in egg sauce No. 1, 57
in egg sauce No. 2, 57
with ricotta cheese Roman style, 58
Lobster fra Diavolo, 87
Loin of pork Bologna style, 113
of pork in red wine, 113

M

Macaroni, see *also under* specific Italian names: Manicotti, Cannelloni, Spaghetti, Ravioli, Linguine, Bucatini, Vermicelli

and cheese casserole, 66
and squab casserole, 66
Bucatini with kidney, 62
pie, 67
pizzaiola, 63
Macaroons, 192
Mackerel fillets Venetian style, 80
Maddalena cake, 181-182
Maître d'hôtel butter, 40
Majestic egg noodles al Triplo Burro, 49-50
Manicotti all'Etrusca, 53
homemade, 51
Maria Luisa salad, 146
Marrons, preserved, 179
Mayonnaise, 37
garlic, 38
with cream, 38
with gelatine, 37
with pickles, 37
Measurements, standard, 230
Meat. See also name of meat
loaf, 91-92
patties, 91
patties Maddalena, 90-91
Meatless tomato sauce, 30
Melon Oriental style, 164
Menus, buffet, 222-224
formal dinners, 226-227
formal luncheons, 225-226
Meringue, Italian, 204
Meringues, Genoese, 196-197
Minestrone Milanese, 22-23
Molded salad, 149
salmon, 87
Mont Blanc Maria Luisa, 185-186
Mornay sauce, 34
Mozzarella in Carozza, 4
Mussel chowder, 29-30
Mussels in anchovy sauce, 10
Mushroom omelet, 75
sauce, 33
soup, 19-20
Mushrooms,
creamed, 133
in olive oil, 214
pickled, 213
stuffed, Piedmont style, 134
Trifolati, 133-134

N

Neapolitan pastry, 190
pie, 202

Noodles, egg,
casserole, 64
green, Bologna style, 50-51
homemade, Bologna style, 50
homemade medium, 49
homemade wide, 49
majestic al Triplo Burro, 49-50
pie Bologna style, 63-64
Rugantino, 50
timbale, 65

O

Omelet
frog legs, 75
mushroom, 75
onion, 76
potato, No. 1, 76
potato, No. 2, 77
spinach, 76
Onion omelet, 76
sauce, 36
soup, 19
stuffed, Hector, 132
One-dish meals, 228-229
Orange cookies, 194-195
Oysters Veneziana, 9

P

Panettone, see White fruit cake 187-188
Parmesan cream spread, 13
Pasta, preparation of, 42-48
Pasticcera cream, 168
Pastry
Neapolitan, 190
short, 190
Patties
meat, 91
meat, Maddalena, 90-91
tunafish, Nizzarda, 86
Peach jelly, 219
Melba, 172-173
Peaches Fenice, 162-163
Maria Luisa, 163
Pear pie Milanese, 250
Pears, rum, 165
Peas
and eggs, 77
Roman style, 129
Pepper relish, 11-12
salad, 153

Peppers and potatoes, 141
  pickled, 215
  Ticinese, 141
Petit fours, 197
Pheasant, Norcia style, 124-125
Pickled cucumbers, 214-215
  eggs, 6
  mixed vegetables, 216
  mushrooms, 213
  peppers, 215
  string beans, 214
Pies
  apple, No. 1, 200-201
  apple, No. 2, 201
  coconut Bavarian cream, 200
  crust, homemade, 199
  crust, quick, 199-200
  Neapolitan, 202
  pear Milanese, 201
  Sicilian, 201-202
  strawberry, 200
Pineapple Veneziana, 166
Pine nut cookies, 192-193
Pink sauce, 35
Pizza dough, 154
  (miniature) di Sciullo, 4-5
  Neapolitan style, 154-155
  with anchovies and mozzarella cheese, 155
  with onions and olives, 155
Pizzaiola sauce, 32-33
Polenta casserole, 73
  ring with chicken livers, 74
  soft, 73
  thick, 73
  with sausage, 74
  see also Corn meal
Pork
  chops, Modena style, 112
  chops, Neapolitan style, 111-112
  in tuna sauce, 7
  loin of, Bologna style, 113
  loin of, in red wine, 113
  roast, Fiorentina, 112
  sausage with grapes, 113
Potato croquettes, 144
  omelet, No. 1, 76
  omelet, No. 2, 77
  ring, 143
  soup, 20
Potatoes and sausage, 144
  Delfino, 142-143
  fried, home style, 142
  Maria Luisa, 143-144
  sweet, and apples, 166
  with cream, 142

Pot roast Lombardy style, 96
Poultry and game, 114-126
  see also name of fowl
Preserved artichoke hearts in olive oil, 215-216
  marrons, 179
  tomatoes, No. 1, 212
  tomatoes, No. 2, 212
  tomato sauce, 213
Preserves, chestnut, 218
Prosciutto and melon, 8
Puddings
  Bavarian cream, 168
  cheese, Roman, 167
  iced zabaglione, 169-170
  Pasticcera cream, 168
  Torino, 169

Q

Quick pie crust, 199-200
Quince jam, 217
  paste, 217-218

R

Rabbit Buongustaio, 125
  Leghorn style, 126
Ravioli Italian style, 55-56
Relishes
  pepper, 11-12
  Sicilian eggplant, 12
Rice alla Milanese, 68-69
  and kidney casserole, 71
  and potato soup, 27
  and shrimp Adriatic style, 72
  and turnip soup, 26
  casserole Genoa style, 71-72
  country style, 69
  croquettes Roman style, 3-4
  Finanziera style, 70
  green, 68
  risotto Fagiano, 70-71
  with mushrooms, 68
  with peas, 27
  with sage, 67
Risotto Fagiano, 70-71
Roast baby lamb, 111
  beef Italian style, 96-97
  capon, truffled, 124
  duck, 120
  pork Fiorentina, 112

Rolled veal with anchovies, 100
   veal with tomato sauce, 100-101
Rolls, homemade milk, 156
   sandwich, 157
Romaine salad all'Italiana, 147
Roman cream, 203-204
Roman cheese pudding, 167
Royal icing, 203
Rum filbert bonbons, 175
   pears, 165

S

Saint Joseph cream puff, 198
Salad, 146-153
   Bella Elena, 150
   Buca Lapi, 149
   cauliflower, Neapolitan style, 151
   combination, Italian style, 147
   country style, 151
   escarole, 146
   fennel, 149
   fennel and celery, 150
   garden, 152
   Maria Luisa, 146
   molded, 148
   pepper, 153
   romaine all'Italiana, 147
   string bean, 152
   three-color, 147
   tomato, 150
   turnip green, 153
Salmon, molded, 87
   stuffed tomatoes, 12-13
Saltimbocca Roman style, 97
Sandwich rolls, 157
Sauces, 31-41
   Bolognese, 33
   brown Chaufroid, 39
   brown stock, 38-39
   butter, maître d'hôtel, 40
   caper, 41
   for fish, 36
   green, Genovese, 34
   horseradish, 36
   housewife's, 40
   hunters', 40-41
   mayonnaise, 37
   mayonnaise, garlic, 38
   mayonnaise with cream, 38
   mayonnaise with gelatine, 37
   mayonnaise with pickles, 37
   Mornay, 34
   mushroom, 33
   onion, 36
   pink, 35
   Pizzaiola, 32-33
   preparation of, 42-43
   tomato, Italian style, 31
   tomato, meatless, 32
   tomato, Neapolitan style, 32
   tomato, Sicilian style, 31
   Venetian, 41
   white, heavy, 35
   white, thin, 35
   white stock, 38
   wine, for fish, 39-40
Sausage and ricotta stuffing (for cannelloni), 51
Sausages, pork, with grapes, 113
Sautéed string beans, 127
Savarin al rum, 188-189
Scrambled eggs with sausage, 77
Shell bean soup, 24
Short pastry, 190
Short ribs Italian style, 89
Shrimps di Sciullo, 83
   grilled, 84
Shrove Tuesday sweet knots, 199
Sicilian eggplant relish, 12
   pie, 201-202
Snails Marchigiana, 7
   St. John's, 8
Snowball bombe, 174-175
Sole, fillet of, Messalina, 82-83
   fillets of, Oltremare, 82
Soufflés,
   cauliflower, 136
   string bean, 129
Soups, 17-30
   bean, 25
   bean, Venetian style, 25
   beef broth, 17
   broth with egg flakes, 18
   broth with toasted croutons, 18
   cabbage and rice Lombardy style, 26
   caps Romagnola style, 20-21
   cauliflower, No. 1, 23
   cauliflower, No. 2, 23-24
   chicken and beef broth, 17
   egg bows in broth, 18
   egg drop, 18
   fish chowder Fano, 29
   fish chowder Lazio, 28
   fish chowder Rimini, 29
   fondue, Piedmont style, 21-22
   lentil, 24
   minestrone Milanese, 22-23
   mushroom, 19-20

mussel chowder, 29-30
onion, 19
Pavese style, 19
potato, 20
rice and potato, 27
rice and turnip, 26
rice with peas, 27
shell bean, 24
spinach, 22
Spaghetti all'Amatriciana, 60
and peas, 61
and truffles Umbria style, 60
Carbonara, 58
chicken Tetrazzini, 65
in tuna sauce, No. 1, 61
in tuna sauce, No. 2, 61-62
Transatlantico, 59
with anchovy sauce, 62
with meat balls, 59-60
Spinach in butter, 130
omelet, 76
soup, 22
with lemon dressing, 130
Spumoni, vanilla, 171-172
Squab and macaroni casserole, 66
Squabs and rice Maria Luisa, 120
on the spit, Maria Luisa, 119-120
Squash, stuffed acorn, 133
Steak Florentine, No. 1, 95
Florentine, No. 2, 95
with caper sauce, 95
Stews
beef, 89-90
beef, Romana, 90
veal, Casalinga, 103-104
veal, with peas, 104-105
veal, with tomato sauce, 104
Stock,
brown, 38-39
white, 38
String bean casserole, 128
bean salad, 152
bean soufflé, 128
String beans,
Italian style, 127
pickled, 214
sautéed, 127
with tomato sauce, 128
Stuffed acorn squash, 133
mushrooms Piedmont style, 134
onion Hector, 132
shoulder of veal, 101-102
tomatoes alla Romana, 132
turkey Lombardy style, 121-122
Stuffings,
for ravioli, 55
sausage and ricotta (for cannelloni), 52
Strawberries in fondant, 117
in wine, 164
Strawberry cup, 173
ice cream Neapolitan style, 172
pie, 200
Sweet chestnuts Lazio, 198
Sweet potatoes and apples, 166

T

Three-color salad, 147
Tomato salad, 150
Tomato sauce,
Italian style, 31
meatless, 32
Neapolitan style, 32
preserved, 213
Sicilian style, 31
Tomatoes,
preserved, No. 1, 212
preserved, No. 2, 212
stuffed, alla Romana, 132
Torino pudding, 169
Tripe Roman style, 105-106
Toscana, 105
Truffled canapés, 3
roast capon, 124
Tuna, molded, 9-10
Tunafish patties Nizzarda, 86
Turkey casserole alla Scarlatta, 123
fillets of, Bolognese, 123
rolls, 118-119
stuffed, Lombardy style, 121-122
Turnip green salad, 153

V

Vanilla butter cream, 204
ice cream, 170
nougat candy, 178
spumoni, 171-172
Veal birds Delizia, 101
cutlets Milanese, 97
in tuna sauce, 6-7
jellied, 103
kidney Madeira, 106
kidneys, creamed, 106
loaf, 91
rolled, with anchovies, 100
rolled, with tomato sauce, 100-101

Saltimbocca Roman style, 97
scaloppini Pizzaiola, 99-100
scaloppini with Marsala, 99
shanks Milanese, 108
shoulder Carabiniera, 102-103
shoulder with mustard sauce, 102
stew Casalinga, 103-104
stew with peas, 104-105
stew with tomato sauce, 104
stuffed shoulder of, 101-102
tripe Roman style, 105-106
tripe Toscana, 105
Valdostana, 99
see also Calf liver
Vegetables, 127-145. See also name of vegetable
mixed, pickled, 216
Venetian cookies, 193-194
sauce, 41
Vermicelli with clams Transatlantico, 62-63

W

Walnut bonbons, 175

White fruit cake, 187-188
lady ice cream, 172
sauce, heavy, 35
sauce, thin, 35
stock, 38
Whiting, baked, in green sauce, 80-81
Wine sauce for fish, 39-40
sherbet Roman style, 173
Wines, 208-211
serving of, 209-210
storing of, 209
to serve with special dishes, 222-227
types of, 210-211
Witch's bombe, 174

Z

Zabaglione, iced, 169-170
Zucchini, baked, with prosciutto, 134
golden, 135
Madeleine, 135
Zuppa Inglese, 185

ITALIAN INDEX OF RECIPES

A

Abbacchio in Brodetto, 109
Agnello Arrosto, 111
Albicocche alla Cardinale, 163-164
Amaretti, 192
Ananas alla Veneziana, 166
Anello di Polenta con Fegatini, 74
Anguilla Carpionata, 11
Anguille in Umido alla Marinara, 87
Anitra alla Nizzarda, 120-121
Anitra Arrosto, 120
Antipasto, 15
Aragosta fra Diavolo, 87
Arrosto di Agnello con Patatine, 110-111
Arrosto di Maiale alla Fiorentina, 112
Asparagi alla Maddalena, 138
Asparagi alla Milanese, 137
Asparagi alla Polonese, 137-138

B

Baccalà alla Benedettina, 85
Baccalà alla Vicentina, 84
Baccalà Biscaglia, 85
Bagna Cauda, 16
Banane Fritte al Rum, 161
Bignè al Formaggio, 13
Biscotti all'Anice, 196
Biscotti all'Arancio, 194-195
Biscotti al Limone, 195
Bistecca alla Fiorentina No. 1, 95
Bistecca alla Fiorentina No. 2, 95
Bistecca alla Salsa di Capperi, 95
Bomba Palla di Neve, 174-175
Bomba Strega, 174
Broccoli alla Romana, 131
Broccoli in Padella, 131
Brodo con Crostini, 18
Brodo con Tagliarini, 18
Brodo con Tripolini, 18
Brodo di Manzo, 17
Brodo Misto, 17
Buccatini con Rognone, 62
Budino all'Italiana, 185
Budino di Ricotta alla Romana, 167
Budino Torinese, 169
Burro alla Maître D'Hôtel, 40

C

Cannelloni, 51
Cannelloni alla Nerone, 52
Cappelletti alla Romagnola, 20-21
Caponatina alla Siciliana, 12
Cappone Tartuffato, 124
Carciofi alla Giudia, 139-140
Carciofi alla Romana, 138
Carciofi con Piselli, 140
Carciofi Dorati, 139
Carciofi Elpidiana, 139
Carciofini sotto Olio, 215-216
Cassata alla Palermitana, 186
Castagnole Laziali, 198
Cavolo alla Casalinga, 144-145
Cavoletti alla Parmigiana, 131
Cavolfiore Dorato, 135
Cenci per il Berlingaccio, 199
Cetriolini in Aceto, 214-215
Ciambella Bolognese, 196
Ciambella di Patate, 143
Ciliege al Cognac, 176
Ciliege Fiammeggiate, 165
Cima di Vitello, 103
Cipolle Ripiene alla Ettore, 132
Confettura di Mellone, 218
Coniglio alla Livornese, 126
Coniglio del Buongustaio, 125
Coppa alle Fragole, 173
Coppa Melba, 172-173
Coscia di Montone al Marsala, 110
Coste all'Italiana, 89
Costolette di Maiale alla Modenese, 112
Costolette di Maiale alla Napoletana, 111-112
Cotognata, 217-218
Cotolette di Agnello Panate, 109
Cotolette di Vitello alla Milanese, 97
Cozze Acciugate, 10
Crema al Burro, 204
Crema al Burro alla Torinese, 205
Crema al Burro Cioccolato, 205
Crema al Burro Nocciole, 205

241

Crema al Burro Vaniglia, 204
Crema Bavarese, 168
Crema di Gorgonzola, 14
Crema di Parmigiano, 13
Crema Pasticcera, 168
Crema Romana, 203-204
Crema Rovesciata Maria Luisa, 167
Croccante di Mandorle, 177-178
Crocchette di Patate, 144
Crocchette di Riso alla Romana, 3-4
Crostata alla Napoletana, 202
Crostata alla Siciliana, 201-202
Crostata Bavarese al Cocco, 200
Crostata di Fragole, 200
Crostata di Mele No. 1, 200-201
Crostata di Mele No. 2, 201
Crostate di Pere alla Milanese, 201
Crostini Caldi ai Tartufi, 3

D

Dolce di Patate e Mele, 166

F

Fagiano alla Norcese, 124-125
Fagiolini all'Agro, 152
Fagiolini all'Italiana, 127
Fagiolini al Pomidoro, 128
Fagiolini in Padella, 127
Fagiolini sotto Aceto, 214
Fagottini di Mellone e Prosciutto, 9
Fegato al Vino, 106-107
Fegato di Pollo, 14
Fegato di Vitello all'Italiana, 108
Fegato di Vitello alla Genovese, 107
Fegato di Vitello alla Salvia, 107
Fettuccine all'Uovo, 49
Filetti di Anitra alla Dino, 121
Filetti di Merluzzo alla Fiorentina, 86
Filetti di Pesce Passara ai Funghi, 80
Filetti di Pesce Passera Gratinati, 79
Filetti di Sgombro alla Veneta, 80
Filetti di Sogliola alla Messalina, 82-83
Filetti di Tacchino alla Bolognese, 123
Filetto alla Chateaubriand, 93
Filetto alla Woronoff, 92-93

Fondant al Cioccolato, 203
Fondo Bianco, 38
Fondo Bruno, 38-39
Fonduta alla Piemontese, 21-22
Fragole al Fondente, 177
Fragole al Vino, 164
Frittata di Cipolle, 76
Frittata di Funghi, 75
Frittata di Patate No. 1, 76
Frittata di Patate No. 2, 77
Frittata di Rane, 75
Frittata di Spinaci, 76
Fritto alla Toscana di Pollo e Funghi, 119
Fritto Misto, 15-16
Funghi alla Panna, 133
Funghi Ripieni alla Piemontese, 134
Funghi sotto Aceto, 213
Funghi sotto Olio, 214
Funghi Trifolati, 133-134

G

Gelatina al Kirsch, 168-169
Gelato al Caffe, 171
Gelato alla Vaniglia, 170
Gelato Dama Bianca, 172
Gelato di Cioccolata, 171
Gelato di Fragole alla Napoletana, 172
Ghiaccia Reale, 203
Giardiniera di Legumi in Aceto, 216
Gnocchi all'Italiana, 56
Grissini, 157

I

Il Fondente per Ghiacciare, 202-203
Imbottini Delizia, 101
Insalata al Bosco, 152
Insalata alla Bella Elena, 150
Insalata Buca Lapi, 149
Insalata di Broccoletti di Rapa, 153
Insalata di Finocchi, 149
Insalata di Finocchi e Sedani, 150
Insalata di Peperoni Arrostiti, 153
Insalata di Pomodori, 150
Insalata di Rinforzo alla Napoletana, 151
Insalata di Scarola, 146
Insalata Maria Luisa, 146
Insalata Mista all'Italiana, 147

Insalata Paesana, 151
Insalata Russa, 148
Insalata Tricolore, 147
Insalata Verde all'Italiana, 147
Involtini di Vitello al Pomidoro, 100-101
Involtini di Vitello alle Acciughe, 100

L

Lasagne Fatte in Casa, 53-54
Lasagne Napoletane all'Antica, 54-55
Linguine con la Ricotta alla Romana, 58
Linguine Strascinate No. 1, 57
Linguine Strascinate No. 2, 57
Lumache di San Giovanni, 8

M

Maestose Fettuccine al Triplo Burro, 49-50
Maiale al Vino Rosso, 113
Maiale al Latte alla Bolognese, 113
Maiale Tonnato, 7
Maionese all'Aglio, 38
Maionese alla Panna, 38
Maionese con Sott'aceti, 37
Mandorle Tostate, 180
Manicotti, 51
Manicotti all'Etrusca, 53
Manzo alla Certosina, 96
Manzo alla Lombarda, 96
Manzo Arrosto all'Italiana, 96-97
Marchesine, 176
Marenga all'Italiana, 204
Marenghe Genovesi, 196-197
Marinara di Anguilla, 10-11
Maritozzi Romani, 158
Marmellata di Cotogne, 217
Marmellata di Marroni, 218
Marmellata di Pesche, 219
Marroni Canditi, 179
Medaglioni alla Arlesiana, 93
Medaglioni alla Carignano, 94
Melanzane alla Parmigiana, 136-137
Melanzane Gratinate, 137
Mele alla Priscilla, 160
Mele Fritte, 141-142
Mele Fritte al Rum, 161
Mele Ripiene, 160-161
Mellone all'Orientale, 164
Merlango Gratinato al Verde, 80-81

Merluzzo alla Mistral, 85-86
Minestra di Cavolfiore No. 1, 23
Minestra di Cavolfiore No. 2, 23-24
Minestra di Fagioli, 25
Minestra di Fagioli Freschi, 24
Minestra di Lenticchie, 24
Minestra di Spinaci, 22
Minestrone Milanese, 22-23
Monte Bianco Maria Luisa, 185-186
Mozzarella in Carozza, 4

N

Noccioline al Rum, 175
Noccioline Mascherate, 176
Noccioline Pralinate, 180
Noci al Cioccolato, 175

O

Occhi di Lupo alla Pizzaiola, 63
Ossibuchi alla Milanese, 108-109
Ostriche alla Veneziana, 9

P

Pan di Genova, 182-183
Pan di Spagna, 182
Pane, 155-156
Pane all'Anice, 197
Pane per Pizza, 154
Panetti di Pollo o Tacchino, 118-119
Panetti per Tartine, 157
Panettone di Milano, 187-188
Panforte di Siena, 189-190
Panini al Latte, 156
Pasta di Mandorle, 191
Pasta e Fagioli Veneta, 25
Pasta Frolla, 190
Pasta Genovese, 181
Pasta Maddalena, 181-182
Pasta per Crostate, 199
Pasta Reale, 191
Pasta Zuccherata, 193
Pastella per Friggere No. 1, 159
Pastella per Friggere No. 2, 159
Pastella per Fritti di Carne, 158
Pasticceria con Pan di Spagna, 197
Pasticcini Napoletani, 190
Pasticcio di Fettuccine, 64
Pasticcio di Maccheroni, 66
Pasticcio di Maccheroni, 67
Pasticcio di Maccheroni e Piccioni, 66

Pasticcio di Tagliatelle alla Bolognese, 63-64
Pastine al Cocco, 195-196
Pastine al Miele, 194
Pastine con i Pignoli, 192-193
Pastine con le Nocciole, 192
Pastine Fantasia alla Milanese, 193
Patate alla Panna, 142
Patate del Delfino, 142-143
Patate Fritte alla Casalinga, 142
Patate Ripiene di Salsiccia, 144
Peperonata, 11-12
Peperonata con le Patate, 141
Peperoni alla Ticinese, 141
Peperoni sotto Aceto, 215
Pere alla Fiamma, 165
Pesce Passera ai Ferri, 79
Pesce Persico alla Massaia, 81
Pesche Fenice, 162-163
Pesche Maria Luisa, 163
Pesto alla Genovese, 34
Petto di Tacchino alla Scarlatta, 123
Piccioncini alla Maria Luisa, 119-120
Piccioncini con Risotto alla Maria Luisa, 120
Piselli alla Romana, 129
Piselli con Uova, 77
Pizza alla di Sciullo, 4-5
Pizza con Acciughe e Mozzarella, 155
Pizza con Cipolle ed Olive, 155
Pizza Napoletana, 154-155
Polenta al Forno, 73
Polenta Dura, 73
Polenta Pasticciata con Salsiccia, 74
Polenta Tenera, 73
Pollo alla Cacciatora Maddalena, 116
Pollo alla Diesola, 115
Pollo alla Finanziera, 118
Pollo alla Ghiottona, 118
Pollo alla Marengo, 117
Pollo alla Panna, 117
Pollo alla Priscilla, 116
Pollo con Peperoni alla Romana, 115
Polpette di Carne Cotta, 91
Polpette di Tonno alla Nizzarda, 86
Polpettine di Manzo e Salsiccia Maddalena, 90-91
Polpettone, 91-92
Pomidori Conservati No. 1, 212
Pomidori Pelati Conservati No. 2, 212

Pomodori Ripieni alla Romana, 132
Pomodori Ripieni di Salmone, 12-13
Prosciutto con Mellone, 8
Punch alla Romana, 173

R

Ragù alla Bolognese, 33
Ravioli o Agnolotti all'Italiana, 55-56
Ripieni per Cannelloni, 51
"Risi e Bisi," 27
Riso alla Genovese, 71-72
Riso con Rognoncini Trifolati, 71
Riso e Patate, 27
Riso e Rape, 26
Riso Verde, 68
Risotto alla Fagiano, 70-71
Risotto alla Finanziera, 70
Risotto alla Milanese, 68-69
Risotto con Funghi, 68
Risotto con Scampi all'Adriatica, 72
Risotto in Cagnone, 67
Risotto Paesano, 69
Rognone di Vitello al Madera, 106
Rognone di Vitello alla Panna, 106

S

Salsa ai Capperi, 41
Salsa ai Funghi, 33
Salsa al Vino Bianco, 39-40
Salsa alla Cipolla, 36
Salsa alla Pizzaiola, 32-33
Salsa Aurora, 35
Salsa Besciamella, 35
Salsa Besciamella Densa, 35
Salsa Chaufroid Scura, 39
Salsa dei Cacciatori, 40-41
Salsa della Massaia, 40
Salsa di Pomodori alla Napoletana, 32
Salsa di Pomodori alla Siciliana, 31
Salsa di Pomidoro, 213
Salsa di Pomodori all'Italiana, 31
Salsa di Pomodori di Magro, 32
Salsa di Rafano, 36
Salsa Maionese, 37
Salsa Maionese alla Gelatina, 37
Salsa Mornay, 34
Salsa per Pesce, 36
Salsa Veneta, 41
Salsiccia con l'Uva, 113
Saltimbocca alla Romana, 97

Savarin al Rum, 188-189
Savoiardi, 195
Scaloppine di Vitello alla Pizzaiola, 99-100
Scaloppine di Vitello al Marsala, 99
Scampi alla di Sciullo, 83
Scampi alla Griglia, 84
Sedano alla Milanese, 130
Seppie alla Veneziana, 81
Seppie al Pomidoro, 81-82
Sfingi di San Giuseppe, 198
Sformato di Patate Maria Luisa, 143-144
Sformato di Tonno, 9-10
Sogliole d'Oltremare, 82
Soufflé di Cavolfiore, 136
Soufflé di Fagiolini, 129
Spaghetti alla Carbonara, 58
Spaghetti all'Amatriciana, 60
Spaghetti al Tonno No. 1, 61
Spaghetti al Tonno No. 2, 61-62
Spaghetti con Piselli, 61
Spaghetti con Polpettine, 59-60
Spaghetti con Tartufi all'Uso d'Umbria, 60
Spaghetti Tetrazzini, 65
Spaghetti Transatlantico, 59
Spaghettini alle Acciughe, 62
Spalla di Vitella Ripiena, 101-102
Spalla di Vitello alla Carabiniera, 102-103
Spalla di Vitello al Senape, 102
Spezzatino di Abbacchio alla Cacciatora, 110
Spezzatino di Pollo alla Cacciatora, 115-116
Spezzatino di Vitella alla Casalinga, 103-104
Spezzatino di Vitello al Pomidoro, 104
Spezzato di Vitello con Piselli, 104-105
Spinaci al Burro, 130
Spinaci all'Olio e Limone, 130
Spuma di Banane, 161-162
Spuma di Salmone, 88
Spumoni alla Vaniglia, 171-172
Stracciatella, 18
Stufatino alla Romana, 90
Stufato di Manzo al Vino Bianco, 89-90

T

Tacchino Ripieno alla Lombarda, 121-122

Tagliatelle alla Rugantino, 50
Tagliatelle all'Uovo, 49
Tagliatelle con Ragù alla Bolognese, 50
Tagliatelle Verdi alla Bolognese, 50-51
Tartufi Neri in Sorpresa, 191
Timballo di Fagiolini, 128
Timballo di Fettuccine, 65
Torrone alla Vaniglia, 178
Torta al Cocco, 183
Torta con Crema al Burro, 183-184
Torta per Compleanno, 184
Tournedos alla Rossini, 94
Trippa alla Romana, 105-106
Trippa in Umido alla Toscana, 105

U

Uova Acciugate, 6
Uova alla Fiorentina, 78
Uova con Pâté, 5
Uova Piccanti, 5
Uova sotto Aceto, 6
Uova Strapazzate con la Salsiccia, 77

V

Valdostana di Vitello, 99
Veneti, 193-194
Vermicelli con le Vongole alla Transatlantico, 62-63
Verzata di Riso alla Lombarda, 26
Vitello Tonnato, 6-7

Z

Zabaglione Gelato, 169-170
Zucche Ripiene, 133
Zucchini alla Maddalena, 135
Zucchini Dorati, 135
Zucchini Gratinate al Prosciutto, 134
Zuppa alla Pavese, 19
Zuppa di Cipolle, 19
Zuppa di Cozze, 29-30
Zuppa di Funghi, 19-20
Zuppa di Patate, 20
Zuppa di Pesce alla Fano, 29
Zuppa di Pesce alla Lazio, 28
Zuppa di Pesce alla Rimini, 29
Zuppa Inglese, 185